E.O.Hoppé's Amerika

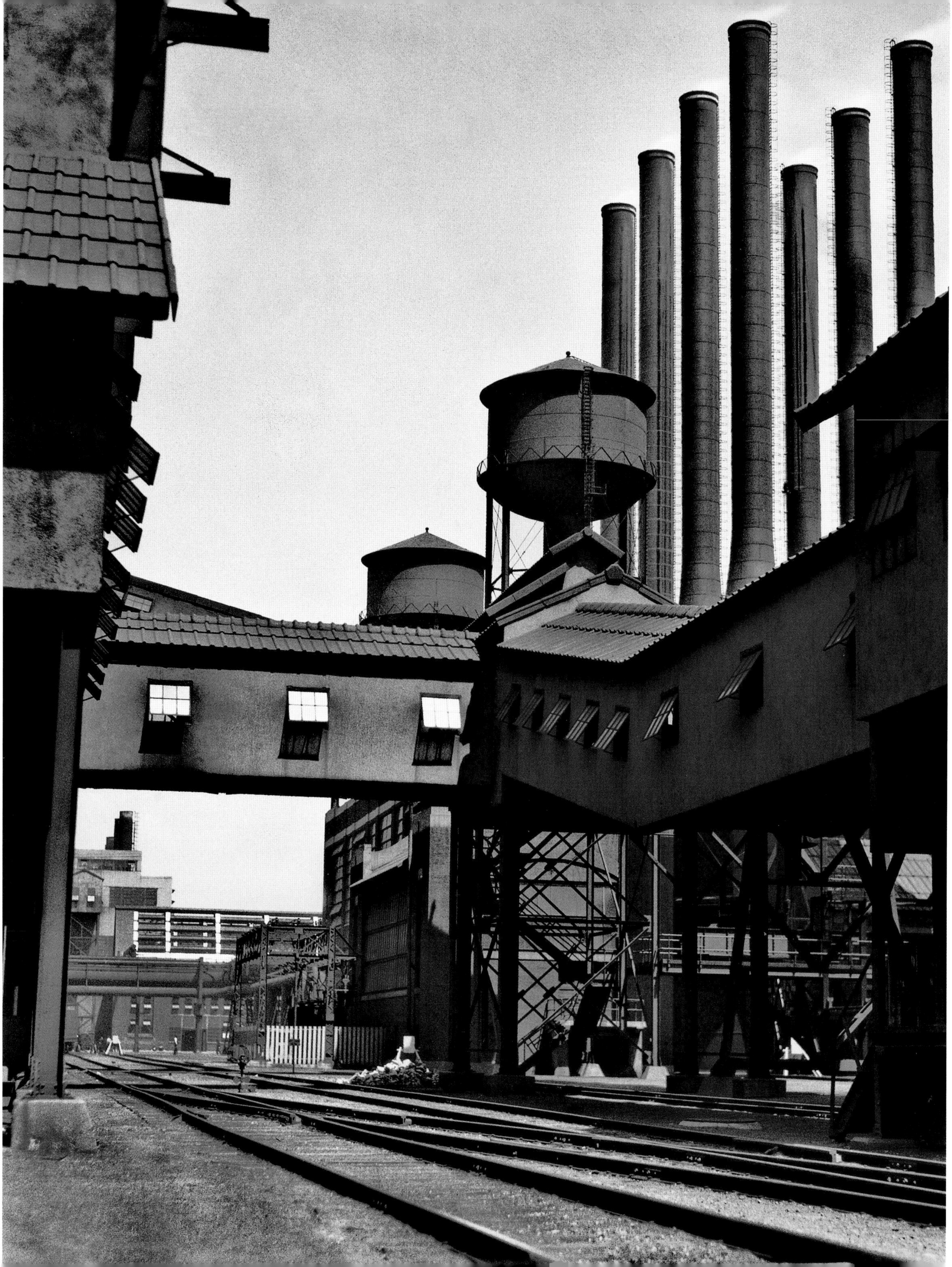

E.O.Hoppé's Amerika

MODERNIST PHOTOGRAPHS FROM THE 1920'S

PHILLIP PRODGER

CURATORIAL ASSISTANCE

IN ASSOCIATION WITH

W. W. NORTON & COMPANY
NEW YORK · LONDON

E.O. Hoppé's Amerika
Modernist Photographs from the 1920's
Phillip Prodger

Printed in Italy
First Edition

The text of this book is composed in Centaur
Book design and composition by Katy Homans
Manufacturing by Mondadori Printing, Verona

Library of Congress Cataloging-in-Publication Data

Prodger, Phillip.
E.O. Hoppé's Amerika : modernist photographs from the 1920s / Phillip Prodger.
p. cm.
ISBN 978-0-393-06544-2 (hardcover)
1. Photography, Artistic. 2. Photography—United States—History—20th century. 3. United States—History—20th century—Pictorial works. 4. Modernism (Art) 5. Hoppé, E. O. (Emil Otto), 1878-1972. I. Title.
TR653.P76 2007
770.97309'04—dc22
2007010231

W.W. Norton & Company, 500 Fifth Avenue, New York, NY 10110
www.wwnorton.com

W.W. Norton & Company Ltd., Castle House, 75/76 Wells Street, London, WIT 3QT

1 2 3 4 5 6 7 8 9 0

Contents

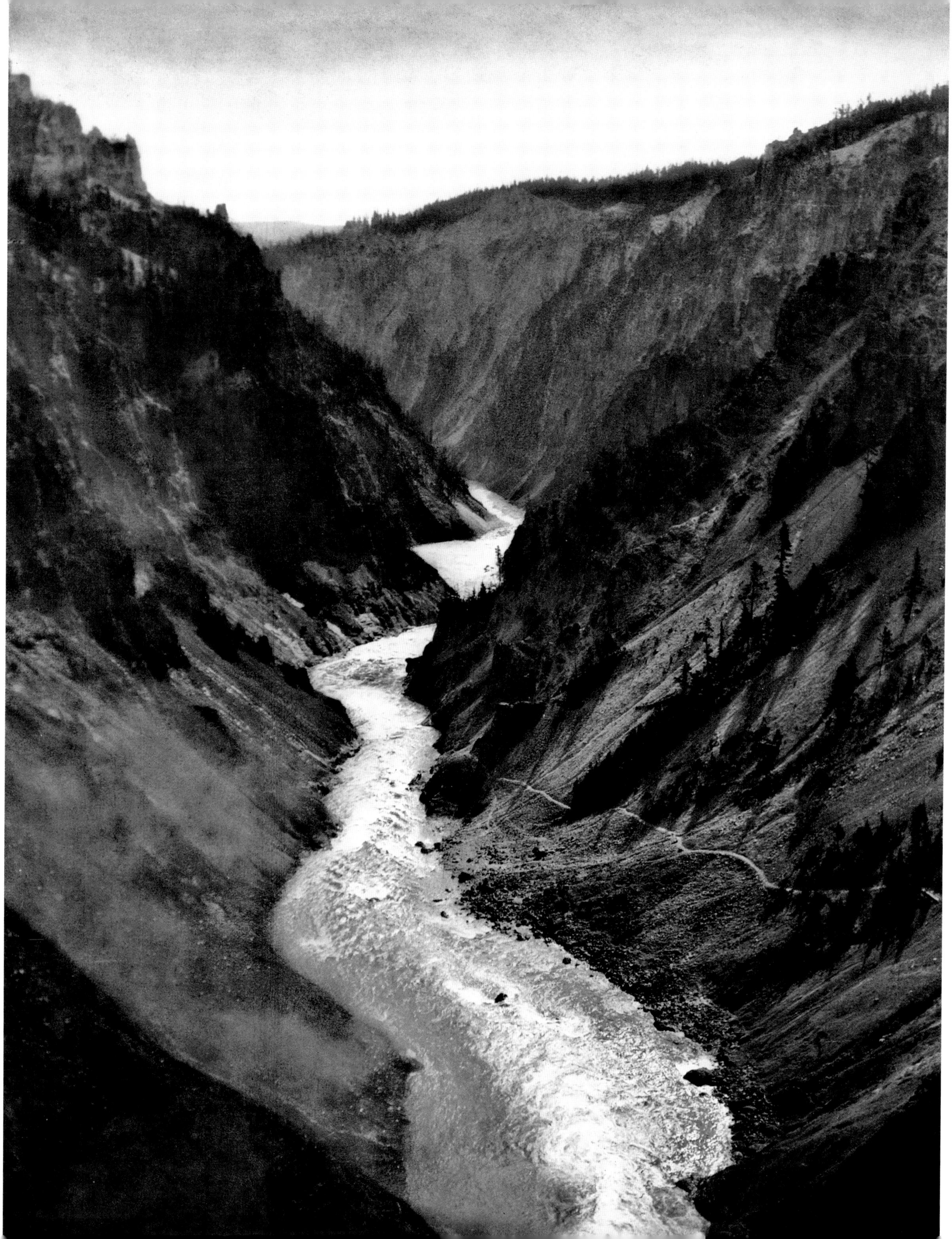

Hoppé's Portrait of America

The German-born British photographer Emil Otto Hoppé sailed for America in 1919, just months after the armistice ending the First World War was signed. "My task," he later wrote, "was to discover the *real* America, at that time unfamiliar to so many people, even Americans."[1] He also understood that the postwar period would bring commercial opportunities. Relations had been disrupted for most of the decade, and Europeans had pent-up curiosity about the American way of life. Powerful and remote, prosperous and introverted, the country was a study in contrasts. Moreover, from 1911 to 1920 nearly six million immigrants had arrived on American shores, most of them from southern and eastern Europe. The people they left behind wanted to see where their compatriots had gone, and those who considered joining them wanted details.

Hoppé's trip of 1919 lasted for two years and was the first of three he would make into the 1920s. At first he produced the kind of photographs he knew best—studio portraits of celebrities and aristocrats—made almost entirely in New York. But as his imagination took hold he ranged farther inland, expanding his project to include pictures of a wide variety of the places and people that make America unique. By the end of his last photographic tour in 1926, Hoppé had succeeded in making a portrait of the entire United States. Just as a great portrait provides a window on a personality, revealing strengths and betraying vulnerabilities, Hoppé's portrait of America conveys the complexities of the nation.

Conceptually, Hoppé was the first photographer to use a survey approach to distill the American experience. Crisscrossing the country by car and rail, he photographed the four corners of the United States, from New Hampshire to the Florida Keys and from Seattle to San Diego, with many points in between. His goal, however, was not just to document what the United States looked like but to capture the character of the American people. Hoppé found little of interest in conventional views and he made few photographs of tourist sites. He was drawn to something more elusive—the realities of day-to-day life in the country, its triumphs, its failings, and the contradictions engendered in its people. And he was determined to find what made America unique at a critical time in its history. He moved easily between the sublime and the prosaic, finding clues in unobvious places. Although he photographed the Brooklyn Bridge, the legendary Ford factory in Detroit, and the Grand Canyon with palpable excitement, he found meaning not just in the majesty of these places but in the pleasing pattern of bolts and girders, the irony of advertising posters, or the geometry of stones on a rocky trail. For Hoppé such details represented life in America on a human scale, the way ordinary people had built it and the way they could see it, too, if only their eyes were sharp enough.

Hoppé's project directly anticipated surveys made by members of the Farm Security Administration (FSA) from 1935–43, which included famed photographers Dorothea Lange (1895–1965),

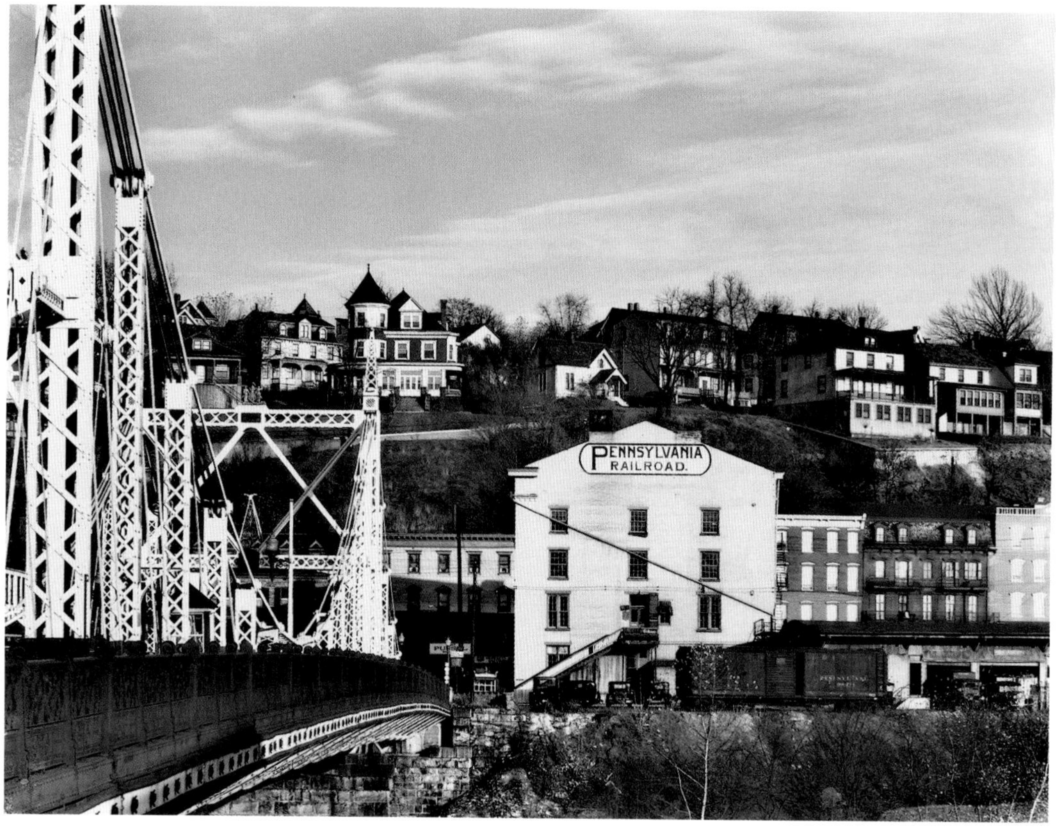

Figure 1. Walker Evans, *Phillipsburg, New Jersey,* 1935

Arthur Rothstein (1915–85), Ben Shahn (1898–1969), and Marion Post Wolcott (1910–90), among others. Above all, it foreshadowed the lyrical photographs of maverick FSA photographer Walker Evans (1903–75), whose 1938 exhibition at the Museum of Modern Art in New York, *American Photographs,* with its accompanying catalogue, constitutes one of the undisputed landmarks in photographic history. The photographs Evans and Hoppé made on their respective surveys bear striking resemblances. Evans's well-known 1935 view of *Phillipsburg, New Jersey* [Figure 1], for example, contains many of the same elements as Hoppé's *Pittsburgh, Pennsylvania, 1926* [Figure 2], made a decade earlier. Both shared appreciation for the haphazard coexistence of architecture and engineering works, the cacophonous lay of the land, and the distinctiveness of the American vernacular. Both used photography to transform the mundane into the noteworthy. Like Evans, and, indeed, Robert Frank (b. 1924) after him, Hoppé attempted to capture the spirit of America, seeing logic in quiet minutiae and significance in recurring motifs. More than thirty years before Frank published *The Americans* in 1958, Hoppé was hard at work photographing unlikely juxtapositions of flags, cars, and conventioneers. Taken individually, Hoppé's American photographs are meaningful. Yet they work even better in sequence, each frame playing off its neighbors.

In the course of his travels, Hoppé produced several thousand images of the United States, a small fraction of which are reproduced in this book. Some are published here for the first time; others Hoppé printed in various journals, magazines, and books. Still more are known from exhibition prints. All are drawn from the Hoppé Archive at Curatorial Assistance in Pasadena. The

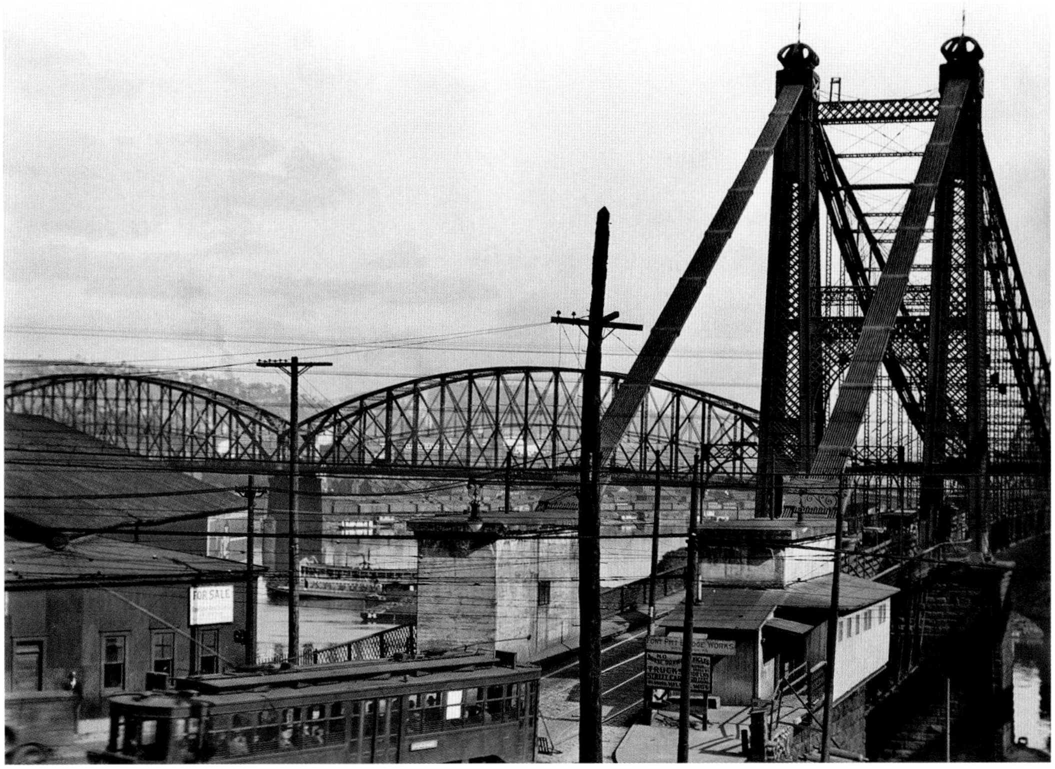

Figure 2. E. O. Hoppé, *Pittsburgh, Pennsylvania, 1926*

selection is designed to show the variety of material in the collection, stressing the original contributions Hoppé made to photographic practice. In spite of the acclaim he enjoyed in his lifetime, he has become a somewhat obscure figure, upstaged by contemporaries such as Alfred Stieglitz (1864–1946), Edward Steichen (1879–1973), and Paul Strand (1890–1976). Yet as the photographs in this volume reveal, Hoppé compares favorably to these renowned figures. In many cases, he engaged subjects that local photographers would not tackle until years later. He was also technically advanced, embracing strategies that were unquestionably avant-garde. Hoppé's American photographs provide compelling evidence for restoring his work to the vanguard of photography in the early twentieth century.

ROMANTIC AMERICA

Unlike Walker Evans and Robert Frank, Hoppé did not travel in anonymity. At the time of his first visit, he was arguably the most famous photographer in the world. He had built his reputation as a portraitist, and this remains the work for which he is best known. At an exhibition at the Wanamaker Gallery in New York in 1921, he showed 117 of his favorites, arranged alphabetically for easy reference.[2] Among the personalities depicted were screen stars Marion Davies and Lillian Gish, authors Thomas Hardy, Henry James, Rudyard Kipling, and H. G. Wells, playwright Maurice Maeterlinck, the poet Ezra Pound, the singer Enrico Caruso and the dancer Alexandra Fedorova, together with a broad assortment of royals, industrialists, artists, and bon vivants. Also included were a portrait of his close friend George Bernard Shaw and a self-portrait, dutifully filed under "S." Hoppé's presence would not have been out of place. He was regarded not just as a celebrity portraitist but also as a celebrity himself. He mixed comfortably in the intellectual and social circles he portrayed. There was an enormous cachet to being photographed by Hoppé, and those with aspirations strived to have him take their portrait. His pictures were unfailingly flattering, and his own fame reassured sitters of their personal prominence. Having their likenesses exhibited in distinguished art galleries certainly did not hurt matters.

Part of Hoppé's appeal undoubtedly lay in his bedside manner. He worked hard to empathize with his clients, reading their poetry and books, seeing their films and performances, and remembering their friends and anniversaries. He would even go so far as to read up on his sitters' hobbies in order to make them more at ease. Hoppé likened a trip to the photographer's studio to visiting the dentist, and he acknowledged that sitters are "nearly always on the defensive, impatient, and thoroughly uncomfortable."[3] To win repeat business and, more important, to take natural portraits, he stressed developing rapport with his sitters. He endeavored to capture the look of genuine engagement on a sitter's face as he or she responded to thoughtful questions or expressed their true character in moments of relaxation. Unlike many of his contemporaries, Hoppé photographed his clients without props or painted backdrops. Occasionally he would have dancers (a favorite subject) pose in costume, some of which he designed himself. Generally, however, he removed distracting attributes and photographed against neutral dark backdrops to enable the personality of the individual to best assert itself.

Hoppé approached the United States as a nation in the same way he approached individuals in the studio. He would never cajole or reproach his subjects but got to know them, teasing out their true nature. Similarly, Hoppé's photographs of America were created on not one but several extended trips. It was his method to ingratiate himself with his sitters, talk with them, engage them, and get them to drop their guard. In the satirical magazine *Punch,* he was described as "the photographer who likes to dine with his sitters," and for good reason.[4] He understood that casual visits could result only in superficial pictures. So he explored the land exhaustively, sought out a wide diversity of Americans and the circumstances in which they lived, and ruminated on the country's past, present, and future. Hoppé reasoned that a photographer can communicate only that which he has first internalized. As he put it, "the prime function of photography [is] absolute reliance on supreme craftsmanship in the expression of individual conception of the subject within the legitimate means of the medium. [. . .] This conception should be based on a clear recognition of the fundamental principles of photography, namely its unchallenged ability to reflect reality."[5] Hoppé plumbed that reality, finding meaning in the gaps between stereotypes. His America was not as others portrayed it but the country as he felt it really was. Without affectation or stylization, the face of his America was to be a window on its soul.

Hoppé's project began, appropriately, with portraiture. He had long been interested in what he called typologies—pictures of representative people from various social strata. In an era in which eugenics had many followers, Hoppé questioned whether it was possible to see a person's destiny inscribed in his or her appearance. He concluded that it was, but not in the sense of genetic predisposition. It was his view that life experience takes a toll on a person's features and that the events of a lifetime shape the way one looks. Hoppé wrote several articles in the 1920s arguing that Americans of European stock were gradually becoming more Native American in appearance.[6] He maintained that the stresses of living in such a vast and unforgiving land were written in the face, and that Indians had long ago achieved a quintessentially "American" look. In the 1920s this view was relatively enlightened, as it implied that no race is intrinsically superior to another, and that conditioning alone creates social standing. The parallels with Shaw's *Pygmalion* (1916) are strong, and it is intriguing to consider Shaw's play in light of his association with Hoppé. Hoppé had photographed London types throughout the 1910s, publishing a number of studies in his 1922 book *Taken from Life.* A larger selection appeared in the volume *London Types: Taken from Life,* appearing in 1926, with an introduction by the novelist William Pett Ridge, known for his satirical stories about working-class life. These efforts coincided exactly with the German photographer August Sander's (1876–1964) famous documents of German types living in the Westerwald, slated for publication in his unfinished volume *Menschen des 20 Jahrhunderts,* or *People of the Twentieth Century.*

Hoppé's first trip to America had been prompted by a proposal to set up a permanent studio on Fifth Avenue in New York by the theater producer A. H. Woods. In a brief letter of 1919, Woods offered to put up the money to create a satellite Hoppé studio in exchange for a fifty percent share in the profits.[7] Hoppé declined the deal as offered on the grounds that it would have required his residency in the city six months a year.[8] However, the proposal started him thinking about the American market and he did eventually open a temporary studio on West Fifty-seventh Street. The plan was to repeat the formula that had proven so successful in London. One by one, New York socialites were paraded through the premises, where they submitted to Hoppé's accomplished lens.

Hoppé was innately restless, and one can only imagine the strain of attending to self-important persons hour after hour, particularly when an exciting and unfamiliar country beckoned at his doorstep. He hinted in his autobiography at the difficulties a portrait photographer endures, confiding that sitters sometimes had to be "handled," and warning inexperienced photographers about the demands of appeasing strong personalities. Typologies and the allure of New York City excited him. Tedious sessions with vain poseurs did not. In his spare moments, Hoppé stole away to the famously dilapidated Bowery district and the Jewish neighborhoods on the Lower East Side. There he made some of the most memorable portraits of his career, a series he referred to as his "Down and Outs." He described these as psychological character studies, part of his investigation of "the by-products and offshoots of the social order."[9] *Jewish Immigrant with Cigarette* [page 45] is representative of these. A middle-aged man, a few graying whiskers streaking his beard, is pictured in full profile against a dark, empty backdrop. He is shown as a bust, his face taking on a sculptural presence, with one bulging vein rising on his forehead like a topographical feature on a map. His head is tipped back slightly, his hair swept away from his cheek, his pronounced brow and aquiline nose creating a bold graphic presence. The effect is accentuated by the partially smoked cigarette protruding at a slight angle from his lips, the end clipped slightly by the edge of the frame, lending the composition a slightly unsettled feel. Though the man is ostensibly destitute, he is imbued with dignity and strength. Only a thin sliver of his shabby clothes betrays his circumstances.

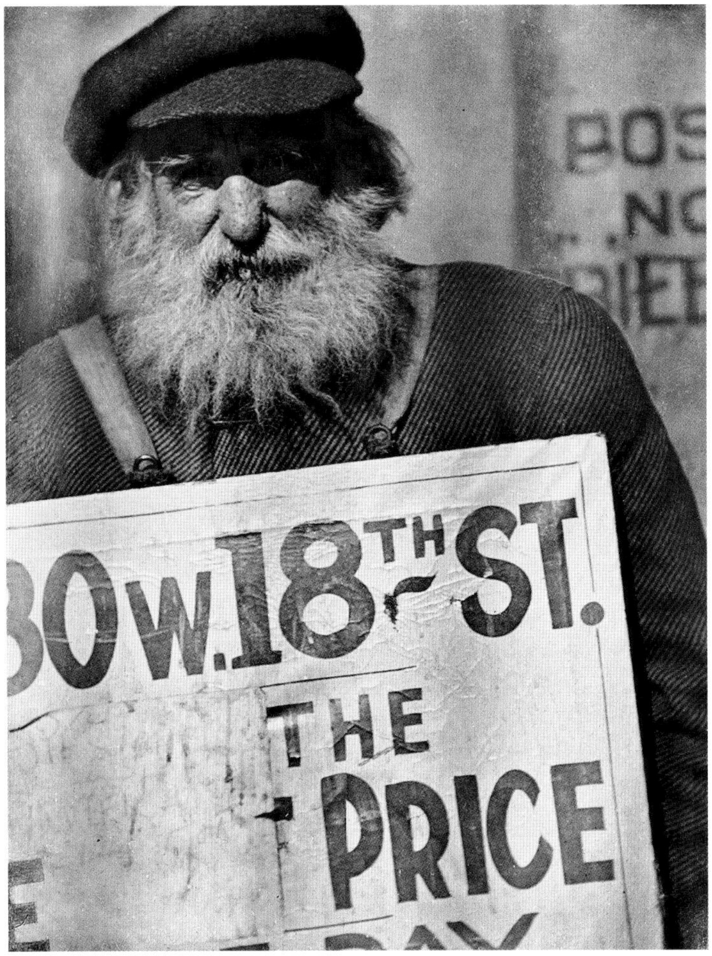

Figure 3. Paul Strand, *Sandwich Man, New York,* 1916

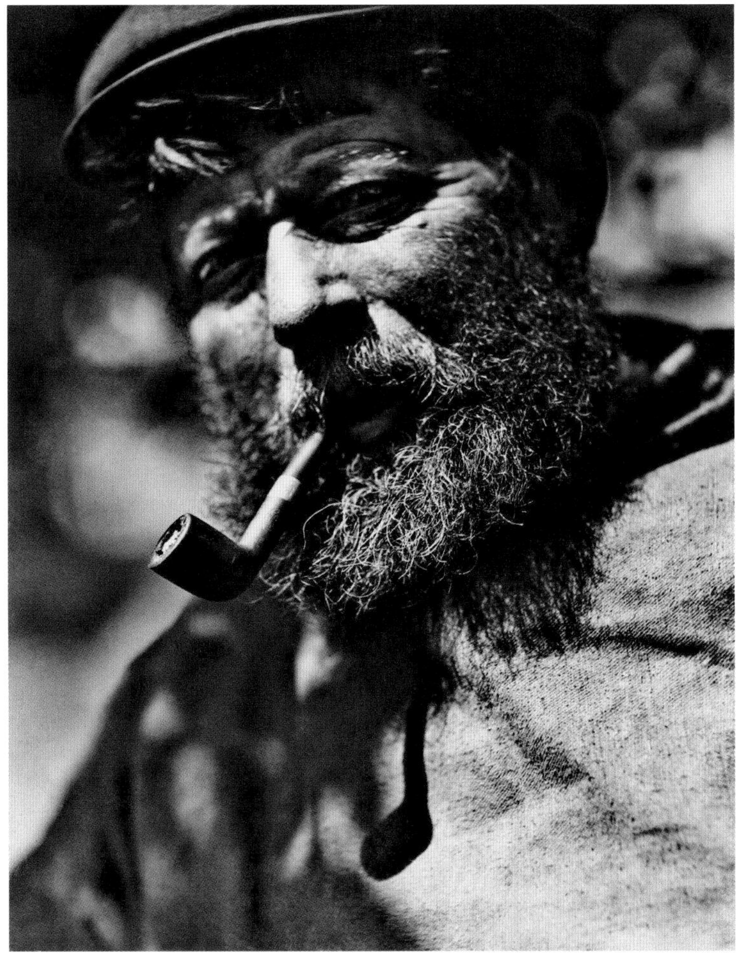

Figure 4. E. O. Hoppé, *Out of Work, New York Type,* c. 1919

Hoppé's "Down and Out" portraits rival photographs Paul Strand also made of poor people on the streets of New York in the mid 1910s. In *Sandwich Man, New York* [Figure 3], Strand photographed an old man reduced to carrying advertisements for a living. The figure is seen from the perspective of a pedestrian on a city street; the radical asymmetry of the composition suggests a scene glimpsed out of the corner of an eye. Fully half of the image is given over to the board itself, the man's face confined to the upper left quarter of the frame. In Strand's conception the subject is a prisoner of his surroundings, a dehumanized spirit carrying an emblem of his condition. The effect is reinforced by the deep shadow cast by his cap, which partly obscures his eyes. Hoppé's approach to a strikingly similar subject [Figure 4] is decidedly different. In *Out of Work, New York Type,* the photographer brings the viewer in close to the subject's face from slightly below, a privileged point of view one would not ordinarily experience in passing. The man is distinct and individual, his partially squinting eyes filled with pathos. The background is intentionally obscure. An out-of-focus swirl of dark and white masses conjures the idea of smoke, while the shadow of his pipe falls perfectly centered across his chest. The mood of Hoppé's portrait is pensive and introspective. Whereas Strand's photograph reads like a film still extracted from a motion picture,

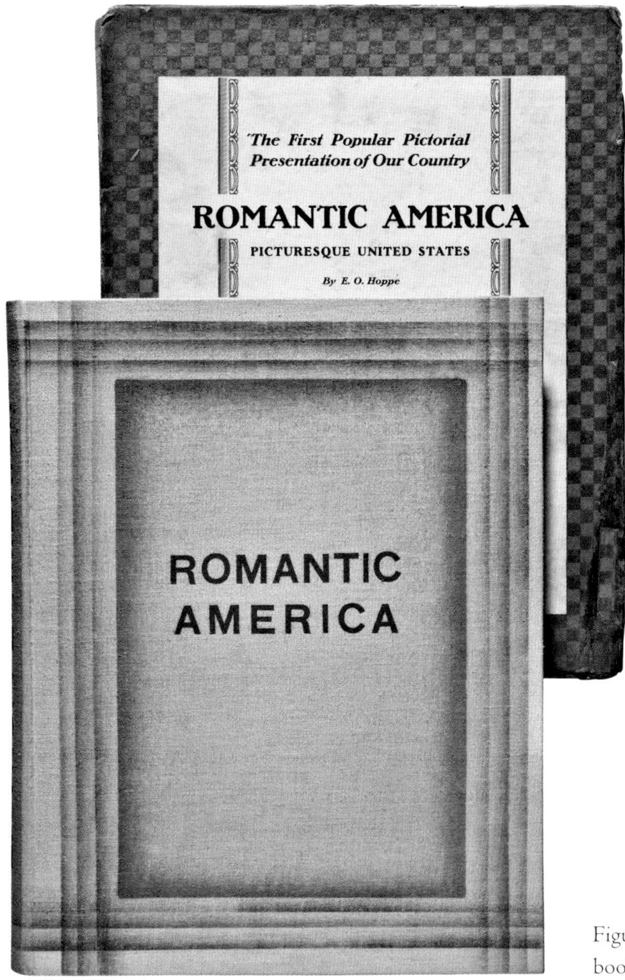

Figure 5. E. O. Hoppé's book *Romantic America,* 1927

Hoppé's interpretation is self-contained. The viewer is encouraged to empathize with the subject as a person.

With his travels around the Lower East Side, Hoppé broadened his explorations of the people and places of New York. His views taken from the interior of the Brooklyn Bridge [pages 48, 49, and 51] are studies in abstraction, the patterning of suspension cables creating playful vortices of space. Hoppé mistakenly claimed to have been the first artist to depict the city of New York as seen from the deck of the bridge, though it is now recognized that the Futurist painter Joseph Stella (1877–1946) preceded him. In the late 1920s, Walker Evans followed a path similar to Hoppé, making wonderfully evocative photographs of the span. Evans almost certainly knew of Hoppé's treatment through his popular book *Romantic America,* published in 1927. Hoppé's appreciation for the bridge was not limited to its design elements, however. He made penetrating photographs looking back at the bridge through city streets, including lonely figures dwarfed by its imposing presence [page 50].

The idea for the book *Romantic America* [Figure 5] was proposed to Hoppé in 1921 by the imprint Orbis Terrarum, which published picture books on popular topics. Travel books were their specialty, and Hoppé was initially retained to photograph in the Caribbean, including Cuba and the British colonies of Jamaica, the Cayman Islands, and British Honduras. He completed that assignment in 1919 and was subsequently invited to produce a volume devoted to the United States. Considering his early explorations in New York, the opportunity was irresistible, and he accepted the commission. The book became the organizing principle of his American photographs and his main undertaking from 1921 to 1926. Touring far beyond the confines of New York, his photographs were taken with the needs of *Romantic America* in mind. Hoppé explained the theme of the book eloquently:

> The march of progress whereby its cities have been built up from virgin unreclaimed land to reach their maturity before the eyes of a single generation is in itself an epic theme impregnated with the spirit of romance; but much further away in anteriority than these few crowded years lies the spirit of America. To the popular idea [...] America has no past, no antiquities, nothing but that which is utterly new; exemplified by a handful of assertive cities such as Chicago or Detroit, or, further towards the Pacific coast, Seattle. Most Europeans who ponder the subject at all, think of America in terms of the project-system: New York City for example is synonymous with skyscrapers, Chicago and stockyards are indelibly associated, Texas and cowboys are condemned to perpetual affinity, and Salt Lake City means venerable bearded men with a multiplicity of wives. Americans themselves are somewhat to be blamed for this misinterpretation of their country's characteristics; unwittingly or with intent they have been at pains to conceal the beauty in infinite variety in which America abounds; they have kept back in the shadow of half-remembered things unparalleled possessions of age-old wonders such as no country on the globe can offer, set out in a land that is a world within a world.[10]

Hoppé applauded the United States as a nation of unbridled industry, of can-do determination free from the burdens of history. As his audience would have expected, many of the 304 plates in *Romantic America* convey the splendor of the country, its picturesque buildings, majestic landscapes, and conspicuous wealth. But he was not uncritical. In Hoppé's America, cracks occasionally appear in the veneer of achievement, and there is an abiding tension between growth and fulfillment. Worrying signs are seen in people and places that progress has left behind.

The title *Romantic America* is partially ironic. Romance implies passion, and Hoppé found this quality in abundance during his travels. He also knew, however, that romance can be misguided, and that the rush for big, new, and modern things does not leave time for circumspection. Hoppé's America is romantic in the same sense that a Chekhov play is comedic. Mistakes are made but the country moves relentlessly forward, sometimes correcting problems with the same dynamism that created them in the first place, and just as often letting them fester. It is a country bound by optimism but riven with paradox. Seen this way, the word "romance" suggests something idealized. The gritty, utilitarian, and occasionally dysfunctional country depicted in Hoppé's photographs is at times manifestly glossed and prettified.

If anyone should have recognized the trappings of false beauty, it was E. O. Hoppé. Much to his consternation, he was considered a leading expert on aesthetics, and his journeys around the United States in the mid-1920s were heralded in the press as the coming of the "connoisseur of pulchritude." This arose partly from his general reputation as an effective portraitist, but mainly it resulted from the publication in 1922 of his *Book of Fair Women.*

The idea behind *Fair Women* was simple. It was a compendium of photographs of women Hoppé considered beautiful, representing various nationalities and races from around the world. Thirty-two women appeared in the book, reproduced in exquisitely printed, tipped-in photogravures. He was intentionally wide-ranging in his selections, including African, Asian, Arab, Pacific Island, Caribbean, European, and North and South American examples. Though the book was clearly intended to appeal to the ogling eyes of male readers, the scheme was nevertheless inventive. In contrast to many nineteenth-century writers who dismissed women of non-Western races as intrinsically unattractive, Hoppé presented a veritable smorgasbord of female loveliness, enabling readers to fantasize about women of different cultures. The idea that one can appreciate beauty in representatives of other races was radical. In any case, the book was provocative and Hoppé received enormous attention for the venture—at times too much.

Hoppé blamed William Randolph Hearst personally for the unwelcome attention he received, but in fairness it *was* a good story. Wherever Hoppé went, newspapers heralded his arrival with bold headlines. Hoppé seldom shied from publicity but he found that journalists wanted to talk of little other than his theories about what distinguished beautiful women. He was interviewed repeatedly on the subject and pressed into judging countless beauty pageants, both in person and using photographs sent to him. Sometimes he was spontaneously forced on stage at the end of a show to identify the most beautiful woman in the audience. He even refused an offer to perform at a Manhattan club, where he was supposed to choose the three most attractive female customers nightly. It was too much of a good thing and, after a while, it seemed to him that his opinions were being trivialized.

To Hoppé's credit, he managed to steer the subject of beauty back to a discussion of American character. In 1927, the same year *Romantic America* appeared, he published the unwittingly Freudian article "Skyscrapers and Women: The Psychology of American Beauty," in the magazine *Eye.*[11] Subtitled, "Environment, Intellect, and Evolution," it went to the heart of his thinking about American character. Women's suffrage had been legalized in the United States with the passage of the Nineteenth Amendment in 1920. In his article Hoppé signaled his sympathy with the movement, arguing that true beauty could be attained only when women asserted their independence and intelligence. "The quickened intellect of American woman chafed at the limitations of conventional usage; this, in its turn, led to revolt and her practical determination began to express itself outside the domestic and social sphere," he wrote. "Keen," "critical," "strong," and "brilliant," the American woman "soon found vent in a feverish thirst for culture [and] unlimited knowledge," he explained. She loses her standing only "if she merely belongs to the ineffectual, idle class," he went on.[12] This was the same position he maintained with Americans of both sexes. Hoppé admired the United States as a crucible of creative energy, a place where the successful were not allowed to slack.

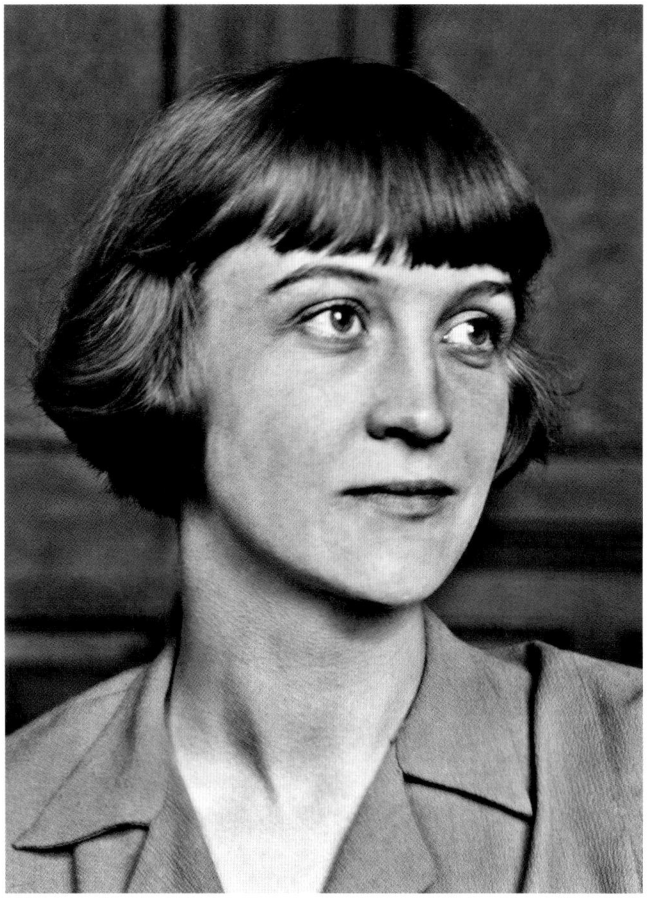

Figure 6. E. O. Hoppé, *Martha Ostenso,* 1927

Hoppé declared ten of his portraits to embody typical American beauty, including an oft-reproduced picture of the novelist Martha Ostenso (1900–63) [Figure 6]. Never mind that she was born in Norway and wrote her best-known novel *Wild Geese* in Winnipeg; to Hoppé she embodied "all the essentials of American Beauty." "What I want to emphasize," he pointed out, "is the quality of striving, or doing, that is written on the American face."[13] For a German publication he expanded on the subject with a portrait of an African-American woman from Harlem [Figure 7], captioned "strongly soulful type, not infrequently found in black churches."[14] She, too, had appeared in the *Book of Fair Women.* Racial discrimination was a reality Hoppé found repugnant in American society, and the pictures in *Romantic America* occasionally address the theme. In his autobiography Hoppé railed against the treatment afforded African-Americans in his presence. For example, when the eminent Harlem Renaissance thinker Hubert Henry Harrison (1883–1927) was forced to use the service elevator to visit his apartment, Hoppé reacted with disgust.[15]

Romantic America, however, was not constrained to a single style or subject. The only concession to uniformity lay in the choice of reproduction. The book was printed in gravure, using cool, silvery inks, imparting a softened, slightly nostalgic look to each image. It is questionable whether this technique was the best choice for the publication, as it tended to mask the muscular, graphic quality of the originals. Though his pictures were bold and modern, the reproduction technique

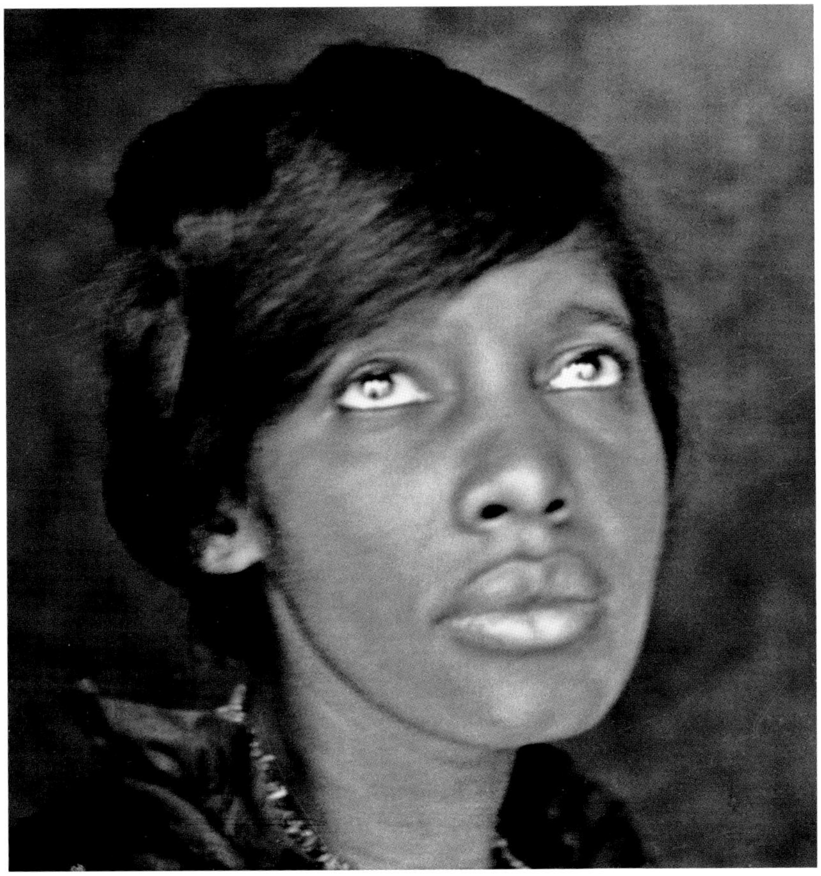

Figure 7. E. O. Hoppé, *African American woman from Harlem, New York*, 1921

he used was old-fashioned and pictorial. Hoppé was one of the first wave of photographers to embrace gelatin-silver bromide paper as an expressive tool, and his original prints make effective use of this new material. Yet, the reproductions in *Romantic America* generally lack the directness of his original photographic prints.

Above all, the book marked a dramatic departure from the studio portraiture for which Hoppé was best known. Portraits were largely omitted from the book, and those people who did appear register as small, faceless figures. Often they are presented in silhouette or shown only from the back. Hoppé marveled at American feats of engineering, and bridges, railways, factories, skyscrapers, and dams make frequent appearances. The belittling relationship of humans to these impersonal structures, whether in California or in New Jersey, New Orleans, or Chicago, is a powerful and enduring theme of the work.

ART OF AN EXPATRIATE

Born in Munich in 1878, Hoppé grew up in Vienna, returning to Munich and continuing to Paris to finish his education. His family was of French Huguenot extraction, which may account for the affectation of the acute "e" at the end of his name, which he used throughout his life. He was said to speak with a "cultured," Austrian accent, which enabled him to enchant even the most aristocratic sitters.[16] Details of his art training are scant but he did receive limited formal instruction and, occasionally, ventured into painting, printmaking, and design as an adult.[17] As a young man Hoppé yearned to be an artist. His sympathetic mother arranged for him to take drawing lessons from the eminent Munich watercolorist Hans von Bartels (1856–1913), which he did for about a year.[18] Von Bartels, in turn, introduced Hoppé to the Bavarian painter Franz von Lenbach (1836–1904), widely recognized as one of the great painters of celebrity portraits in the nineteenth century. His father, a successful banker, opposed his pursuit of a career in art and steered him into the finance sector. This evidently remained a touchy subject; although in the draft of his autobiography, preserved in the Hoppé Archive, Hoppé described himself as having had "a certain facility with the pencil" and "enthusiastically deciding to make painting my career," he also described his father's opposition to his wishes, recounting that he "pleaded in vain" with him to allow him to pursue his interests.[19] In the published version of his autobiography, called *Hundred Thousand Exposures* (1945), these passages were dropped, perhaps in deference to his father's memory.

In 1897, after two years of compulsory service in the German army, Hoppé began working in banking more or less constantly for the next ten years, first in Munich and Berlin. Around 1900 Hoppé's parents decided to send him to Shanghai to work for two years with his uncle Gaspard, who ran an export firm. Some historians describe him as having planned to join the Shanghai Banking Corporation, although this cannot be confirmed.[20] In any case, he never made it as far as China. Breaking his journey in London, Hoppé fell in love with Marion Bliersbach, the sister of a German financier who lived in the city. They married, and from then on England became his permanent home. He continued to make his living working for German banks; various reports have him working at both Deutsche Bank and Lombard in London.

According to Hoppé, in 1903, at age twenty-five, he met the British photographer John Cimon Warburg (1867–1931), who made a strong impression. Warburg, Hoppé would later explain, demonstrated what a "pliable instrument the camera can be in discerning hands."[21] Like Hoppé, Warburg dabbled in painting. He also excelled in the use of autochrome plates, the first fully automatic color process, and made photographs with a decidedly Japoniste flavor.[22] Warburg undoubtedly influenced the younger Hoppé, and his technique of juxtaposing a foregrounded object with a distant background became a signature of Hoppé's art, as did the flattening of space Warburg apparently absorbed from Japanese ukiyo-e prints.

Inspired by Warburg, Hoppé purchased his first professional camera, a Goerz-Anschutz model that he later described as "a solid mahogany affair, formidable as a Howitzer."[23] Soon he joined the Royal Photographic Society, and for the next four years Hoppé exhibited regularly in salons and amateur exhibitions, although photography remained strictly a hobby. He may or may not have perceived this as a sacrifice. In Germany amateur photography was held up as an ideal. The influential scholar Alfred Lichtwark, for example, argued that amateurs were superior to commercial practitioners because they worked only for the love of their art and not as slaves to external, market pressures.[24] The tension between fine art and commercial photography preoccupied Hoppé throughout his career.

Gradually, Hoppé's success in amateur exhibitions convinced him he could turn his photography into a viable business. This idea was cemented after he won a £100 first prize in a contest sponsored by the *Daily Mail* in 1907. It was such a large sum that, combined with other sales and winnings, his income from photography suddenly equaled his banker's salary. Emboldened, but nevertheless cautious, he drew up an elaborate ledger detailing his financial picture and dispatched his wife to Germany to meet with his father and explain his desire to leave banking and set up a photographic studio. His father relented and Hoppé opened a studio in collaboration with E. F. Griffin in Baron's Court later that year. Hoppé's business grew rapidly, and in 1911 he moved to new premises in Baker Street. Finally, in 1913 he moved into the former house and studio of the Pre-Raphaelite painter John Everett Millais (1829–96). This illustrious address became a calling card of sorts, attracting the most fashionable sitters in London as well as many international visitors.

Hoppé's reputation blossomed early in his photographic career. In 1909 he cofounded the London Salon of Photography, that same year joining Sir Benjamin Stone (1838–1914) to represent Great Britain at the International Exhibition of Photography at Dresden. Stone, who specialized in documentary photographs of traditional customs and festivals in British villages, was highly regarded himself, having won the grand prize in photography at the Saint Louis World's Fair of 1904, among other honors.[25] In 1910 Hoppé was given his first one-man show at the Royal Photographic Society. By 1913 he was showing at the prestigious Goupil Gallery in London. In 1916 he became a contributor to the new magazine *Vogue*. Business boomed.

Hoppé's cosmopolitan upbringing had a strong bearing on his success as a photographer. He adapted quickly to people of other cultures and empathized with writers, performers, politicians, and businessmen for whom travel was a way of life. His father's enduring skepticism about art combined with his education in banking ensured his attention to profitability. Hoppé never lost sight of financial considerations, and he was highly effective in promoting his work. He was also extraordinarily industrious, emerging rapidly not just as one of London's most talented photographers but also as one of the most prolific. Hoppé admired the industriousness of the Americans because he shared their entrepreneurial fire. Moreover, the perseverance, efficiency, and commercial common sense that propelled his London studio ensured the success of his American work.

Hoppé's life history had another, less obvious effect on his photography. Although he admired the United States enormously and mixed freely with her people, he was always something of an outsider in the country. To him America was ultimately a foreign land, and he used his camera as a tool to investigate its strangeness. Through his travels he familiarized himself with the country, and the process of discovery this entailed is evident in his photographs. Like a physician giving a medical exam, his first instinct was to study the patient's anatomy, examining the organs that make it tick and identifying its maladies. Photography was his scalpel. Hoppé's photographs of America are clearly empathetic, but few are straightforwardly admiring. He remained impartial and detached. Growing up in four different cultures enabled him to approach a new country with near sociological objectivity, and his range of international experience ensured he was not easily impressed. He saw the country for what it was: ingenious, autonomous, and feisty but occasionally crude, raw, and provincial.

The role of the United States in the First World War undoubtedly shaped his perception. Hoppé's family had connections on both sides. His adolescence had been spent in the Axis powers

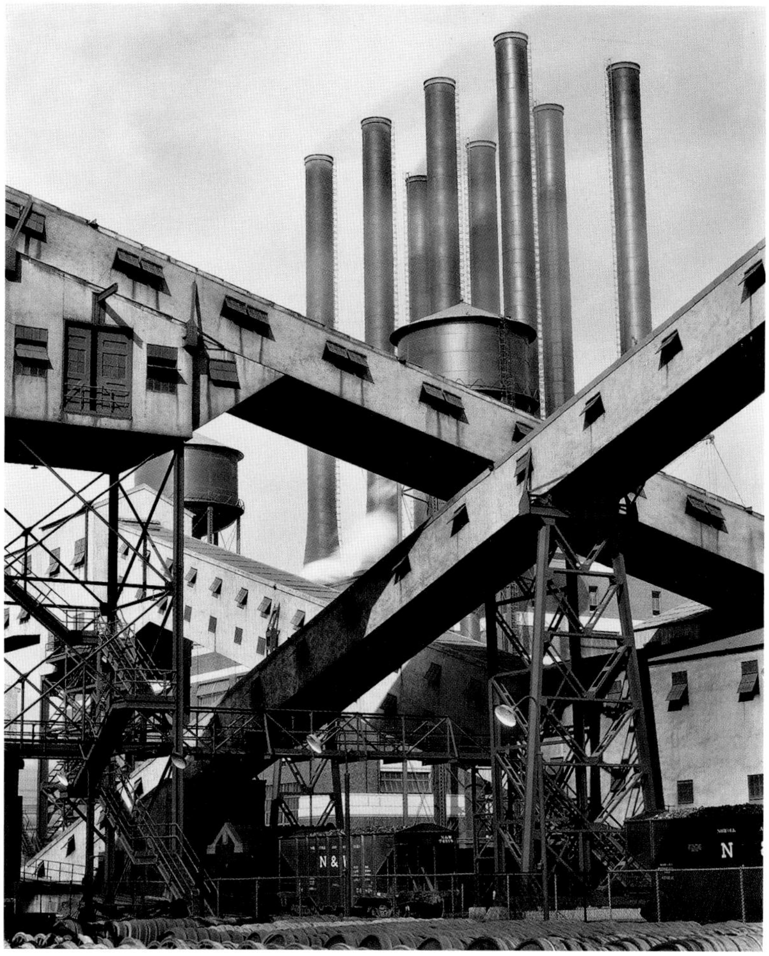

Figure 8. Charles Sheeler, *Criss-Crossed Conveyors, Ford Plant*, 1927

of Germany and Austria-Hungary, and his family continued to live in central Europe. But his adult life belonged to Allied Britain, and his ancestry was French. Politically he kept a low profile but he might well have felt America's economic might to be vaguely threatening. There is an element of apprehension in Hoppé's photographs, reflecting the menace he must have perceived in unbridled power. Hoppé made many photographs of factories in New York, Michigan, and Pennsylvania but conspicuously avoided depictions of military installations and equipment, though these became dominant themes in travels he made in Germany in the 1930s. In place of air force installations he showed seaplanes, and instead of gun emplacements he showed Model T Fords.

Nowhere is Hoppé's ambivalence toward American industry more evident than in the series he made at Detroit's Ford motor works in 1926. Hoppé visited one year before the artist Charles Sheeler (1883–1965), whose photographs and paintings of the site have become icons of American modernism. In Sheeler's *Criss-Crossed Conveyors*, [Figure 8], smokestacks stand proud and tall, seemingly indomitable in the background, as conveyors slice diagonally across the frame in confident gestures. Sheeler's Ford factory is an expression of design, a harmonic assembly of elements arranged with rationality and purpose. Hoppé shows the same conveyors much as a shift supervisor might see them: a cascade of forms in chaotic rhythm, punctuated by the steel beams of the vertical staircase

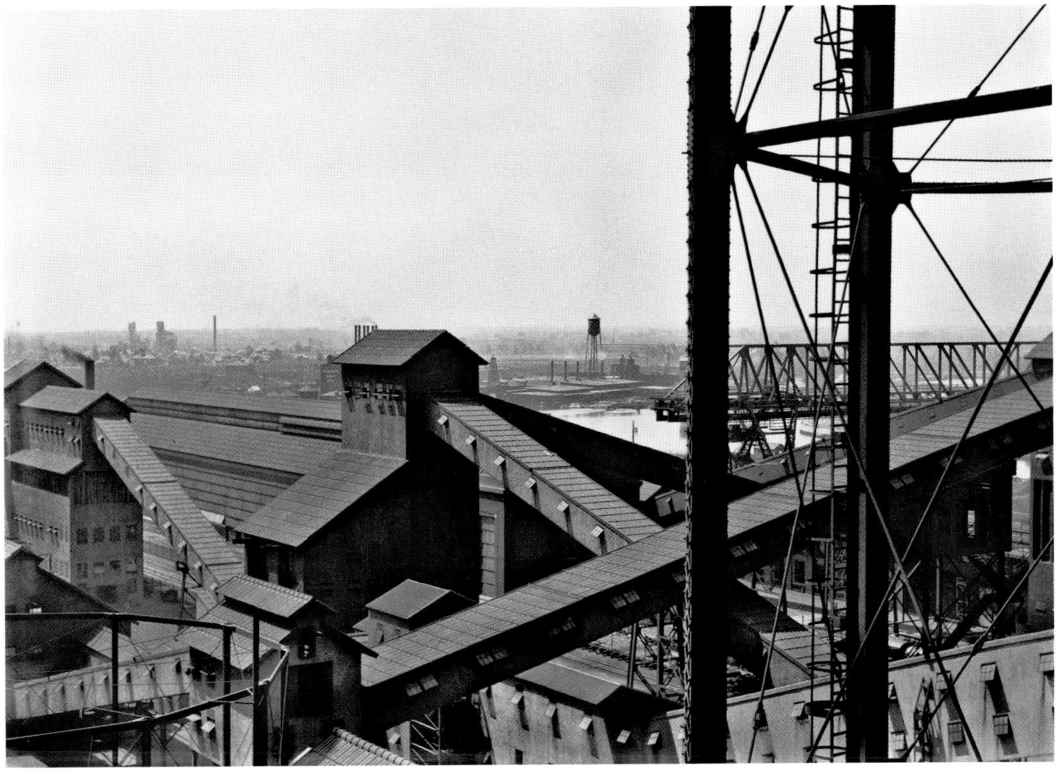

Figure 9. E. O. Hoppé, *Crossed Conveyers, Ford Factory, Detroit, Michigan,* 1926

in the right foreground and the partial ring of a circular tank in the lower left [Figure 9]. Unlike Sheeler he also gives the scene context, admitting the distant landscape on the horizon, giving the viewer a sense of the flatness of the land and the presence of other factories in the distance.

The graphic boldness of Sheeler's interpretation is accentuated by the perspectival correctness of the scene, as he used the adjustments on his camera to ensure the smokestacks appear straight and parallel, though to the naked eye they would have seemed to converge in the distance. By comparison, Hoppé's photograph of the same eight smokestacks [page 111] allows conventional optics to take over. His towers seem to lean toward the middle of the composition, creating a visual crescendo at top center. They are gently unsettling to the eye, their asymmetry accentuated by the single smokestack at right funneling black smoke in contrast to the white smoke rising from the others. Sheeler was associated with a movement that came to be known as Precisionism. Precisionists such as Sheeler and Charles Demuth (1883–1935) welcomed industrial architecture as ushering in a new age of progress. The visual similarities between Hoppé's photographs and Precisionist paintings of the period are striking; Hoppé's *The Shredded Wheat Company's Grain Elevator at Niagara Falls, New York,* 1926, [page 119] looks almost like a pastiche of Sheeler's friend Charles Demuth's (1883–1935) celebrated painting *My Egypt,* 1927 [Museum of Modern Art, New York], though it was made a year

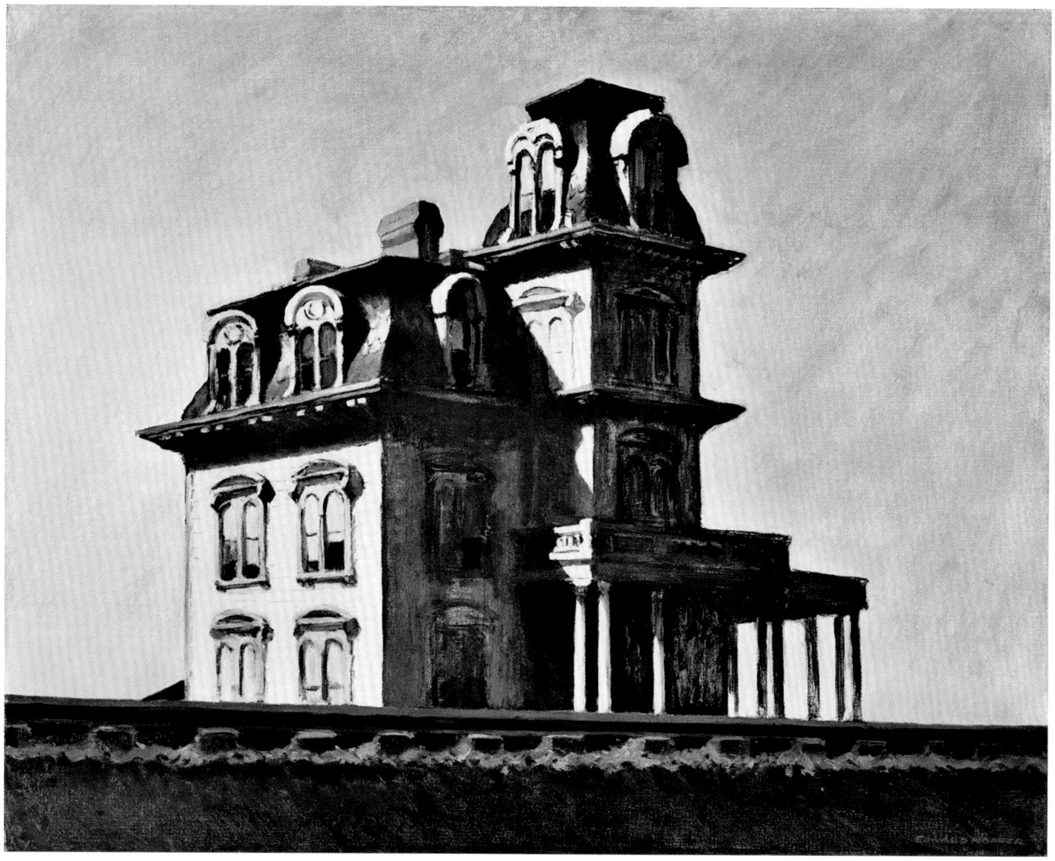

Figure 10. Edward Hopper, *House by the Railroad,* 1925 (original in color)

earlier. Hoppé, however, was no cheerleader for the machine aesthetic, though he could make graphic arrangements when it pleased him. [page 106], for example, contains a riot of patterns and converging lines. *Coal Loading, Ford Factory, Detroit, Michigan* [page 107], by contrast, presents a more enigmatic interpretation of the factory. Gorgeous, billowing clouds of steam jet from the side of a building while a worker stands barely noticeable underneath. He presents his back to the viewer, small and alone, the nature of his work invisible. Hoppé shows the figure alien and disconnected from the powerful forces at work nearby. He accepted the impressiveness of the space but questioned its human impact. In this image, the ambiguity of progress asserts itself.

In Hoppé's America, humans are often dwarfed by their collective accomplishments. Isolation and anonymity are strong undercurrents of the work. Hoppé was amazed at the speed with which the country's architectural jewels had been erected, but he recognized the costs of unbridled growth. In *Signal Hill, Los Angeles,* 1926 [page 143], he photographed a development of similar-looking tract houses sprawling over a rise in the land. On the ridge behind them, a forest of oil derricks clutters the horizon. People are absent from the scene except for a solitary figure standing at the front door of the single house pointing toward the viewer. It is the only evidence of social interaction in the scene. The figure gives the picture scale, but it also serves as a warning of the potential pitfalls of suburban living. The individual is supremely isolated, the only evidence of human presence in an otherwise completely artificial environment.

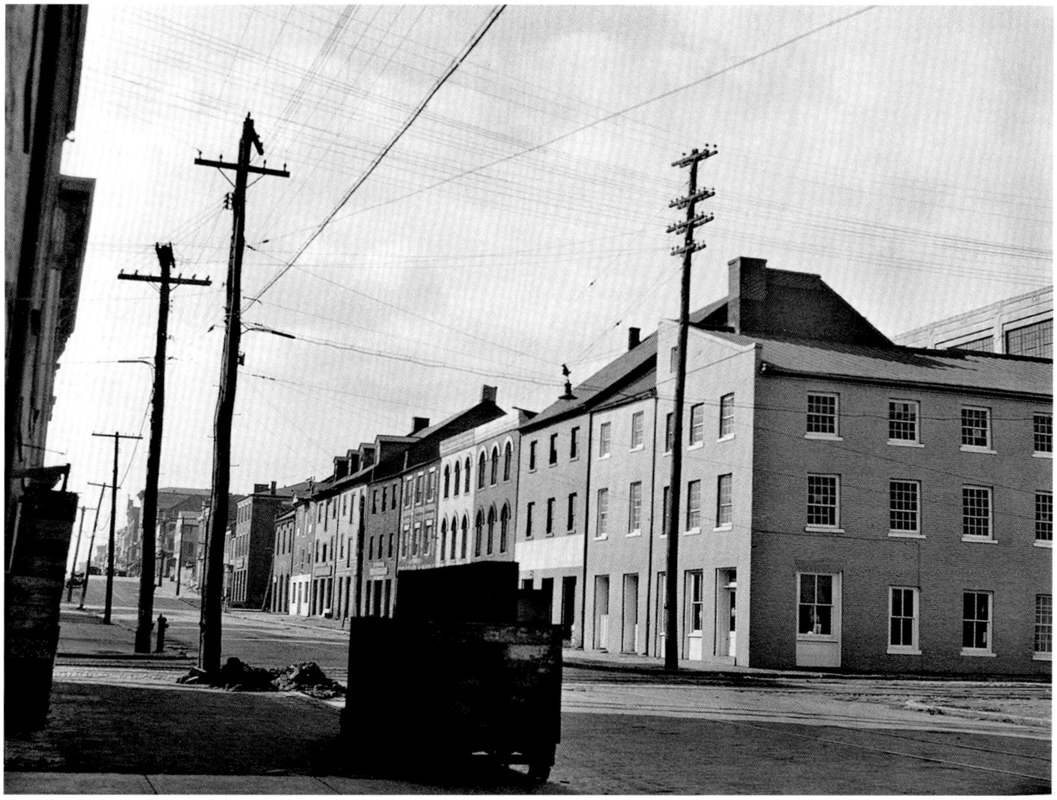

Figure 11. E. O. Hoppé, *Alexandria, Virginia,* 1926

Farther down the road Hoppé photographed the derricks themselves, their forms spreading like bacteria in a petri dish [page 142]. It is a bold graphic composition conveying the commercial exploitation of the area. In Hoppé's conception, the natural areas of the Los Angeles basin have been taken over by industry. Homes and derricks echo each other's presence—the featureless swarm of drilling platforms gives the houses behind them a similar, uniform presence. Hoppé's American photographs contain many examples of this sort of furtive critique. Figures on the beach congregate as groups rather than individuals. On Venice beach [page 151], they gather in blissful ignorance of the oil storage tank behind them, while one man, clad in a suit, tie, and riding cap, stands apart in the right foreground, looking out to sea. A figure stands at the base of a dam in New York [page 77] as though single-handedly holding back the waters behind him. In *Superior City, Arizona,* 1926, mining houses are scattered across a hillside in numbing conformity [page 135]. Even a dizzying array of mailboxes on a street corner [page 130] reinforces the theme. America was known as a land of freedom and independence. How ironic, Hoppé must have thought, that Americans should use their liberty to associate in featureless groups.

Hoppé viewed the United States as a kind of machine within which each area has a clearly defined role. In his edits for *Romantic America,* he was occasionally guilty of perpetuating stereotypes. Each region became a cog in a wheel: New York and Philadelphia were trade centers and Boston a center of learning. The Pacific Northwest was a lumber capital, the Midwest a hub of agriculture

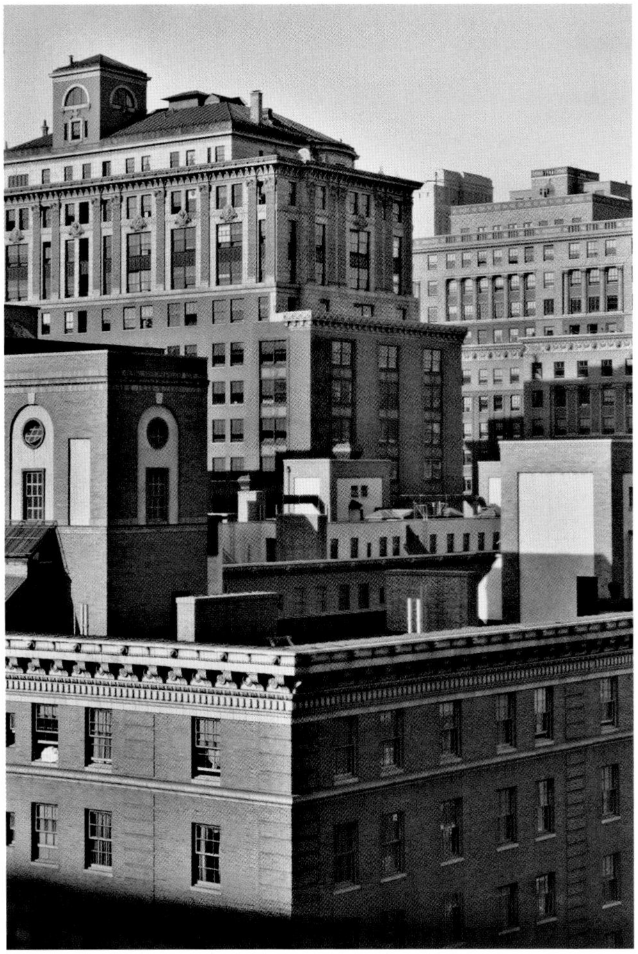

Figure 12. E. O. Hoppé, *New York City Rooftops from the Shelton Hotel,* 1925

and mining. Florida existed for entertainment. Though Hoppé accepted these generalizations, he also drew connections between them where he could. Cars, for example, appear in every region, whether on a beach, in an elevated parking garage, on a busy shopping street, or parked in front of a tidy suburban home. Hoppé's picture of junked cars on the back of a Hollywood film lot [page 145] is especially effective; their hollow abandoned shells appear strewn in a field behind the wooden buttresses that support the facade of a film set.

The occasional melancholy of Hoppé's photographs is reminiscent of the prints and paintings of Edward Hopper (1882–1967), whose career was beginning to gather steam in the 1920s. Hopper was a protégé of the Ashcan school painter Robert Henri (1865–1929), whom Hoppé knew and photographed; his portrait of Henri was one of the exhibits in Hoppé's Wanamaker exhibition of 1921. Both Hopper and Hoppé vested their pictures with an emotional charge; often it is the absence of people that gives their pictures meaning. The only evidence of human occupation in Hopper's *House by the Railroad,* 1925 [Figure 10], for example, is the partially drawn window blinds on the left side of the house. The railroad track in the foreground, passing ridiculously close to the front door, adds piquancy. As in Hoppé's photographs, the industrial cohabits with the residential. Hopper's elegiac air is occasionally matched in Hoppé's photographs. In *Alexandria, Virginia,*

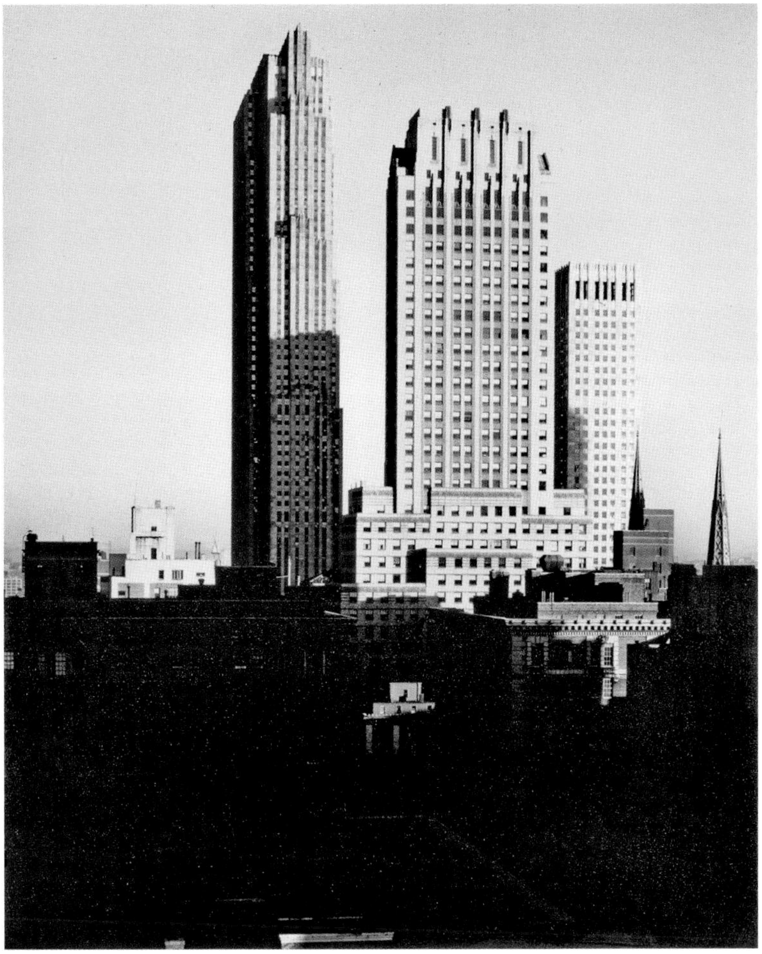

Figure 13. Alfred Stieglitz, *From the Shelton, West,* 1935

1926 [Figure 11], the emptiness of the scene gives it weight. Rows of desolate apartment buildings butt up against the curb; no pedestrians or vehicles pass in the street below. The only indication of activity is the telegraph wires strung between the buildings and a dumpster Hoppé placed squarely in the foreground. Like Hopper's railroad tracks, the composition features context, speaking to actions felt but not seen.

Like Hopper, Hoppé understood the feeling of estrangement life in modern America could cause. Hopper, in particular, repeatedly explored the theme in his depictions of hotel interiors, as in his often-reproduced *Hotel Room,* 1931 [Museo Thyssen-Bornemisza, Madrid]. Hotel residents are almost inherently disconnected from their environment; Hopper found pathos in the experience of staying in impersonal places far from home. The twentieth-century economy required its share of traveling salesmen, buyers, and contractors. As an itinerant photographer, Hoppé would have appreciated the personal toll the demands of travel could have. In his *New York City Rooftops from the Shelton Hotel,* 1925 [Figure 12], Hoppé articulated this motif. At the time of its completion in 1924, the Shelton was the tallest skyscraper in New York: an emblem of progress in a booming city, and the most conspicuous building in the New York City skyline prior to the building of the Empire State Building in 1931. It was built as a 'bachelor' hotel, mainly catering to single male residents. Shooting from a hotel window, Hoppé disregarded the building's majestic profile, instead showing the world as it might look to one of its many residents. The rectangular forms of neighboring buildings recede accordion-like into the distance, light cascading across their facades. Long shadows contribute to the moody atmosphere, at the same time conjuring the view a resident might have in the morning or evening, the hours he is most likely to be at home. It is a completely artificial environment, with little evidence of human occupation except for a few partially opened windows. As with many of Hoppé's photographs, it is a picture about progress tinged with sadness.

At the time of Hoppé's *New York City Rooftops from the Shelton Hotel,* the idea to photograph from a hotel window was almost without precedent. At the very least, titling a picture as a view from a hotel was innovative. In an extraordinary convergence, Alfred Stieglitz and Georgia O'Keeffe (1887–1986) moved into the Shelton in 1925, the same year Hoppé made his picture. Stieglitz, at least, was well-known to Hoppé, and it is tantalizing to consider whether Hoppé would have made his picture during or as a result of a visit to Stieglitz and O'Keeffe's new apartment, or indeed, from one of their windows on the thirtieth floor. Shortly after Hoppé made his view, both O'Keeffe and Stieglitz began to make pictures of New York as seen from the Shelton. Stieglitz began photographing from his windows in 1927, continuing to explore the changing cityscape below him into the 1930s. The best of Stieglitz's photographs, such as his *From the Shelton, West,* 1935 [Figure 13], share Hoppé's sympathetic gaze. The totemic modernism of the buildings, the melancholy raking shadows playing across the scene, and the self-contained artificial environment all suggest a parallel appreciation for poignant architectural themes.

Though Hoppé admired the American spirit of enterprise, he toured the country as a foreigner would. Living from a suitcase for months on end, speaking with an Austrian lilt and dressing in bespoke suits, he never completely fit in. He was also an urbanite, most at ease photographing industrial scenes and city canyons and not so sure-footed in nature. This became especially noticeable when he arrived in the Southwest. He struggled to make visual sense of the desert, which had a quality of light and proportion utterly unfamiliar to him. The contact sheets in the Hoppé Archive show him casting about for ideas; he spent more time trying to photograph Arizona than any other place. Hoppé enjoyed the window within a window effect, the visual counterpunch of having one prominent item in the foreground and another behind. This was not so easy to accomplish surrounded by empty vistas. Those of his Southwest pictures that succeed best convey his feelings of awe and disorientation.

HOPPÉ'S MODERNISM

Romantic America was designed to provide orientation; it is a visual atlas meant to help readers become familiar with the people and places of the United States. But it is also a travelogue made by an individual photographer touring the country in a specific period of time. Hoppé was learning about the country as he traveled, and this element of discovery is visible in his photographs. He did not use the camera merely to make static records but to transmit the experience of being in a place. He often photographed on the street, approaching situations as a pedestrian would. He usually set up his camera to match the point of view of an ordinary person. Such visual conceits help give his pictures intimacy. Nevertheless, Hoppé consistently structured his pictures in dramatic and surprising ways, allowing them to express the overwhelming sensory experience of engaging a new situation. Hoppé's American photographs are distinguished by this tension—between wanting to orient the viewer while simultaneously expressing the disorientation the photographer himself sometimes felt. This was a precocious idea in the 1920s and one of several modernist tendencies in Hoppé's work.

At the turn of the twentieth century, photography was dominated by a movement known as Pictorialism. Sometimes called the Aesthetic Movement in photography or Photographic Impressionism, Pictorialism was a push to create photographs that looked like prints, drawings, and paintings. Though the movement began in Europe it quickly spread around the globe.[26] To achieve their aims of making "painterly" photographs, Pictorialists rejected store-bought photographic papers such as albumen, collodion, and gelatin silver, opting instead for a variety of handmade processes. One popular technique involved mixing pigments into a light-sensitive oil or gum solution; the result could then be painted on paper with a brush. Using this method, a simple black-and-white photograph could be transformed into any other color; various shades of red, sepia, blue, and brown were common. Depending on the paper chosen, the photograph could also be made on virtually any surface, from coarse stock to thin Japanese tissue. Because the artist applied the emulsion by brush, he or she could control its application, building up certain areas or leaving visible brushstrokes for effect. The exposed emulsion was fragile until it dried, so the artist could manipulate the surface further by rubbing or spraying away sections with water while it was still wet. The techniques Pictorialists used are distinctive and their photographs are easily recognized. Typically they are soft focus, colorful, and nostalgic with strong decorative qualities. Some of the most successful Pictorial photographs are easily mistaken for prints or drawings.

With the upheavals caused by the conclusion of the First World War and the flu pandemic of 1918–19, attitudes toward photography changed. Though Pictorialism had arisen from cutting-edge ideas about the plasticity of photographic media, it was increasingly out of step with the times. The public no longer demanded warm and fuzzy pictures, and as a result photographers embraced a harder-edged look. This new look is described as modernist.

Modernism was not confined to photography. All the arts—from dance to literature, from painting to filmmaking—experienced dramatic changes after the war. In each of these fields modernism took on different character, though there were common threads. Modernists returned to the basics of their media and attempted to make art true to the means that produce it. In the case of photography this meant accepting the unique qualities of photographic imagery and not trying to make photographs that looked like something else. Modernists embraced the way camera and lens organize space. The peculiarities of photographic vision became part of the modernist vocabulary: the camera's omniscient, undifferentiated gaze, its capacity to register extremes of focus (especially sharp focus) and detail, its ability to render three-dimensional space into two dimensions in linear perspective, and its ability to register motion and blur in ways the naked eye cannot. There was no unifying canon of modernism, and various factions arose practicing their own brands of modernist photography. However, modernists were generally drawn to the designs

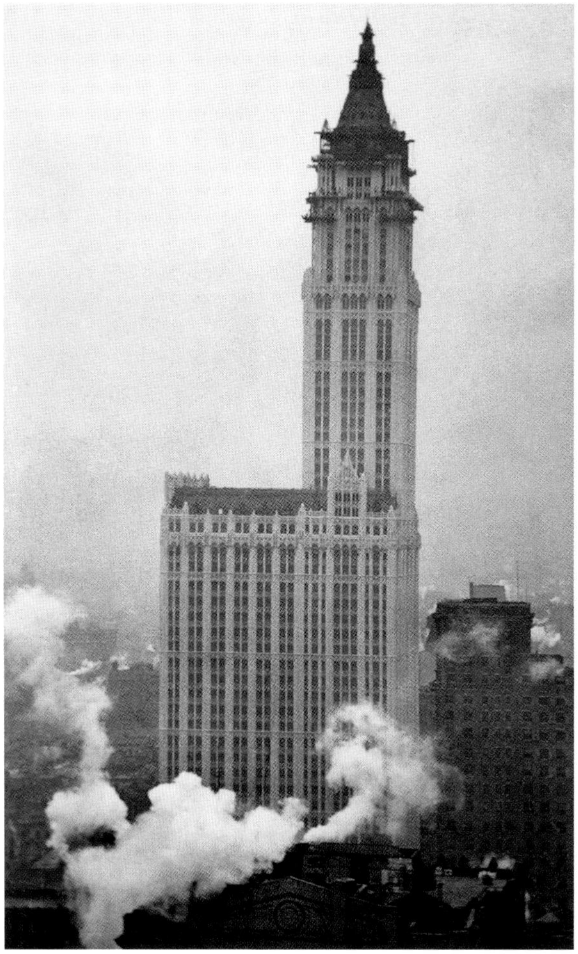

Figure 14. Alvin Langdon Coburn, *Woolworth Building, New York,* c. 1912

that emerged in their pictures. Patterns of light and dark, masses of form, and pleasing delineations of space are recurring motifs in modernist photography.

Hoppé was one of a group of photographers who successfully made the transition from Pictorialism into modernism. Many Pictorialists failed to remain relevant in the 1920s, continuing to make old-fashioned pictures or dropping out of the field. Conversely, many of the new wave of photographers distanced themselves from in Pictorial photography. To them, it represented the obsolete ideas of an earlier generation. An influential group straddled both movements, however, benefiting from the liberating atmosphere of Pictorial photography and joining young modernists in trying to construct new approaches to art. Among those who began as successful Pictorialists and became eminent modernists were Alfred Stieglitz, Edward Steichen, and Paul Strand in the United States, Pierre Dubreuil (1872–1944) in France, František Drtikol (1883–1961) in Czechoslovakia, and Alvin Langdon Coburn (1882–1966) and E. O. Hoppé in Britain. In 1920 Hoppé praised the blend of skills the new generation brought to the field: "The much chaffed 'smudgy' photograph has had the very important result of leading photography from being a mere science to a superb craft. The stupid exaggerations are melting away, and today there is an achievement in photography that is very remarkable.'"[27]

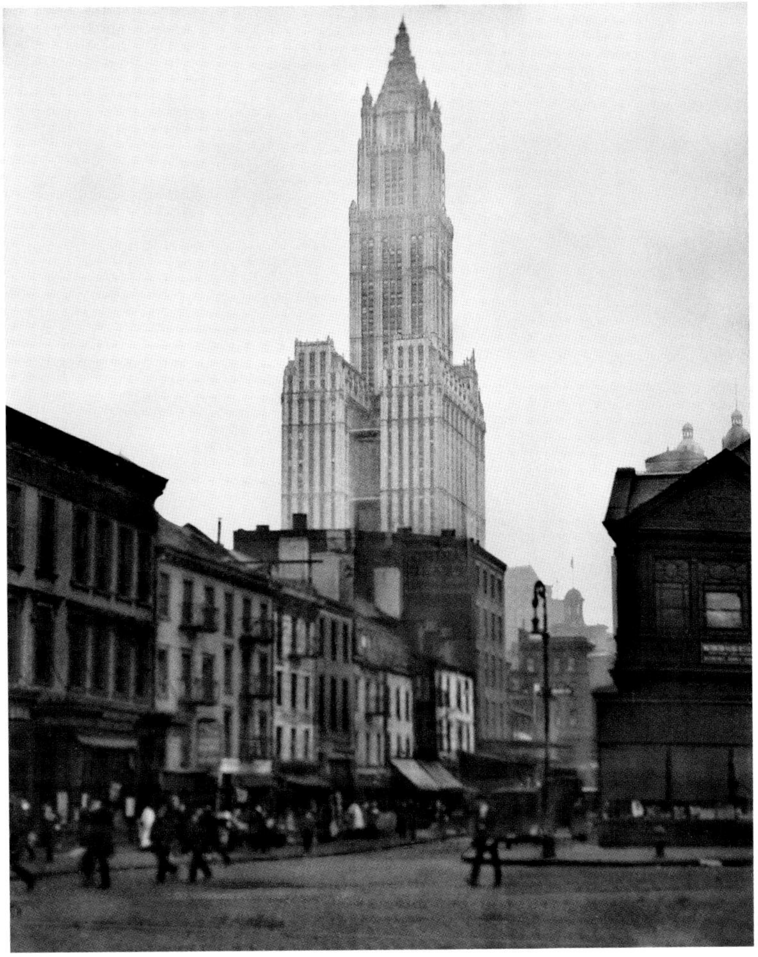

Figure 15. E. O. Hoppé, *Woolworth Building, New York City*, 1921

The art historian Mark Haworth-Booth has described Hoppé as the "missing link" in England between purist Pictorial photographers such as Frederick Evans (1853–1943) and the unabashedly modernist Bill Brandt (1904–83).[28] Like his friend Coburn (himself an American émigré), Hoppé made the transition to modernism without repudiating Pictorialism completely; his modernist works are often accented with Pictorialist sensitivity. Coburn's *Woolworth Building, New York* [Figure 14], is an excellent example of this. The depiction of the building is frank and unadorned in modernist fashion; the graphic reverse "L" shape of the building pronounces itself against a neutral sky. Regular rows of windows add to the building's visual interest, another common modern motif. Meanwhile, the ethereal puffs of smoke drifting across the bottom of the picture give it a romantic quality at odds with strict modernism.

Writing after the Second World War, Hoppé advised young photographers to search for meaning in the patterns created by architecture. "Abounding opportunities can be found," he assured, "to picture the rhythm and design of very ordinary, everyday things, which ninety-nine persons out of every hundred are probably passing every hour of every day without noticing them, because they are so familiar with them that they would consider it a sheer waste of time to give them a second glance. It is one of the chief delights of photography that it creates a spirit of adventure and sharpens the powers of observation. So many people miss the significance of little things and are thereby robbed of a fundamental key to beauty."[29] He used two photographs of staircases by his protégé Ferenc Berko (1916–2000) to illustrate his point. Berko himself embodied an interesting connection with American photography; he worked under Hoppé in the 1930s and, after the Second World War accepted an invitation from experimental photographer László Moholy-Nagy (1895–1946) to teach film at the influential Institute of Design in Chicago.[30]

Hoppé must have had Coburn's magnificent portrayal in mind when he made his own interpretation of the *Woolworth Building* in 1921 [Figure 15]. Deceptively simple in appearance, it was actually made using a complicated combination of methods. At the time this picture was made, he is known to have used a Graflex, a popular brand of press camera. Press cameras were pared-down versions of the classic studio cameras of the nineteenth century, used mainly by journalists for newspaper and magazine work. More traditional cameras are sometimes called bellows cameras. To understand how Hoppé used his press camera, it helps to know a little about the bellows version. A bellows camera is bulky, but its design is simple. It consists of two boards: a lens board at the front and a film board at the back. These boards are connected by an accordion of leather or lightproof fabric. The operator focuses the camera by moving the boards closer or farther away from each other; the lightproof accordion stretches to accommodate the move. But a bellows camera has another important feature. The boards can be tilted, raised, or swung in relation to each other to create visual effects. The most common application of this is perspectival correction. By raising the front board, for example, a photographer can take pictures of tall structures while looking upward at them from ground level, compensating for the convergence of lines that would occur in an ordinary point-and-shoot camera. This is often applied when photographing architecture. Walker Evans used this technique frequently, and his work is distinguished by the clean, parallel lines seen in his pictures of buildings. These parallel lines were created artificially by raising the camera front.

Tilting the front or back boards or swinging the boards left and right affects focus. A skilled photographer can use this principle to control areas of fuzziness in a picture—making the side, top, or bottom of a picture blurry while leaving the rest sharp. Hoppé regularly used such maneuvers for visual effect. He sometimes intentionally threw areas of the picture out of focus to add visual intensity by swinging the front board left or right. However, he was constrained by the limits of his press camera, which works slightly differently from a bellows camera. The back board of a press camera is fixed, making it lighter and easier to load and unload film. The front board still has the normal swings and tilts, although its range of motion is not as extensive as with a bellows camera. This is a trade-off: the photographer sacrifices some artistic control in exchange for convenience and portability.

These details make Hoppé's magnificent *Woolworth Building* all the more remarkable. In this picture, artificial focus was used at two ends of the composition: the bottom and top both are slightly out of focus while the center is sharp. This is all but impossible to achieve using a standard press camera with a fixed back. Most likely, Hoppé created the image by tilting the front of the camera to leave just one edge of the frame slightly unfocused. In this case, it was probably the foreground, because its relative closeness would have made it easier to control. The result would have been a negative with blur on just the bottom half of the image. To create the out-of-focus section at the top, he probably relied on an additional trick in the darkroom. Using the enlarger as a kind of improvised bellows camera, he could have tilted its lens board to throw the second section out of focus on the print. This would have resulted in the extraordinary appearance of his *Woolworth Building* picture, in which only the center third of the image is optically sharp.

Why did Hoppé go to so much trouble? One simple explanation is that it was fun, a star turn to his colleagues who understood the difficulties involved in making such a picture. But Hoppé did not make photographs merely to impress insiders. His *Woolworth Building* has an unexpected band of focus across the center because that was how he wished to show it to viewers. Hoppé's composition mimics the way one might experience the scene. Looking up at a skyscraper, activities in the foreground fall into peripheral vision. A skyscraper is too large to take in all in at once; accordingly, Hoppé directed the viewer to the center of the building, the only part of the photograph in sharp focus. He allowed the tip of the skyscraper to dissolve slightly in the distance, beyond the field of the observer's vision, or perhaps even shrouded in mist. In either case, Hoppé's *Woolworth Building* presents a radical handling of depth of field unprecedented in photographic history.[31] By photographing not just the way the building looks but the way it is seen, Hoppé conveyed the sheer size of the structure.

Because of the atmospheric quality of his studio portraits, and perhaps also as a result of the softness of the gravures he used to reproduce his pictures in books, Hoppé was sometimes labeled a "pictorial" photographer. However, as his American pictures reveal, he was actually one of the preeminent modernists of the 1920s. Hoppé accepted the word "pictorial" to describe his work, but only as he defined the term. He rejected any association with the Pictorial photography movement. In the context of his own work, Hoppé considered "pictorial photography" to mean simply the art of making photographs worthy of being displayed. In a 1955 speech before the Pictorial Group of the Royal Photographic Society, he clarified this point. Criticizing pre-1914 Pictorialism as hopelessly sentimental, he described Pictorial photographs as "depressing travesties," "gloomy," "false," and "artificial." He went on to declare his refusal "to join in the idol-worship with which a few gallant troopers continue to glorify the productions of some admittedly capable photographers of the past."[32] Reality, he went on, is the one true currency of photography. The role of the photographer is to gather visual information from the world at large. "Making pictures with the camera has nothing in common with painting," he asserted.[33] Instead, Hoppé believed, photography should be a direct, immediate reflection of experience. In one particularly striking passage, he explained:

> When observing a scene or looking at an object, the first impression is the optical one. It may only last for a moment, but may immediately and subconsciously stimulate in the artist a mental reaction which will vary in accordance with the mood he happens to be in at that instant. He takes, as it were, a mental photograph of the subject, and there comes into play an emotional element which causes him to conjure up something which is factually non-existent, but which he conceives despite the evidence

> of his eyes. His visualization is of the spirit, and his mood or emotional state will determine the manner in which the subject will be rendered. If the emotional element, which has influenced the character of the pictorial representation, has the effect of arousing in the spectator a reaction akin to that felt by the artist, the latter has created a piece of work in which the imagination has supplanted reality.[34]

For Hoppé, the camera served as a conduit, transmitting information from object to artist to viewer. The photographer's job was to aim the camera effectively and to choose the moment to depress the shutter, simultaneously controlling depth of field and exposure time. Controls that were true to camera and lens, such as the tilts, swings, and focal calculations evident in his *Woolworth Building* photograph, were considered acceptable. Painterly affectations were not. The idea that the camera can act as a proxy for human experience is a distinctly modern conception. Modern photographers devoted themselves to exploring the unique properties of photographic vision. Hoppé believed that the camera should be allowed to speak, and that effective photographs could be made only when the artist accepts the camera as a means to negotiate his or her surroundings.

As he traveled around America, Hoppé adapted his style to his environment. His early streetscapes of New York show the influence of the British Vorticists, the short-lived group of neo-Cubist writers and artists who congregated in London prior to the outbreak of the First World War. As the name suggests, Vorticists reduced their compositions to abstract arrangements of vectors, lines, and angles. Triangular forms were valued for their formal dynamics; attracted by the aesthetics of the machine, Vorticists tried to convey a feeling of motion in their art. Led by the writer and painter Wyndham Lewis (1882–1957), the group was associated with the poets Ezra Pound and T. S. Eliot, both of whom Hoppé photographed, as well as with Hoppé's friend Alvin Langdon Coburn. Around 1916 Coburn began making photographs through a kaleidoscopic arrangement of mirrors: he called the results "vortographs." Though he decided that he quickly exhausted the possibilities of vortography, Coburn's experiments are widely recognized as having had a lasting effect on the progression of modern art.

Hoppé's photographs of the towering buildings and vast city canyons of New York reflect the Vorticist influence. In *New York Skyscraper*, c. 1919 [page 58], the central building is framed between the strong black mass of an overhang on the right and the shadowy structure on the left. The building is seen through a thin sliver of light projecting from the sky, its jagged angles narrowing to an abrupt point at the bottom right of the picture. As was often the case in Hoppé's photographs, he did not bother to artificially adjust perspective, preferring to allow the scene to skew inward, seemingly collapsing upon itself. He then boldly reinterpreted the scene, printing the same composition in the inverted *New York Skyscraper (negative)* c. 1919 [page 59]. The main difference between the two compositions, beyond the obvious negative-positive reversal, is the addition of a dark triangle on the left, connecting the tip of the shaft of light with the top right corner and creating an undulating zigzag the full length of the composition. The idea of presenting an obvious negative as a finished work of art is rare in the history of photography; Hoppé's work predates the negative abstractions of Moholy-Nagy and other Bauhaus photographers later in the

1920s. Brazenly experimental, it represents an extreme of Hoppé's thinking, but it nevertheless demonstrates his sensitivity to graphic problems and his willingness to try radical new techniques.

Hoppé's photographs of urban and industrial America are among his most graphic works. He often portrayed cities with the same deep chiaroscuro lighting he favored in his studio portraits. Brightly illuminated streets contrast with moody shadows, silhouetted figures emerge from darkness and signs dissolve into partial illegibility. In *Snow at Boston Station, Massachusetts* [page 81], for example, the viewer looks out from a subterranean tunnel at figures trudging through the snow. At left, a female figure stands with her back to the photographer, perfectly framed by two vertical columns. Blurry horizontal lines, apparently of a windowpane, stretch from left to right across the image, contributing to the feeling of mystery.

Hoppé used a long lens, which had a tendency to flatten the picture plane. Short lenses are often used by street photographers because they admit more light than long lenses, making them suitable for dim conditions. They also provide a relatively wide angle of view. Long lenses such as the ones used by Hoppé tend to magnify the subject, allowing the photographer to shoot from farther away. Because they admit less light than a short lens, however, the long lens requires wider apertures to expose the film, resulting in a shorter range of focus. The use of a longer than normal lens was one of the distinguishing elements of Hoppé's studio portraiture; the slimming effect of longer lenses flattered sitters, and Hoppé enjoyed the ability to control depth of field across the face. Often in Hoppé's portraits the front of the face is sharply focused, though the hair and ears are not. This gave his pictures gravitas, calling to mind similar strategies employed in portraits by the nineteenth-century photographer Julia Margaret Cameron (1815–79), whom he admired.[35] As he traveled about the United States, Hoppé may have equipped his camera with just such a portrait lens, which would account for the distinctive appearance of his American photographs. Using a longer than normal lens was also a tendency of his Japoniste friend John Warburg. Interestingly, Hoppé enjoyed considerable popularity in Japan; his Goupil Gallery exhibition of 1922 was bought in its entirety by a Japanese photographic museum, which published a catalogue of the show.[36] His innovative handling of space may partially account for his success in that country, as the flat, graphic nature of his pictures suggested the ingenious handling of perspective in Japanese prints.

Through Hoppé's lens, objects often jut across the picture plane in unexpected ways. In *In the West Street District, New York*, 1921 [page 126], for example, nearly a third of the picture is given over to the swooping forms of overhead bridges. They serve to organize the space, dividing it into a wedgelike view of skyscrapers and a strip of a city scene below. The curving shape of the horizontal bridge softens the image, giving it an almost playful air. Similarly, in *Stock Yards, Chicago, Illinois*, 1926 [page 125] Hoppé showed two trucks loaded with cattle in front of row upon row of rectangular pens. The regular geometry of the photograph is punctured by an arch of molding in the upper right. Hoppé enjoyed such illusionistic *repoussoir* effects, achieved by placing an incongruous item in the foreground or shooting through one object at another (the art term *repoussoir* describes the technique of placing an item in the extreme foreground of a picture to provide contrast with items in the background). In *Delaware Bridge, Wilmington*, 1926 [page 83], a distant landscape is visible through a "Z" of bridge girders, providing a bold graphic contrast to the smoke rising beyond.

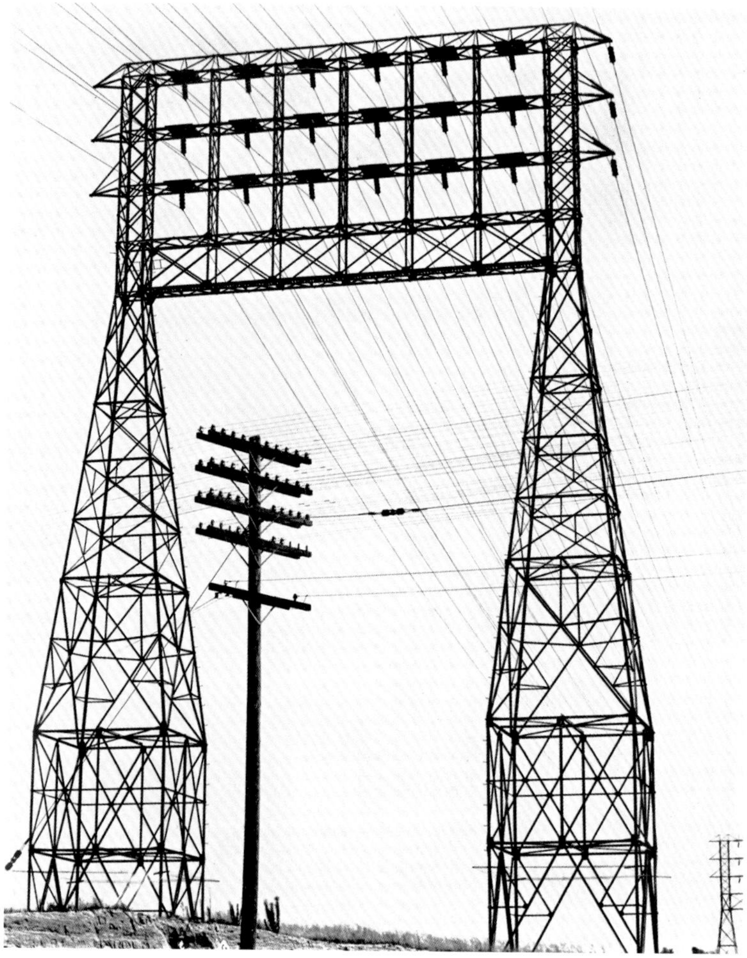

Figure 16. Edward Weston, *Power lines, Lincoln Boulevard, Los Angeles,* c. 1930

Such abrupt juxtapositions made interesting designs, but they also set the tone of Hoppé's American photographs. By placing unexpected objects in his pictures, Hoppé created a feeling of spontaneity—a sense of things appearing before the camera the way they might appear to the eye. The viewer sometimes has the sensation of being overwhelmed by his surroundings, like a drowning man catching a final glimpse of his situation before he goes under. Many of Hoppé's photographs are effective precisely because they seem slightly unresolved. The edgy asymmetry of his American work is one of the qualities that make his photographs unique. Hoppé was able to use modernist conceits to conjure the experience of discovery in a fresh and exciting place. Like the photographs themselves, Hoppé's America is daring and original.

It is fascinating to see Hoppé, as he journeyed around the country, engage the same subjects as his American modernist colleagues, often from identical vantage points. In Los Angeles, Edward Weston (1886–1958) photographed electrical towers on Lincoln Boulevard [Figure 16], while Hoppé, independently, made his own photographs of exactly the same towers [Figure 17]. Weston brought his camera in closer to the subject and photographed from an oblique angle, using the opening between the legs of one tower to frame a distant telegraph pole. Hoppé photographed his towers straight on and from a slight remove, emphasizing the geometric balance of the design. In

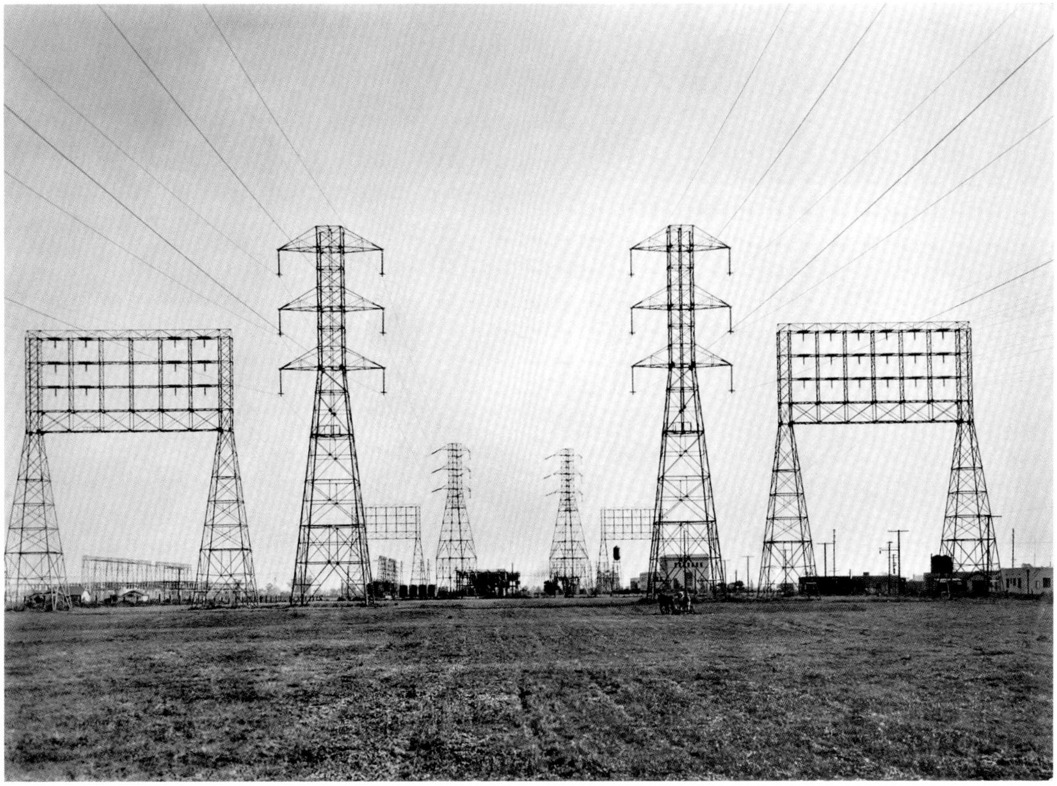

Figure 17. E. O. Hoppé, *Edison Wireless, Electrical Pylons, Los Angeles,* 1926

Weston's photograph, intersecting wires ground the towers and connect them to each other. In Hoppé's version, delicate wisps of wire recede into the upper corners of the picture.

Hoppé also followed the same path as Ansel Adams (1902–84) in the Yosemite Valley.[37] Adams's first volume of photographs of the valley, *Parmelian Prints of the High Sierras,* was published in 1927, the same year as Hoppé's *Romantic America.* Within months of each other, Adams and Hoppé both were making pictures of Half Dome from Glacier Point. Adams's celebrated early view [Figure 18], shows the scene in autumn or early winter, snow gathering on the crests of the mountains. Interestingly, to make his picture Adams used the same *repoussoir* technique that Hoppé used so effectively, placing a tree in the foreground and allowing its branches to blot out the skyline. Hoppé's photograph *Half Dome, Yosemite National Park, California,* 1926, [Figure 19] takes a different tack, contrasting the distant mountain with a stone outcrop. Photographing in summer, the bare rock of the escarpment below Half Dome echoes the texture of the outcrop, and the curved shape of the stones appears to cradle the distant monolith.

Hoppé was enormously sensitive to visual parallels of this type. His *Bridge and Smoke Trail, Key West, Florida,* [page 103], for example, is a modernist tour de force, exhibiting many of the qualities that make Hoppé's photography so special. A print of this image is currently in the collections of

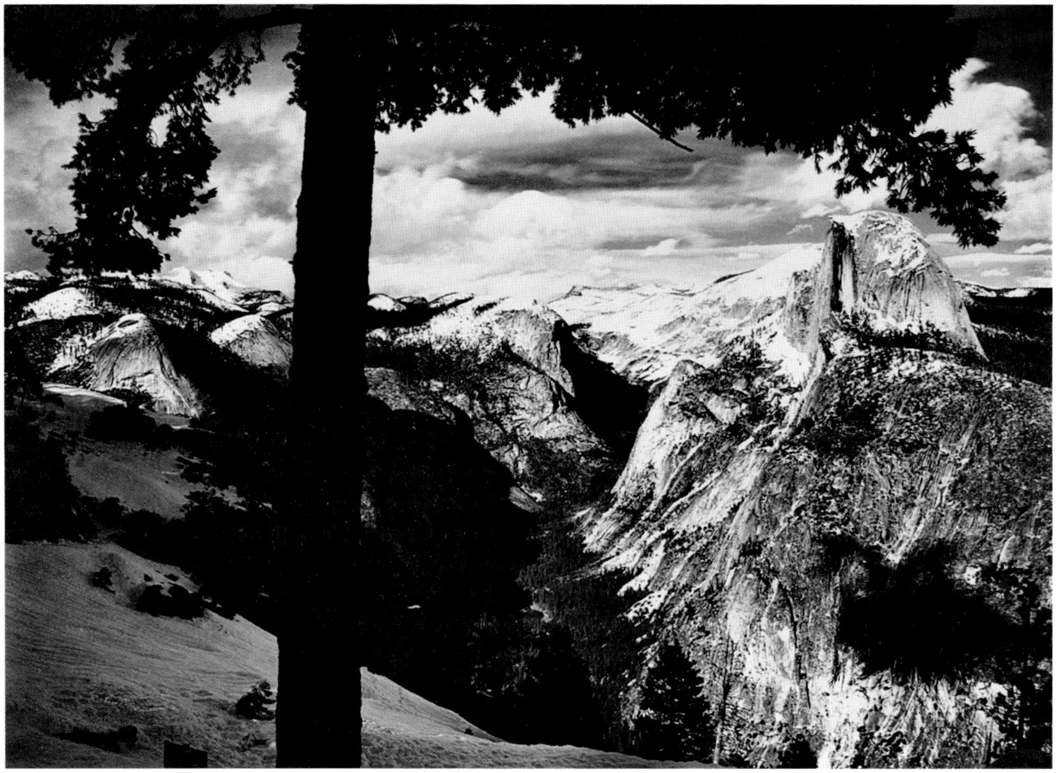

Figure 18. Ansel Adams, *From Glacier Point,* c. 1923

the Victoria and Albert Museum, London. The plunging foreshortening of the bridge filling the left third of the composition provides spatial context and gives the picture a sensation of spontaneity. Hoppé controlled depth of field exactly, leaving the front rail out of focus, and the back rail sharp. Shadows cast by the rails fall across the deck of the bridge, adding mood. Meanwhile, in the far distance, a train proceeds from left to right across the horizon, its elongated form announced by the trail of smoke rising from the locomotive. Hoppé took his photograph just as the train was about to enter a row of trees. The front of the train barely kisses them, while the black trail of smoke exactly matches the shape of the tree line. The sheer formal elegance of the picture demonstrates Hoppé's exquisite attention to detail and the sophistication of which he was capable. To find analogues to the synchronous composition and graphic refinement of *Bridge and Smoke Trail, Key West, Florida,* one must turn to landmarks of American modernist photography such as Alfred Stieglitz's *The Steerage* (1907), or Paul Strand's *White Fence, Port Kent* (1916).

The extent of Hoppé's influence on American modern photography may never by fully understood. Hoppé certainly met the eminent American photographers of his generation, and they knew his work from exhibitions and books. Unlike many of his contemporaries, Hoppé was a prolific author. He produced twenty-seven books and portfolios in his lifetime, and to this day his

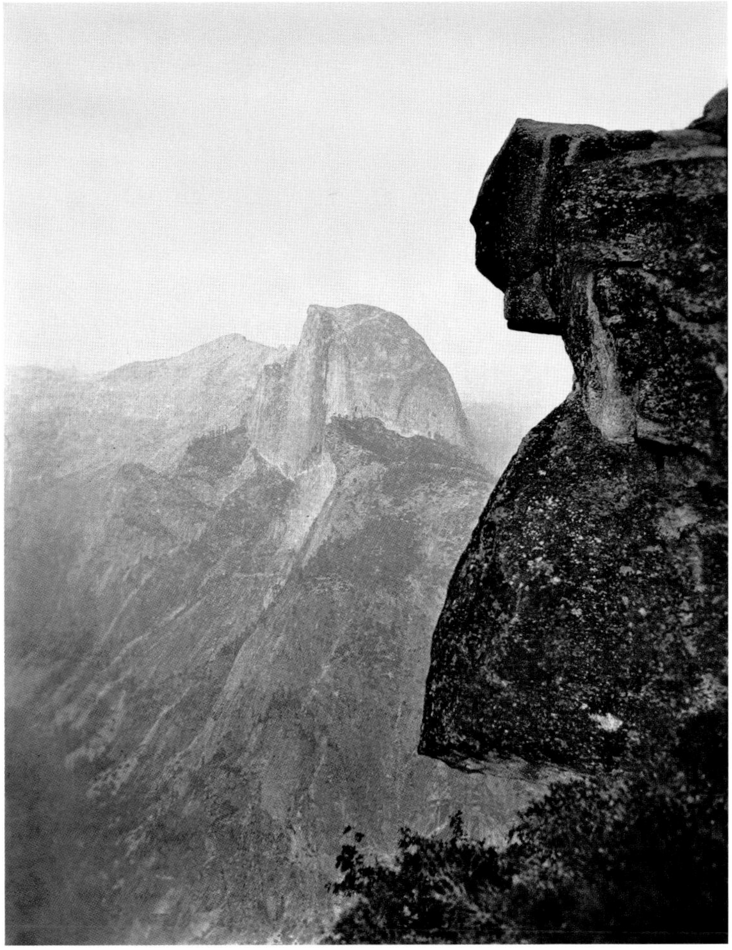

Figure 19. E. O. Hoppé, *Half Dome and the Sierra Nevada from Glacier Point, Yosemite, California*, 1926

work is perhaps best known from published sources. This approach had the advantage of spreading Hoppé's photography to a broad audience, which included fellow artists.

In New York Hoppé befriended the American photographer Pirie MacDonald (1867–1942), whose likeness was one of the 117 portraits Hoppé included in his Wanamaker exhibition of 1921. MacDonald was well connected in New York photographic circles and curated the American section of the Dresden International Exhibition of Photography in 1909.[38] The Dresden exhibition featured the work of Stieglitz, and Hoppé had curated the British section in partnership with Benjamin Stone. During his time in New York Hoppé also became acquainted with Gertrude Käsebier (1852–1934), who contacted him upon seeing the Wanamaker exhibition. "I experienced great pleasure and stimulus in viewing your photographs," she wrote. "I found in them sincerity, psychology, simplicity, technical excellence, and artistry."[39]

Several years later Hoppé made it a point to compliment Käsebier on an exhibition of her photographs in Washington D.C. "I cannot find words to express the pleasure your letter has given me," she replied. "Coming from you, I know that you know what you were saying about my prints . . . Thank you. I wish I knew what you liked best in my work and what you liked least. I like your work always. Your technique and point of view."[40]

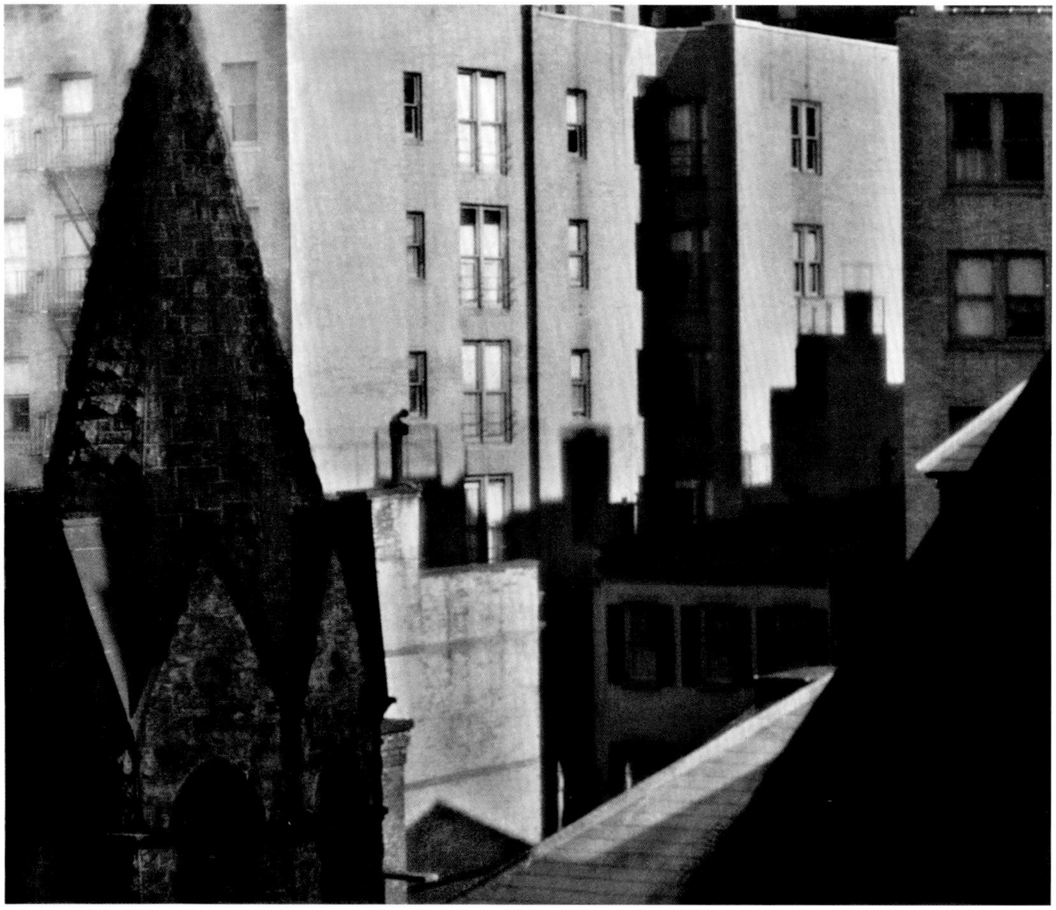

Figure 20. E. O. Hoppé, *Rooftops, Apartments, New York City* (View from E. O. Hoppé's studio on West 57th Street), 1921

Not all American photographers were so sanguine. Alfred Stieglitz, in particular, was notoriously prickly about rival photographers, especially when they refused to recognize critical issues in photography as he perceived them. For his part, Hoppé was unfailingly utilitarian in his approach, counseling whatever means necessary to achieve compelling effects. Though he did publish a credo, it was fiercely libertarian in its advice. "I am indifferent to academic discussion whether photography is an art or craft," he stated, "I consider the prime function of photography to be absolute reliance on supreme craftsmanship in the expression of individual conception of the subject within the legitimate means of the medium."[41] In other words, photographers should strive to make good pictures, in whatever way they see fit, while remaining true to the medium. To Stieglitz, Hoppé's position was no less than a license for mediocrity. It was anathema to Stieglitz, who felt photography lacked direction.

Hoppé's omission from the pages of Stieglitz's publication *Camera Work* is conspicuous, considering the similarity of his work to that of others in Stieglitz's Photo-Secession group. Alvin Langdon Coburn, for example, whose work overlaps closely with that of Hoppé, had photographs published repeatedly in *Camera Work*, as did Gertrude Käsebier, who was emphatic in her praise of Hoppé. Moreover, the Photo-Secessionists shared a similar expatriate background. Hoppé and Stieglitz both were German émigrés (Hoppé having arrived in London via Munich, Berlin, and Austria).

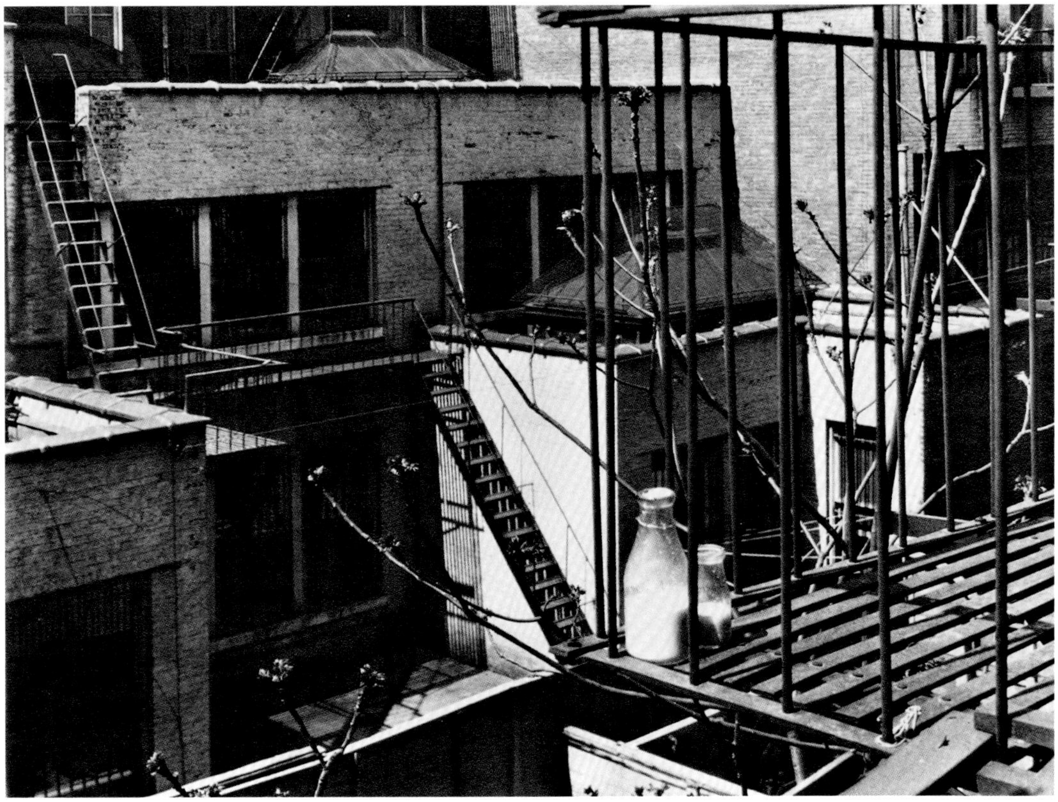

Figure 21. Edward Steichen, *Milk Bottles, Spring, New York*, 1915

Nearly all Stieglitz's associates were European exports: Steichen hailed from Luxembourg, Coburn was Anglo-American, Frank Eugene (1893–1982) was German-American, and Paul Haviland (1880–1950) came from France. In addition, Stieglitz leaned heavily toward photographers of German and Austrian background, such as the so-called Viennese Trifolium of Hugo Henneberg (1863–1918), Hans Watzek (1848–1903), and Heinrich Kühn (1866–1944). In any case, it is unclear whether Hoppé specifically declined to associate with the Photo-Secessionists, whether Stieglitz refused to invite him, or whether their distance was mutually imposed.

It is possible poor relations between Hoppé and Stieglitz originated at the time of Hoppé's Wanamaker exhibition in 1921. Hoppé invited the avant-garde painter and printmaker Max Weber (1881–1961) to write the introduction to his gallery guide. Weber was a student of the Arts and Crafts designer Arthur Wesley Dow (1857–1922) and had helped found the Clarence White School of Photography in Maine in 1910. He was also an associate of Stieglitz, exhibiting at his Gallery 291 in 1910 and 1911. Weber initially turned down Hoppé's request to write the introduction, but relented after persistent requests. As soon as the guide was published, Stieglitz took Weber to task. "Of course I have known Hoppé's work for years," Stieglitz affirmed. Weber had begun his essay by stressing that he would discuss only Hoppé's photographs, not his drawings and designs. These lines were printed in capital letters. With this, Stieglitz became indignant. "I came away quite bewildered by your writing—your forward for the Exhibition. First of all the large type of the first two lines! Why this introduction. To any intelligent person it virtually discounts all that comes thereafter. Or one feels a trick may have been played somewhere. Of course the photographs remain what they actually are no matter what may be written of them or said about them. But I can't understand the painter and designer Hoppé being separated in spirit if not performance from the photographer Hoppé."[43] Philosophically, it irritated Stieglitz whenever critics separated photography from other media. It suggested that photography was inferior to other art forms. Moreover, he steadfastly believed that it is necessary to consider an artist's output in every medium when assessing his or her success.

Stieglitz's assessment of the exhibition was characteristically withering. Writing to Weber, he went on: "Some of the photographs are very good pictorially—above all very effective. Some are very mediocre—thin to meaningless. Yours [i.e., Hoppé's portrait of Weber], and Flagg's [the illustrator James Montgomery Flagg (1877–1960)] are certainly of no merit as photographs, and as portraits, virtually meaningless. But that may be merely my reaction—my opinion based upon my study of life and its actual achievements. I write you because I don't quite understand and perhaps a trick was put over on you."[42]

Stieglitz's criticism caused Weber to become infuriated with Hoppé. Weber sent him a long and scathing letter, restating Stieglitz's points, but without naming Stiegltiz himself. He accused Hoppé of treachery. Hoppé wrote back defending himself:

> Your letter is unworthy of you and its grossly abusive tone totally uncalled for. What right do you have to state as facts what your own morose imagination fabricates? It is obvious that the attacks upon you of which you accuse so many, are largely a matter of hallucination on your part. I am convinced it has become a fixed idea with you to suspect everyone of base motives. Several of the very people of whom you have spoken so disparagingly to us, I have met since and I am positive they bear you no ill-feeling.[44]

But the damage had been done. Weber countered by calling Hoppé "strange," "evasive," and "repulsive," describing his agreement to write the foreword as "distasteful and degrading."[45] He accused Hoppé of substituting inferior works in the exhibition that Weber had never seen, thereby damaging his reputation. Weber was legendary for his mercurial temper, and Stieglitz's provocation was like knowingly poking a hornet's nest. It is not known if Stieglitz intentionally hoped to alienate Hoppé. However irrational the perceived slight, Weber became resolutely opposed to Hoppé and his work. The rift between the two artists undoubtedly soured Hoppé's welcome in some circles.

Regardless of politics, there is no denying the convergence between Hoppé's American photographs and those of his better-known colleagues. The extent of their mutual influence, however, is difficult to quantify. When Hoppé leaned out the window of his Fifty-seventh Street studio to make his evocative picture of shadows falling across city buildings [Figure 20] did he have Steichen's *Milk Bottles* of 1915 [Figure 21] in mind? Did Steichen absorb the lessons of Hoppé's pictorial strategies in the portraits he submitted to *Vogue*? The influence probably extended in both directions. Hoppé was an extraordinarily urbane photographer who knew and appreciated the work of his peers. He was also one of the important influences in the evolution of modernist photography in the 1920s. His work was well known among serious American photographers and, indeed, among photographers internationally.

To the victor go the spoils, and in the case of art the victor is the one who makes his or her way into the history books. The process by which this happens is complex, unpredictable, and can be unfair. Over time, decisions made by historians become self-perpetuating, because young photographers learn of their predecessors' works through exhibitions, books, and catalogues. The birth of modernism in photography is currently ascribed to an iconic group of artists that rightly includes Stieglitz and his colleagues. Ironically, as the photographs in this book reveal, the wonderful inventiveness of their photography was anticipated and in some cases possibly inspired by a figure whose name has now fallen partially into obscurity. Hoppé deserves better. As he eloquently put it, "It comes just to this, that whatever we intensely feel and love will reveal to us its inner powers in a way that can never be obtained by the one who treats his medium as merely the mechanism of expression. The camera is, in itself, of course, purely mechanical, but it can be made the vehicle for the revelation of true art, according to the one who manipulates it."[46]

Plates

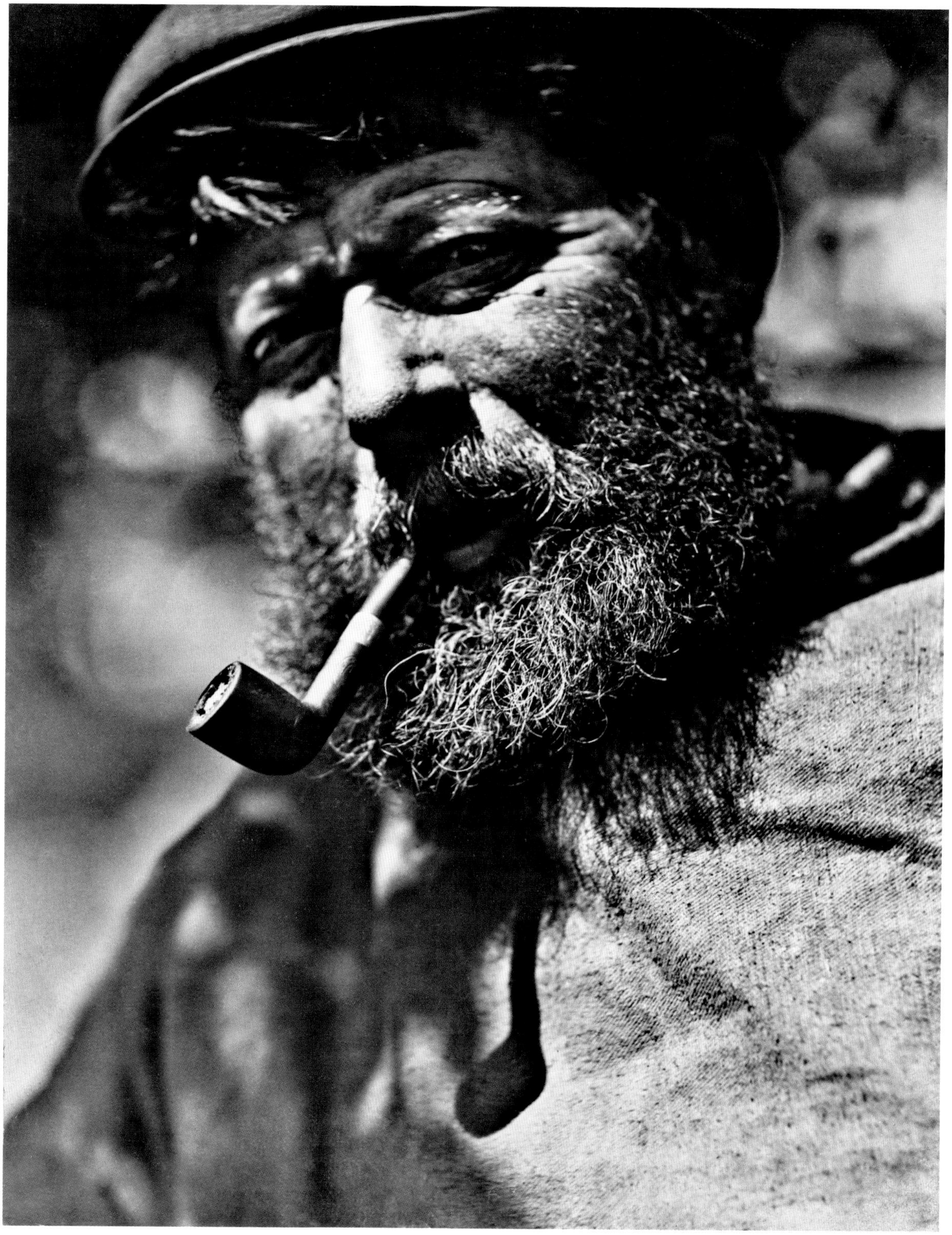

Out of Work, New York City, c. 1919

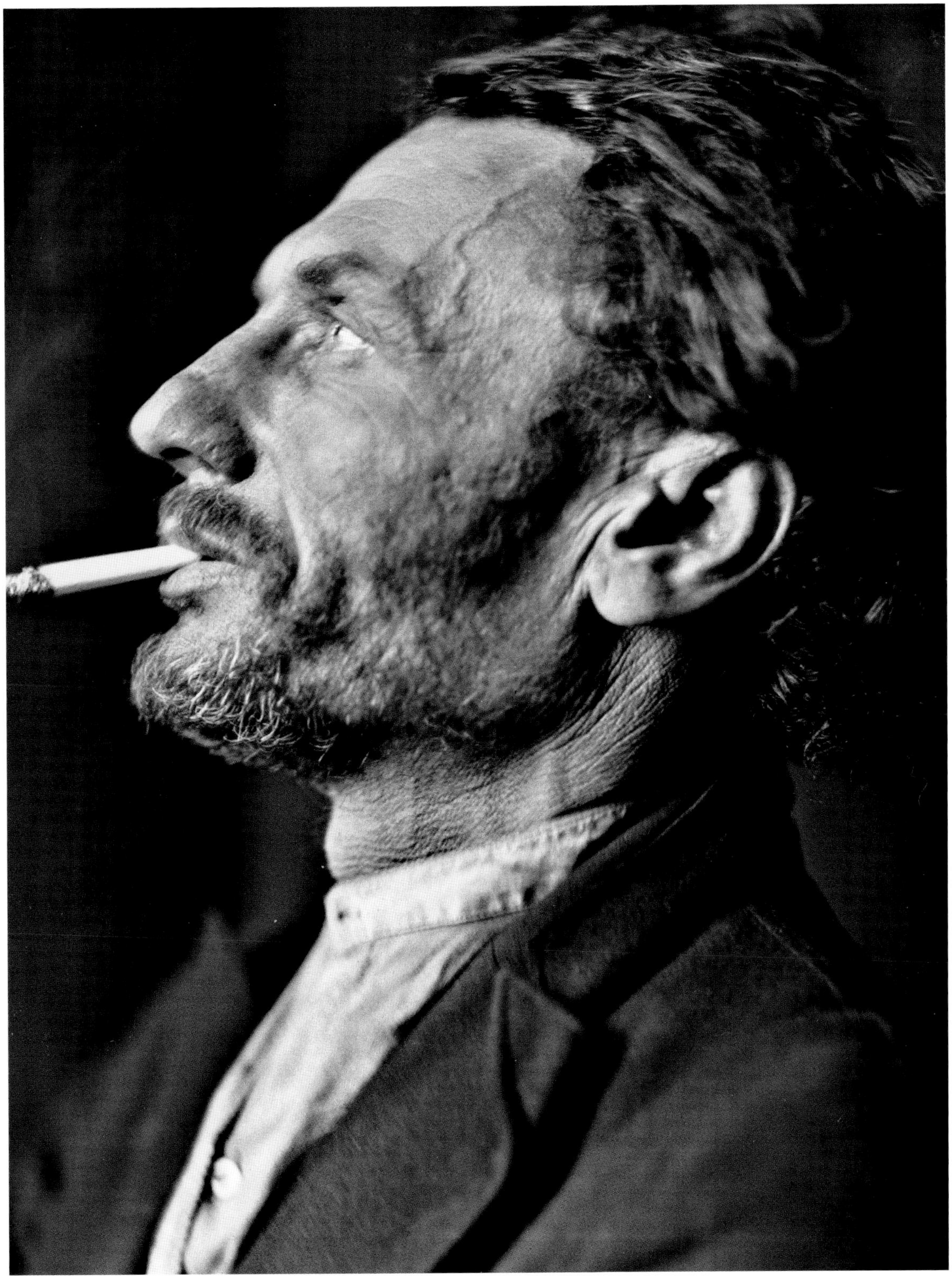

Jewish immigrant with cigarette, New York City, c. 1919

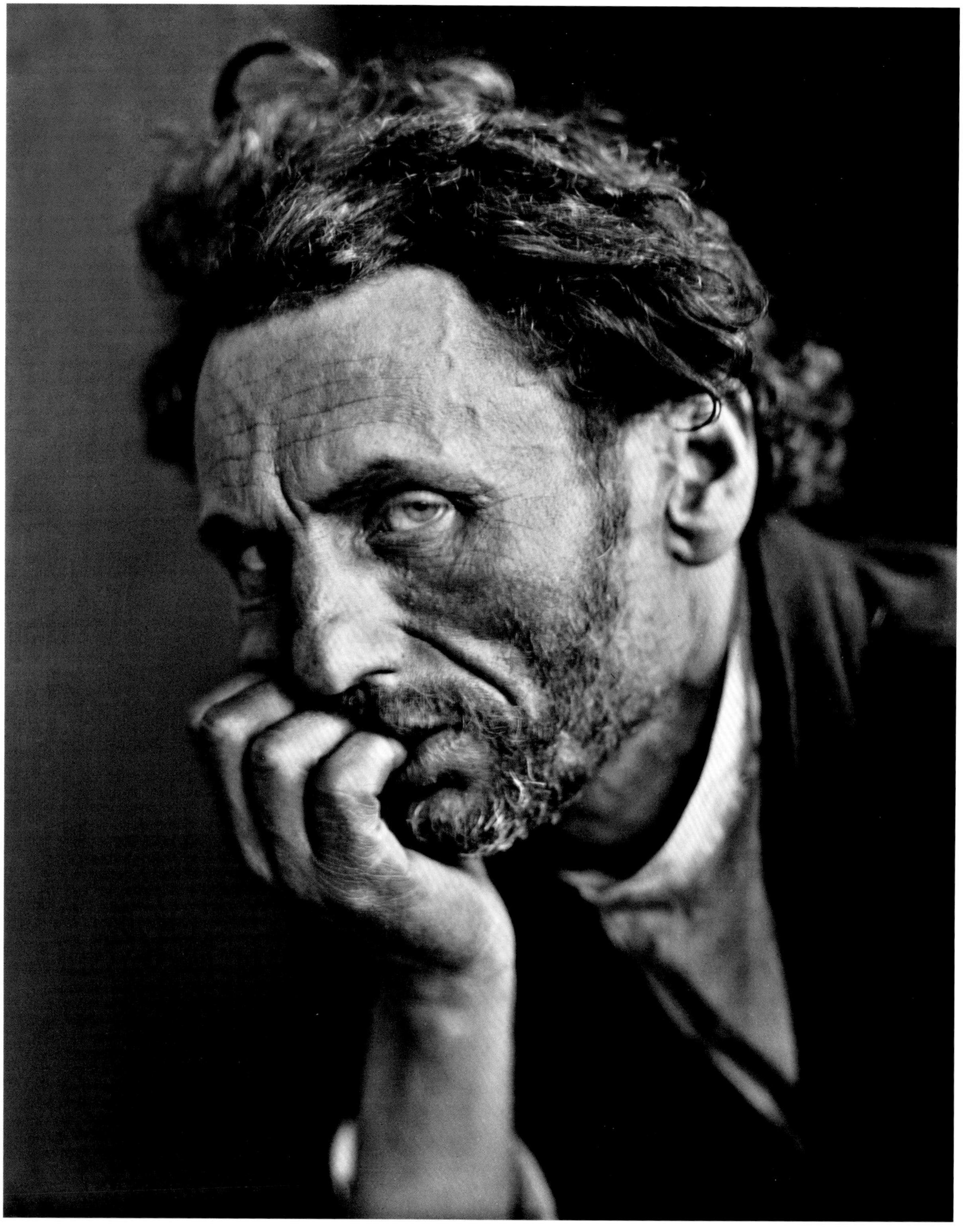

Jewish immigrant, New York City, c. 1919

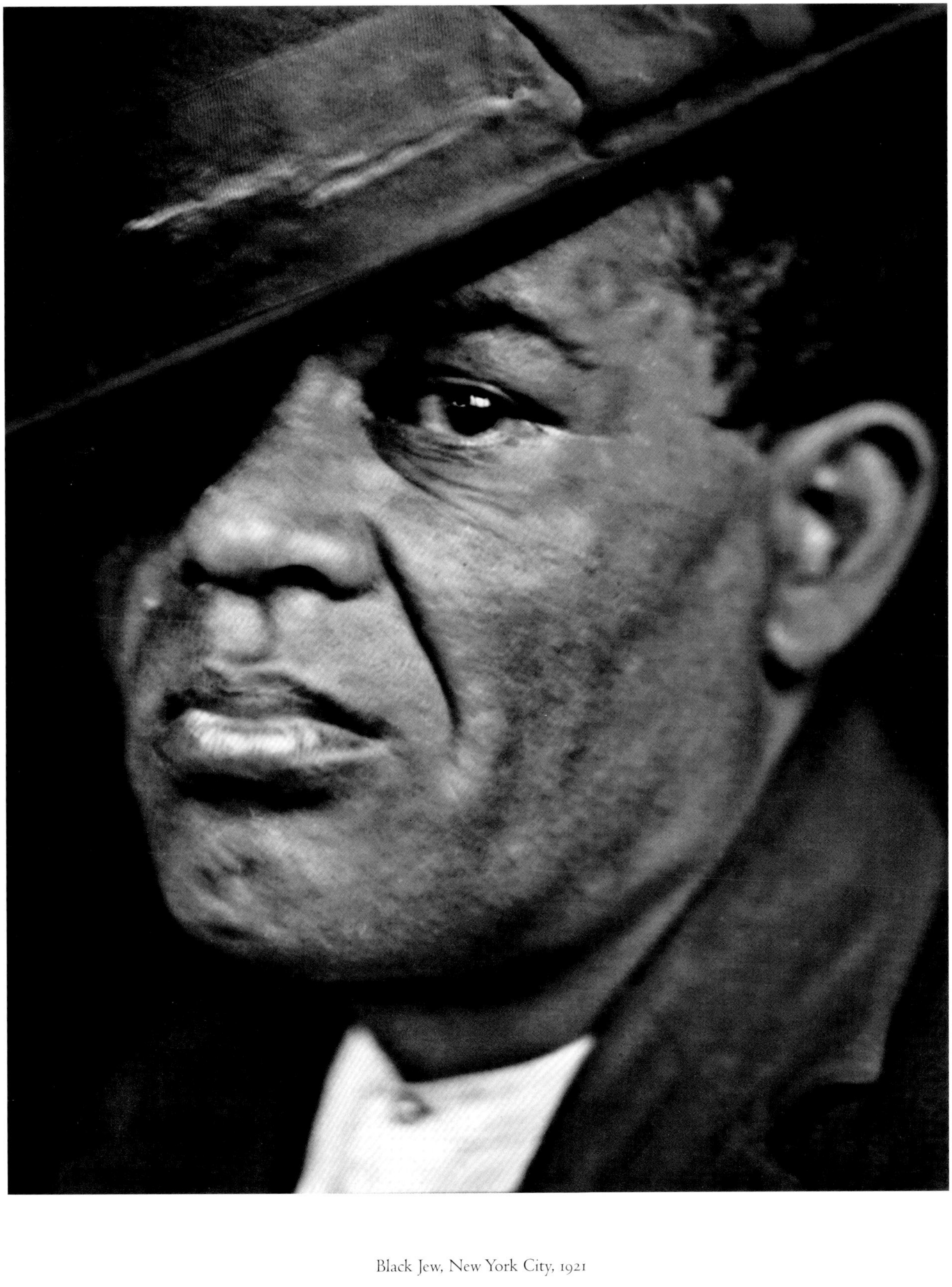

Black Jew, New York City, 1921

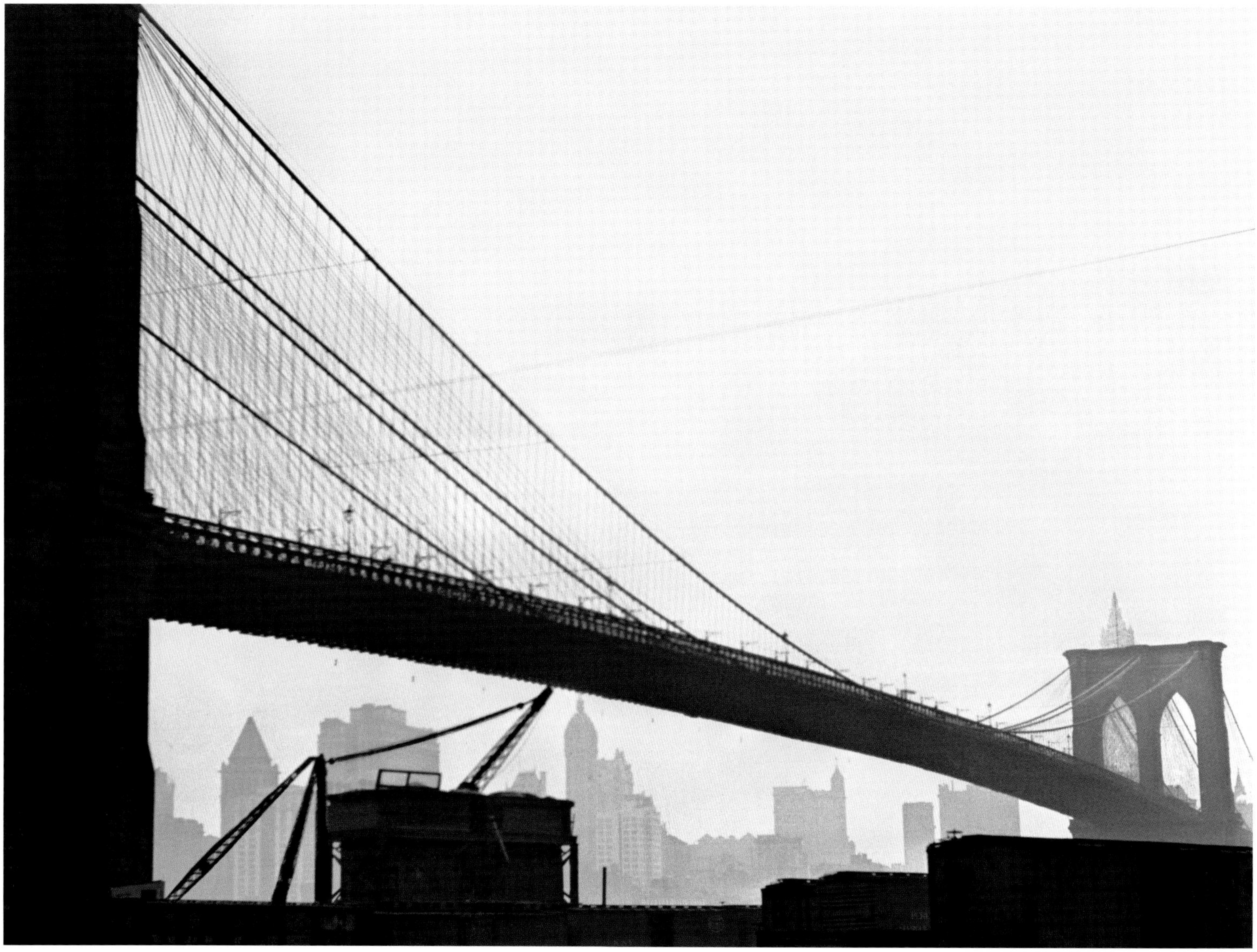

Span of the Brooklyn Bridge, New York City, 1921

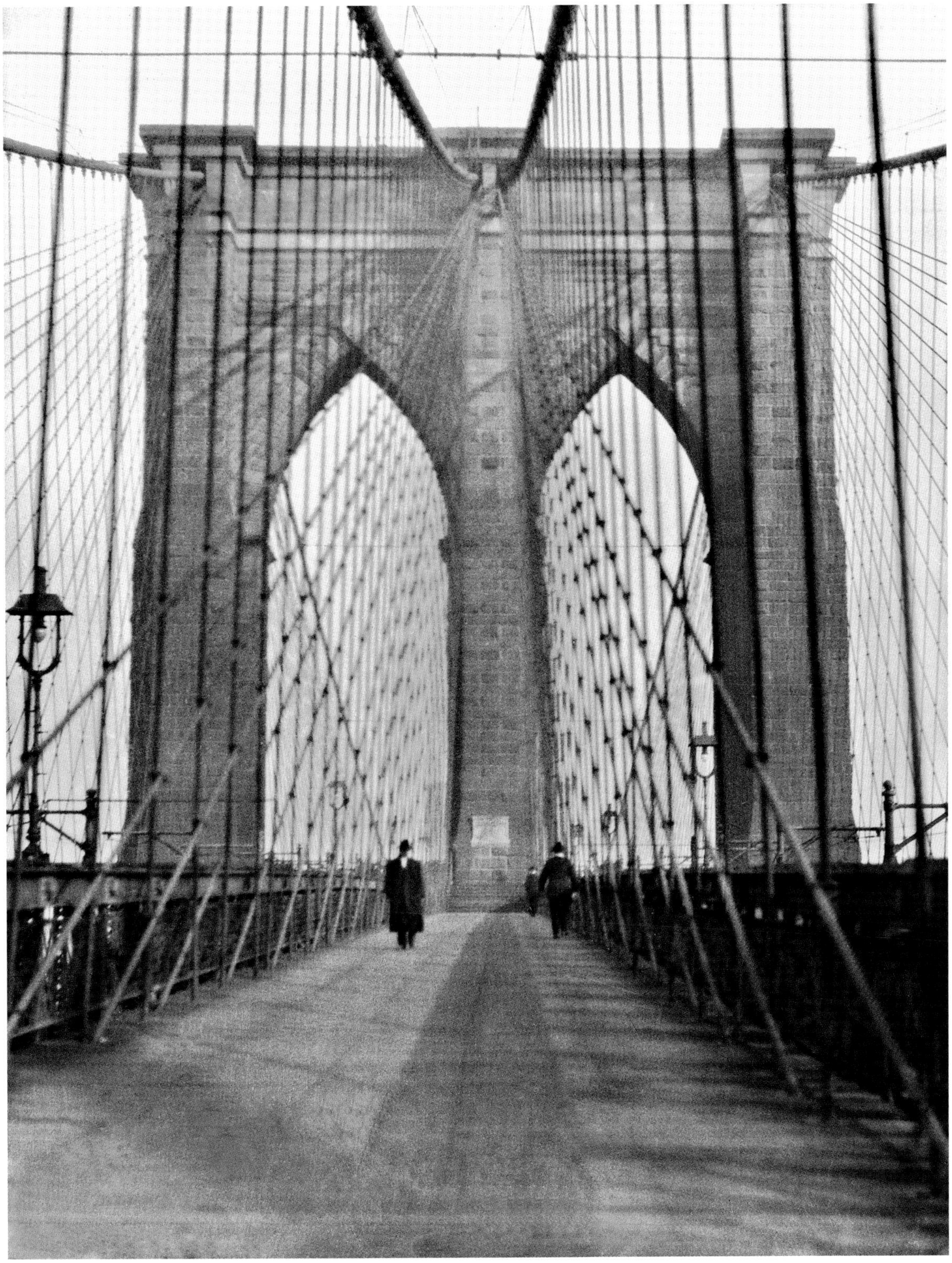

On the Brooklyn Bridge, New York City, 1921

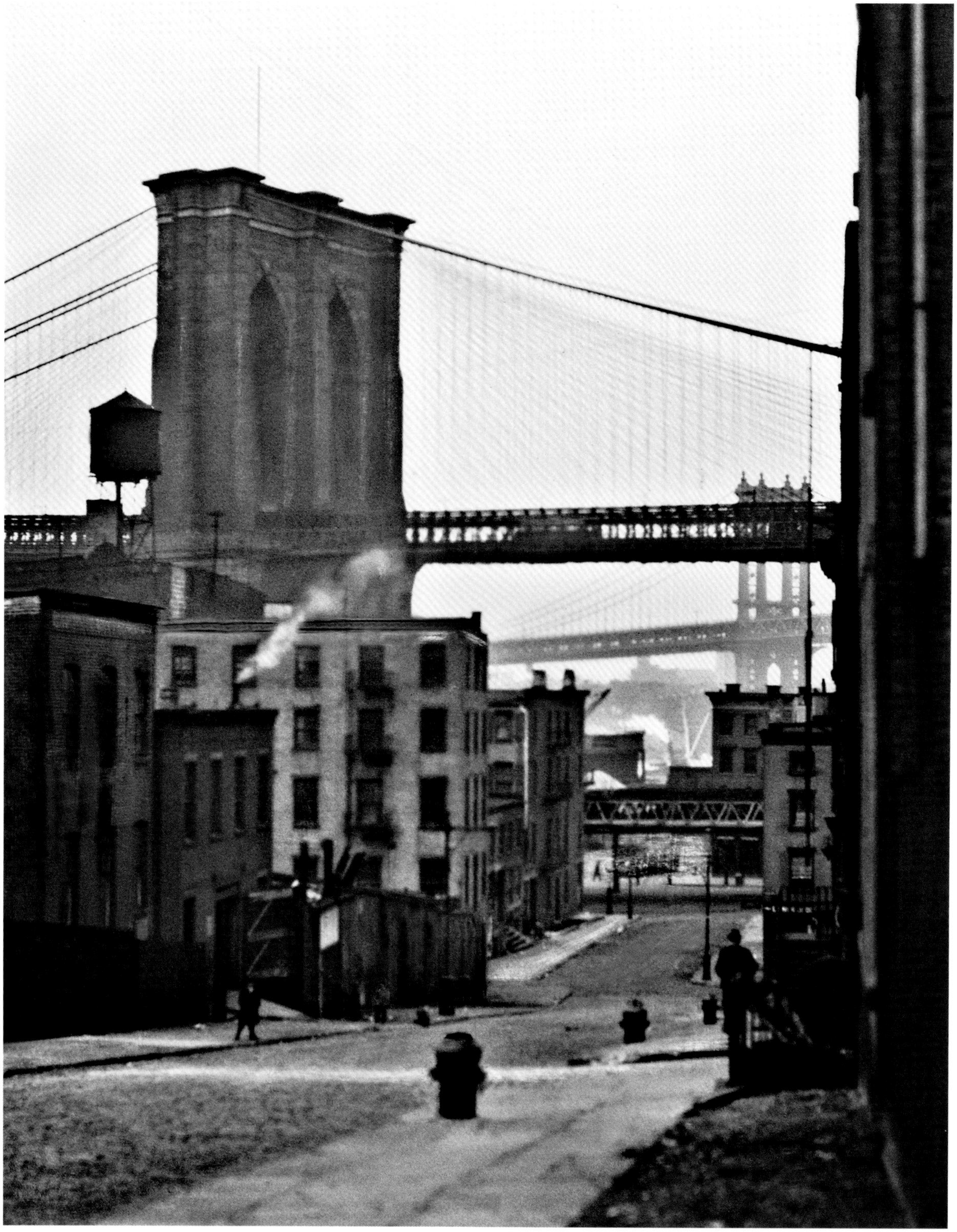

Brooklyn Bridge from East Side, New York, 1921

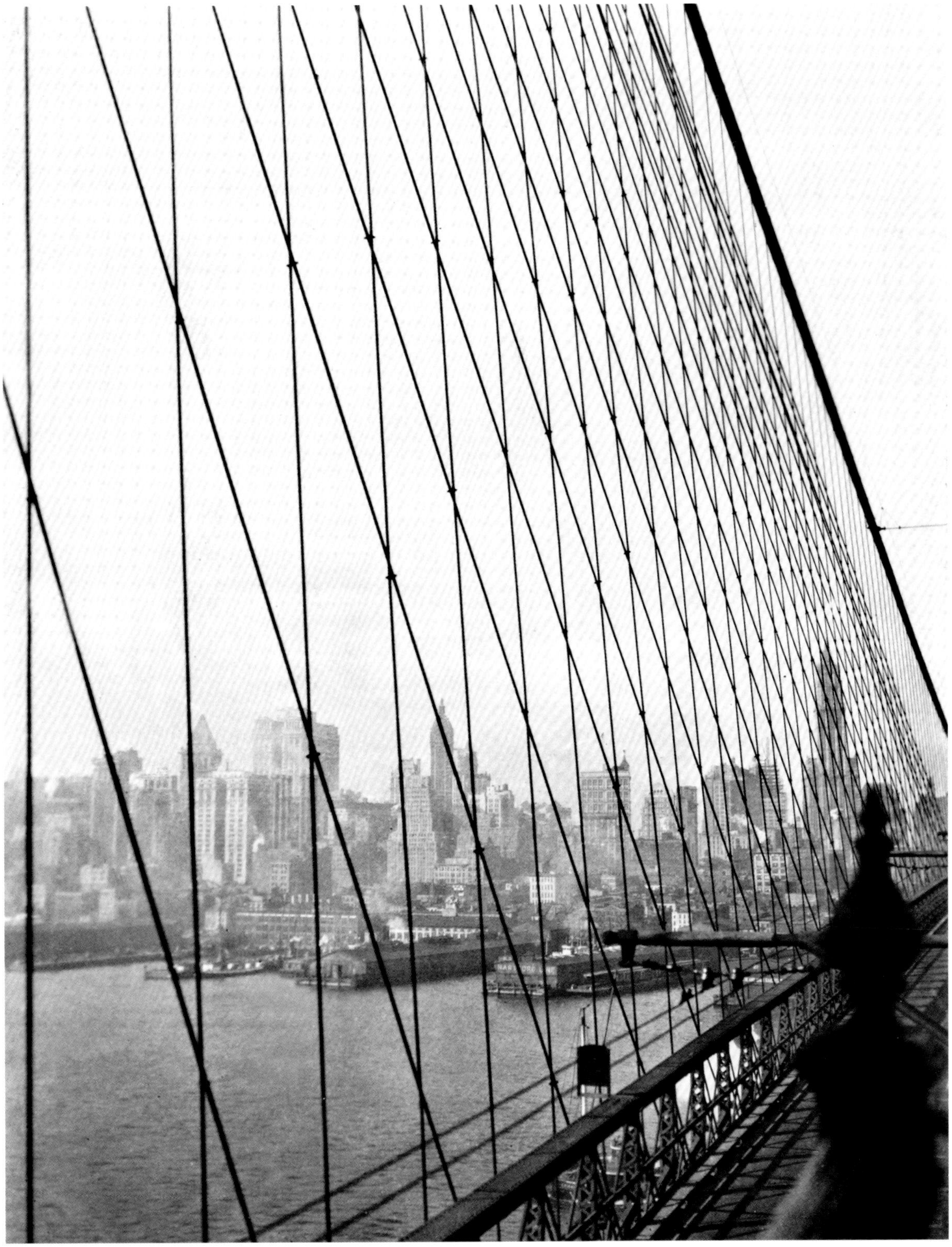

Manhattan Skyline from Brooklyn Bridge, New York City, 1921

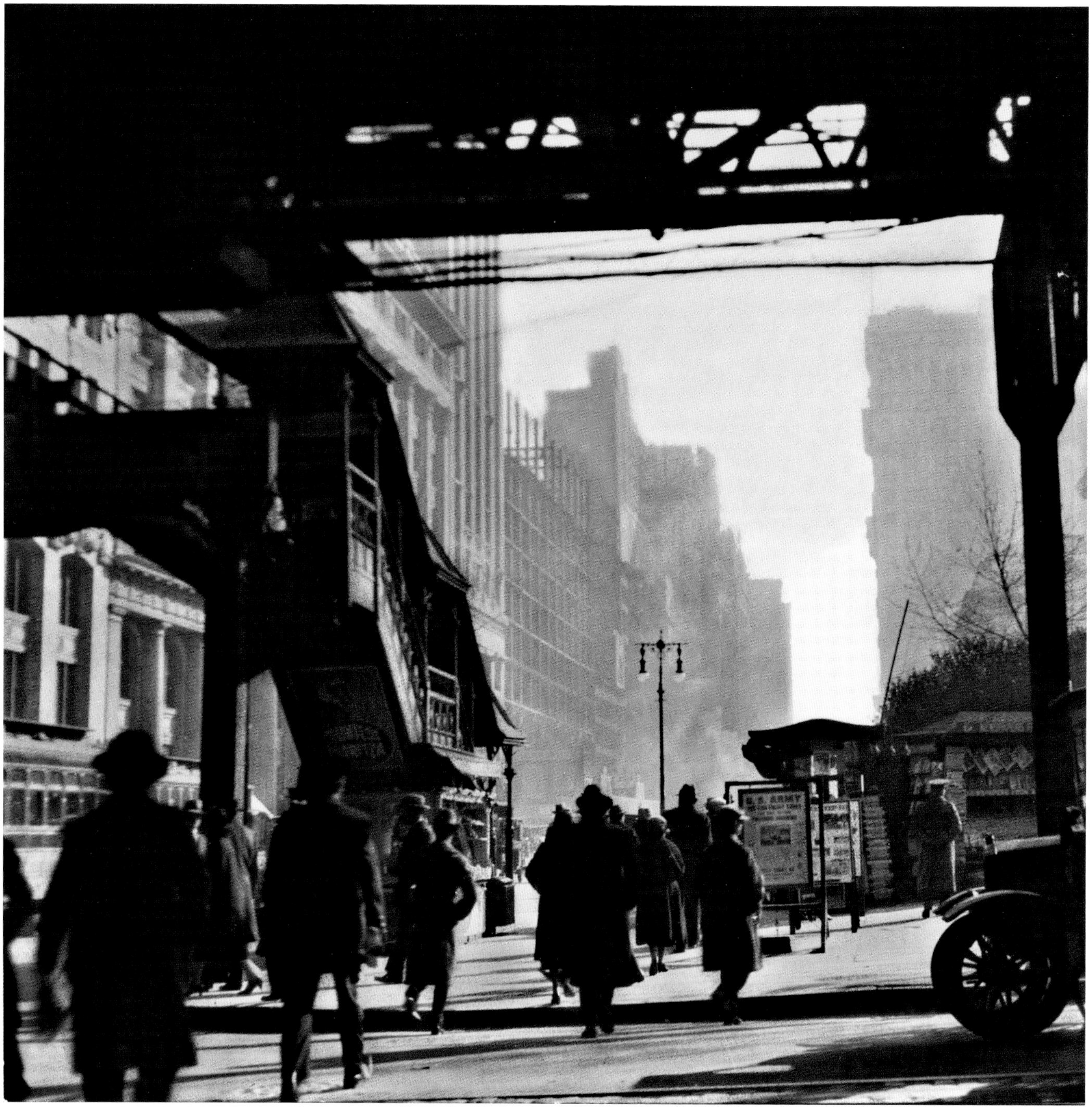

Sixth Avenue at 42nd Street, New York City, 1921

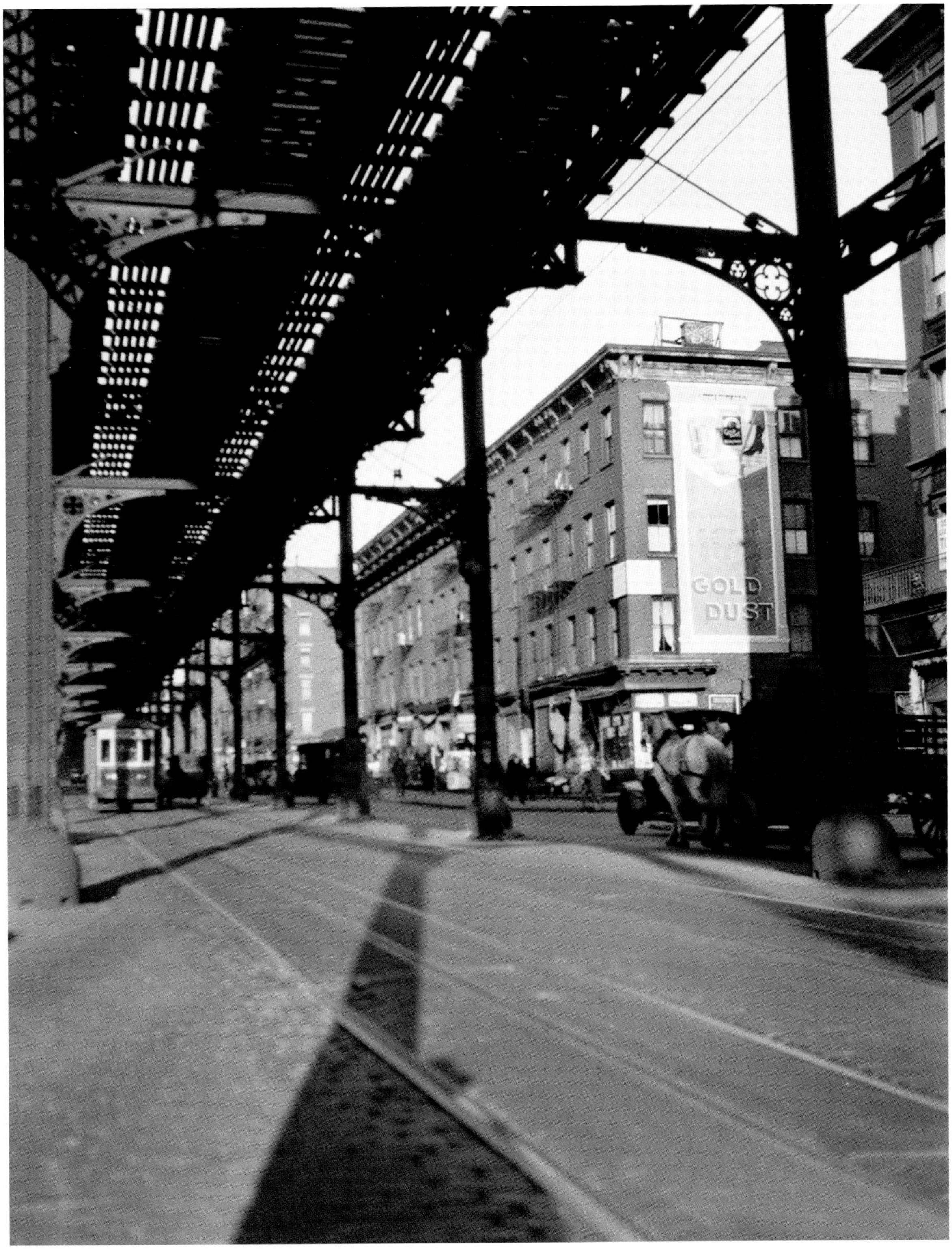

City Street with El, New York City, 1921

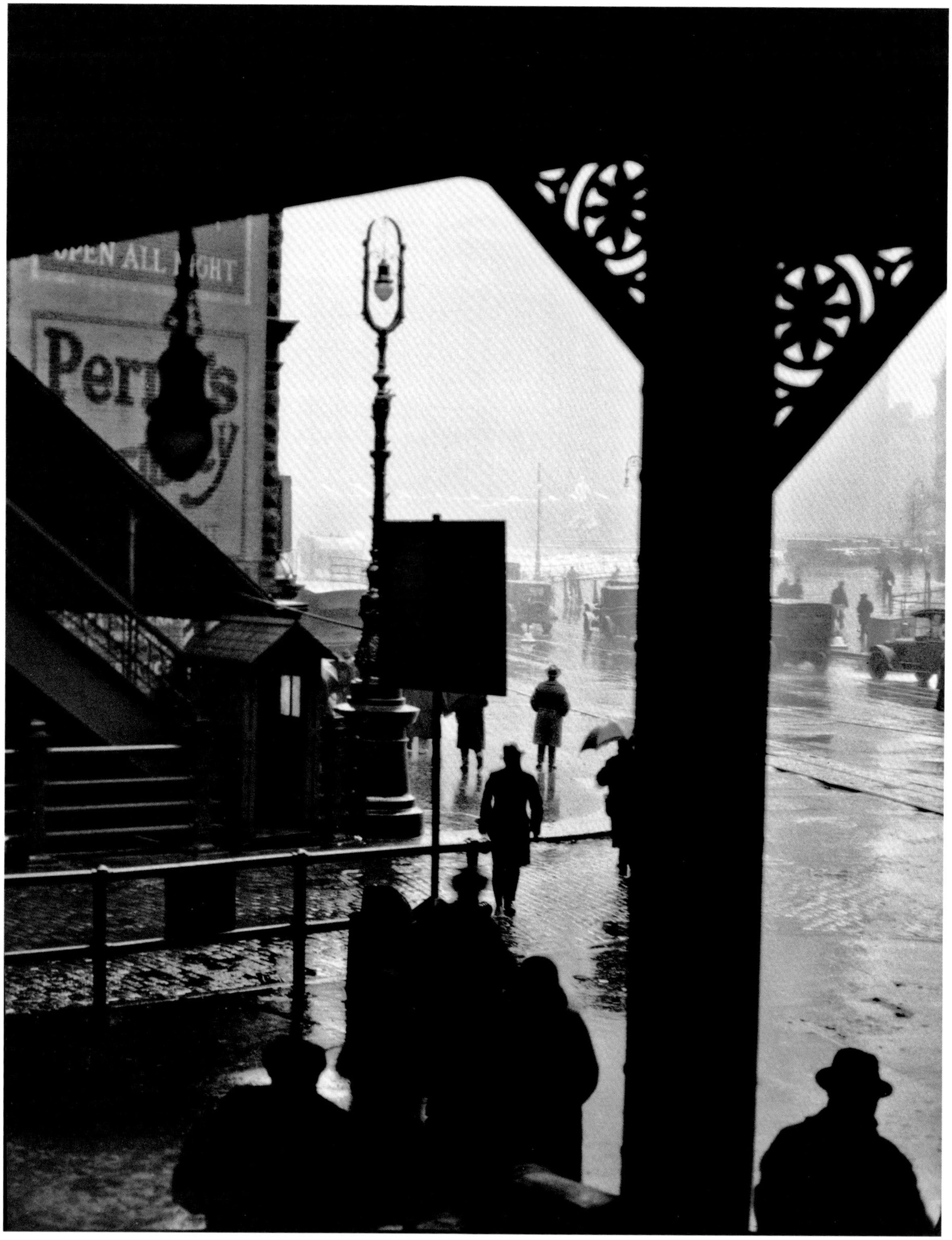

Under the El Railway Bridge, New York City, 1921

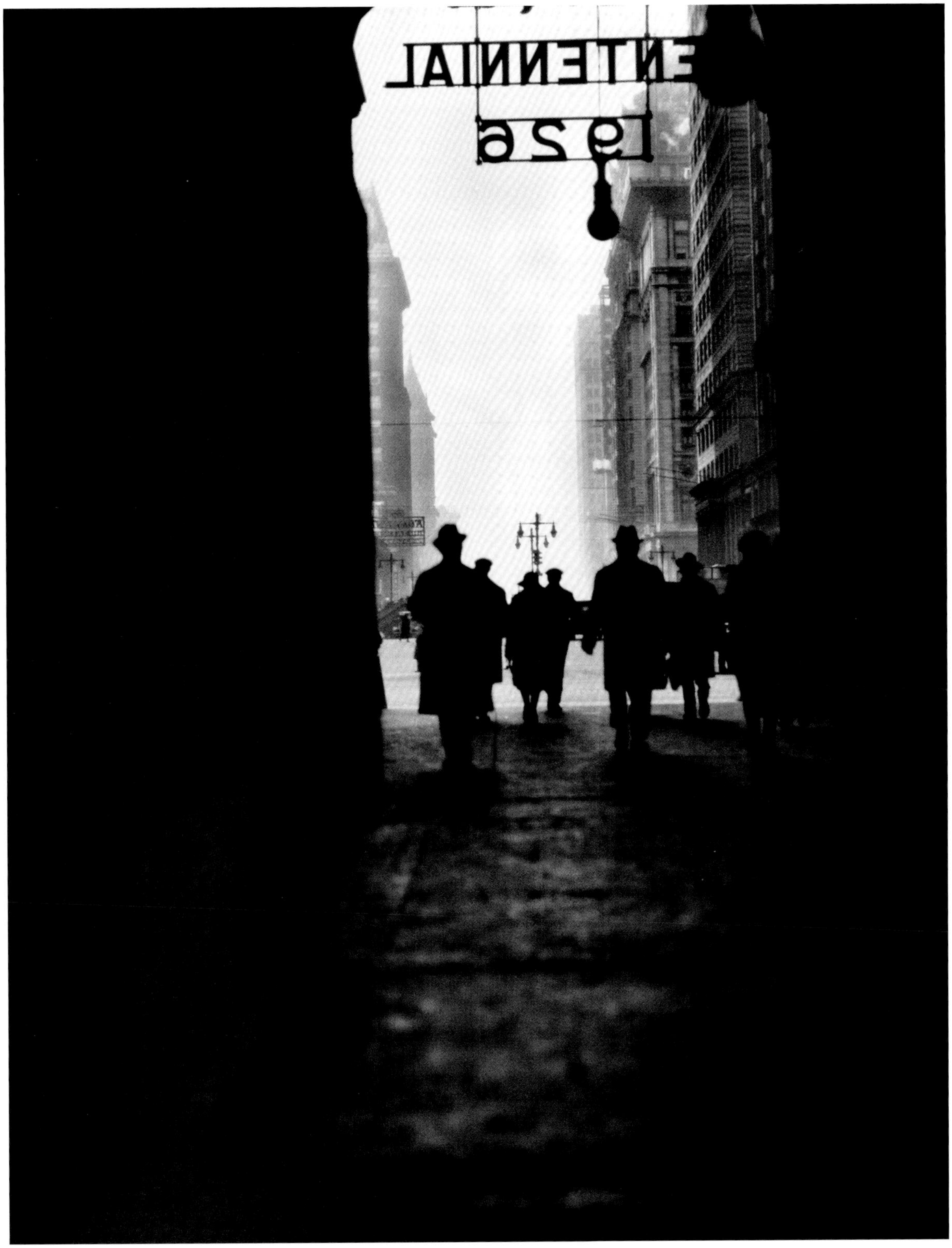

Sesquintennial Signage, Philadelphia, Pennsylvania, 1926

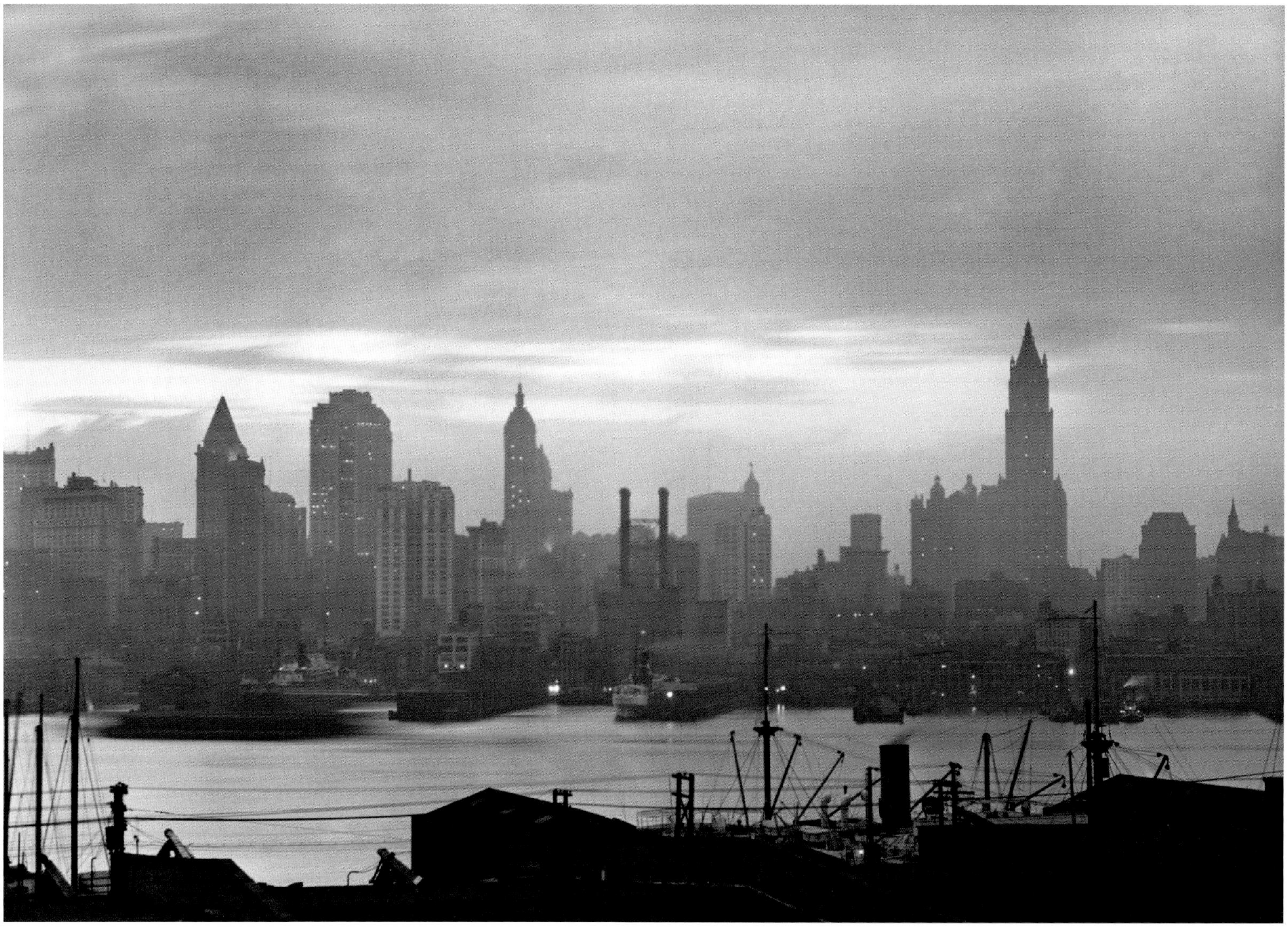

Skyline and Waterfront, New York City, 1921

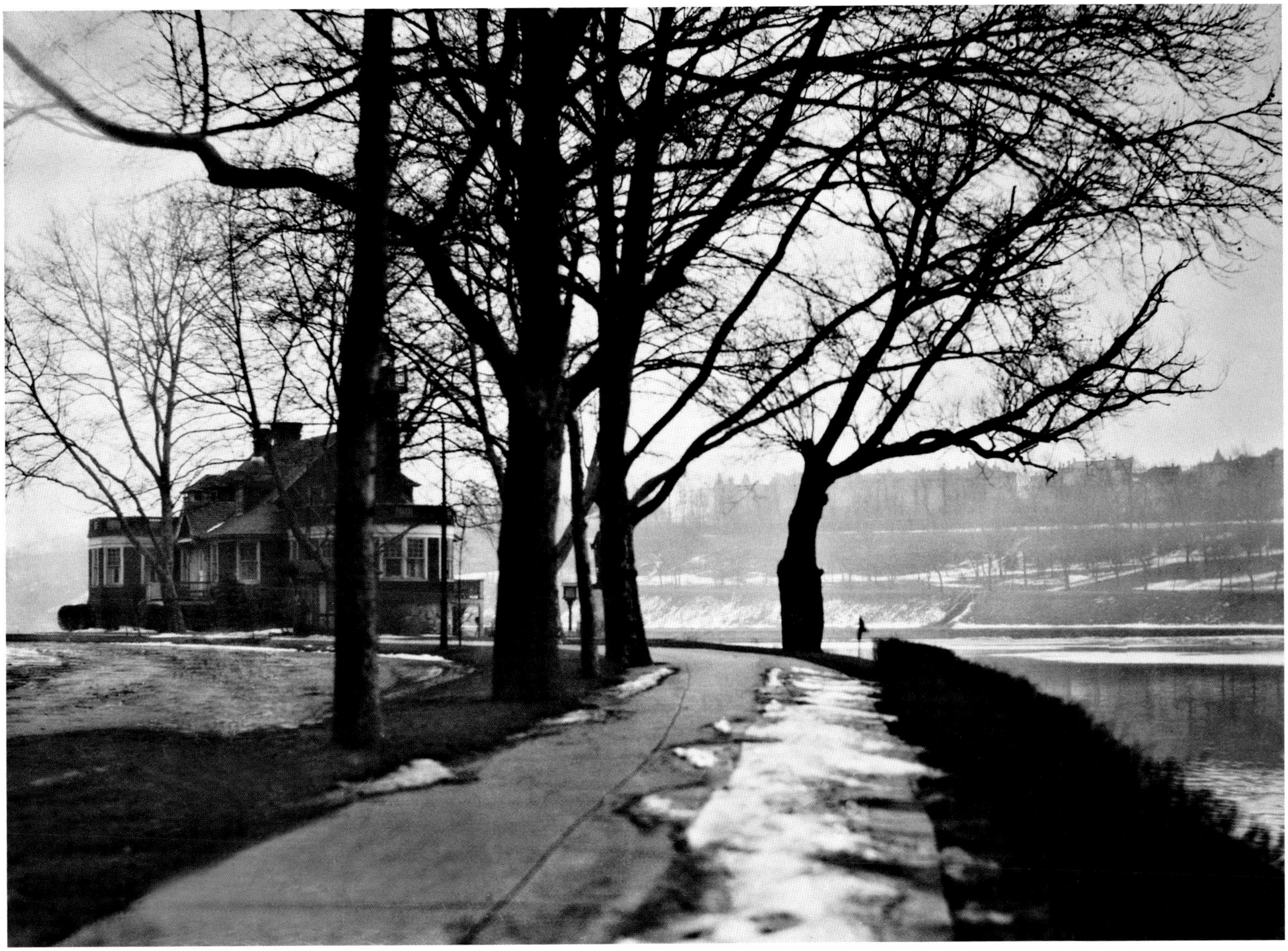

Winter Scene, Philadelphia, Pennsylvania, 1926

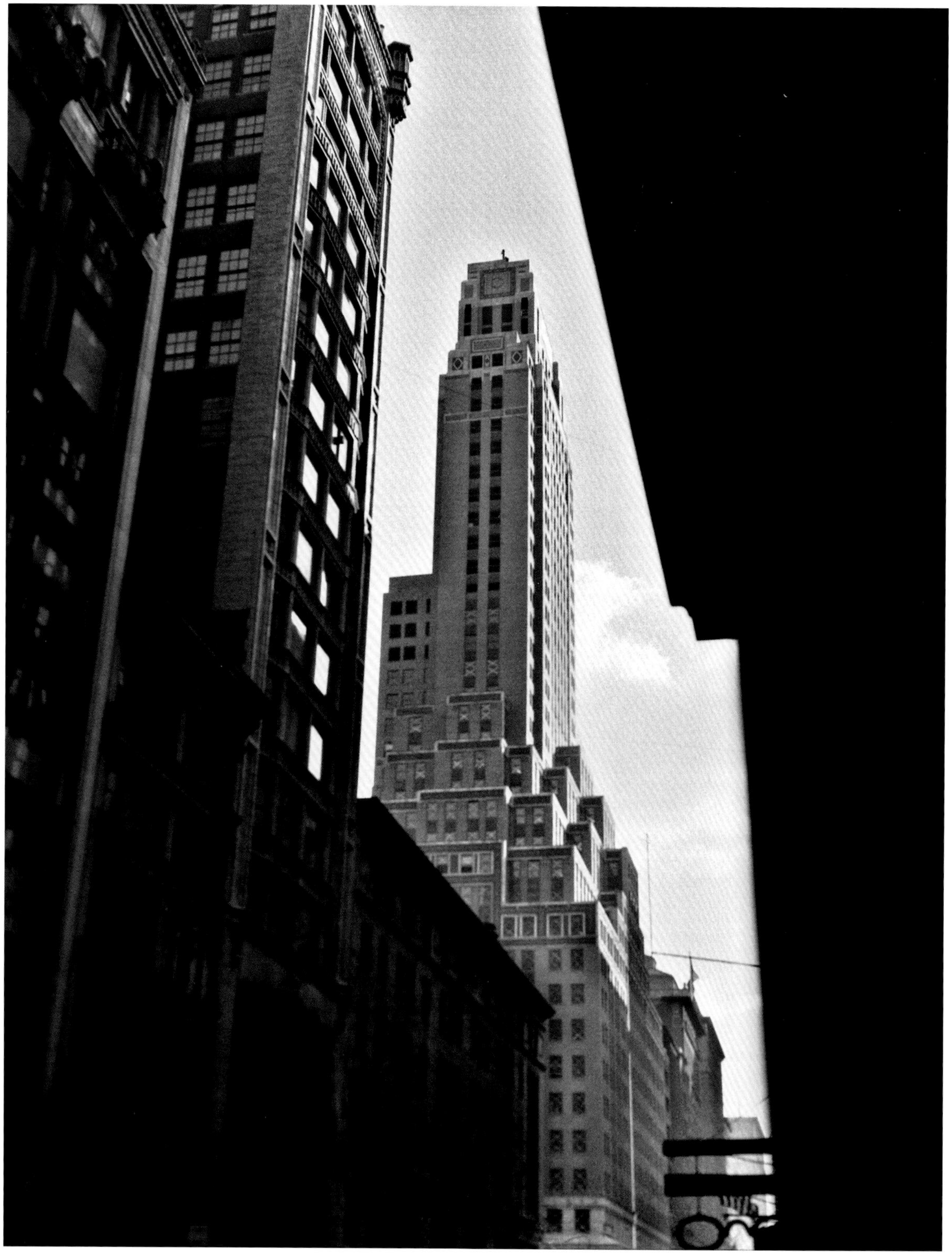

New York Skyscraper, 1921

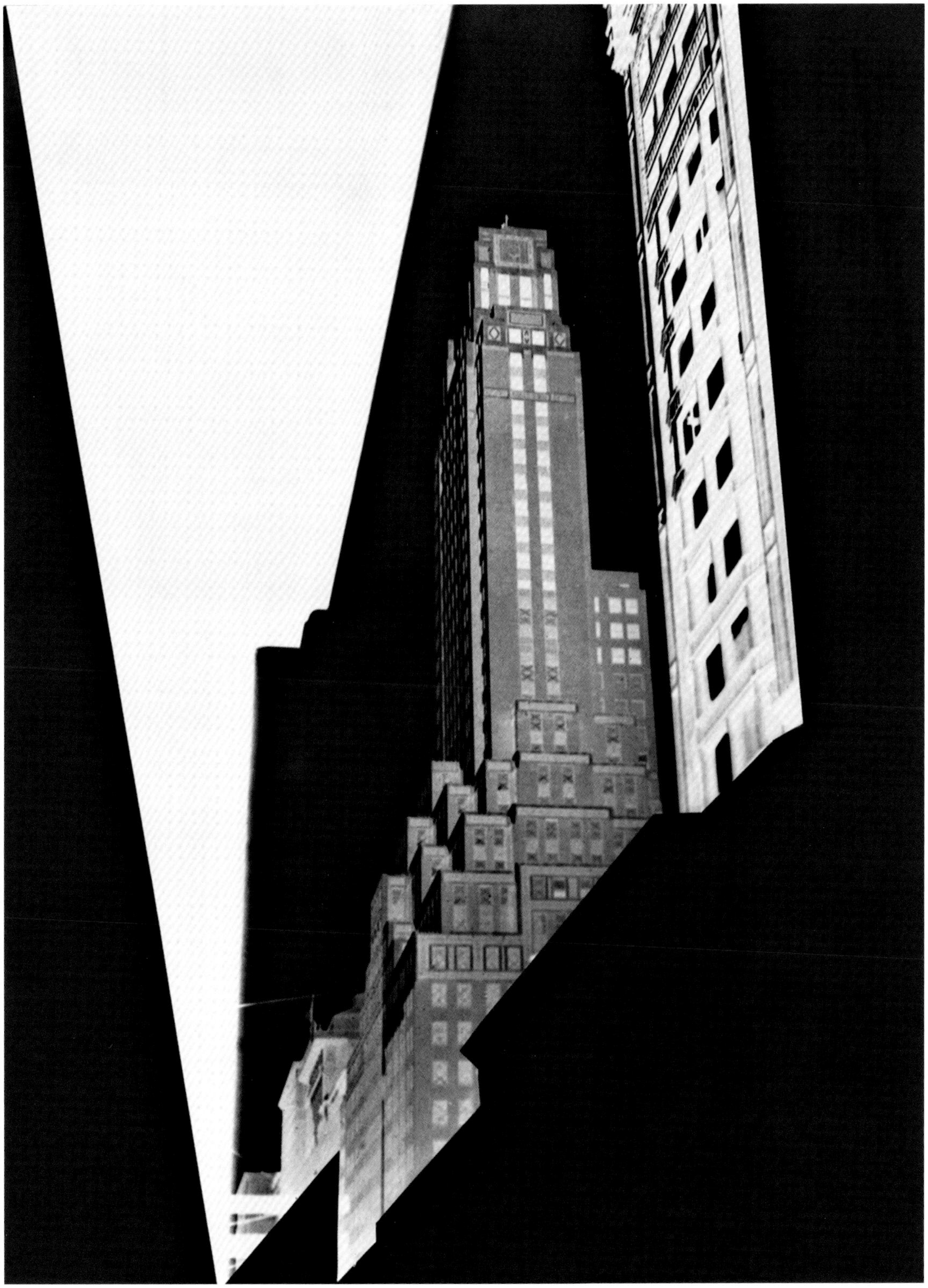

New York Skyscraper (negative), 1921

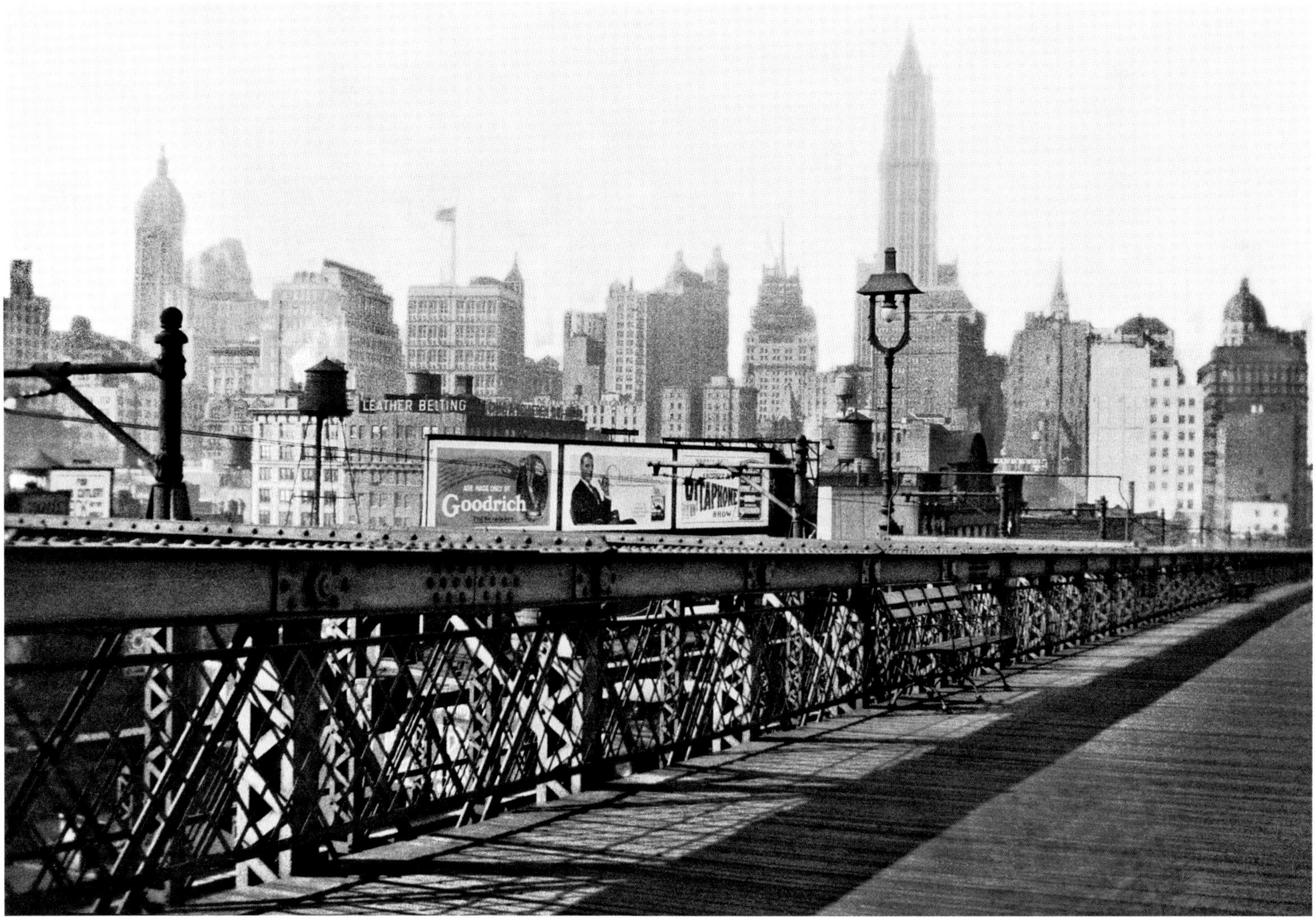

Manhattan from the Brooklyn Bridge, New York City, 1925

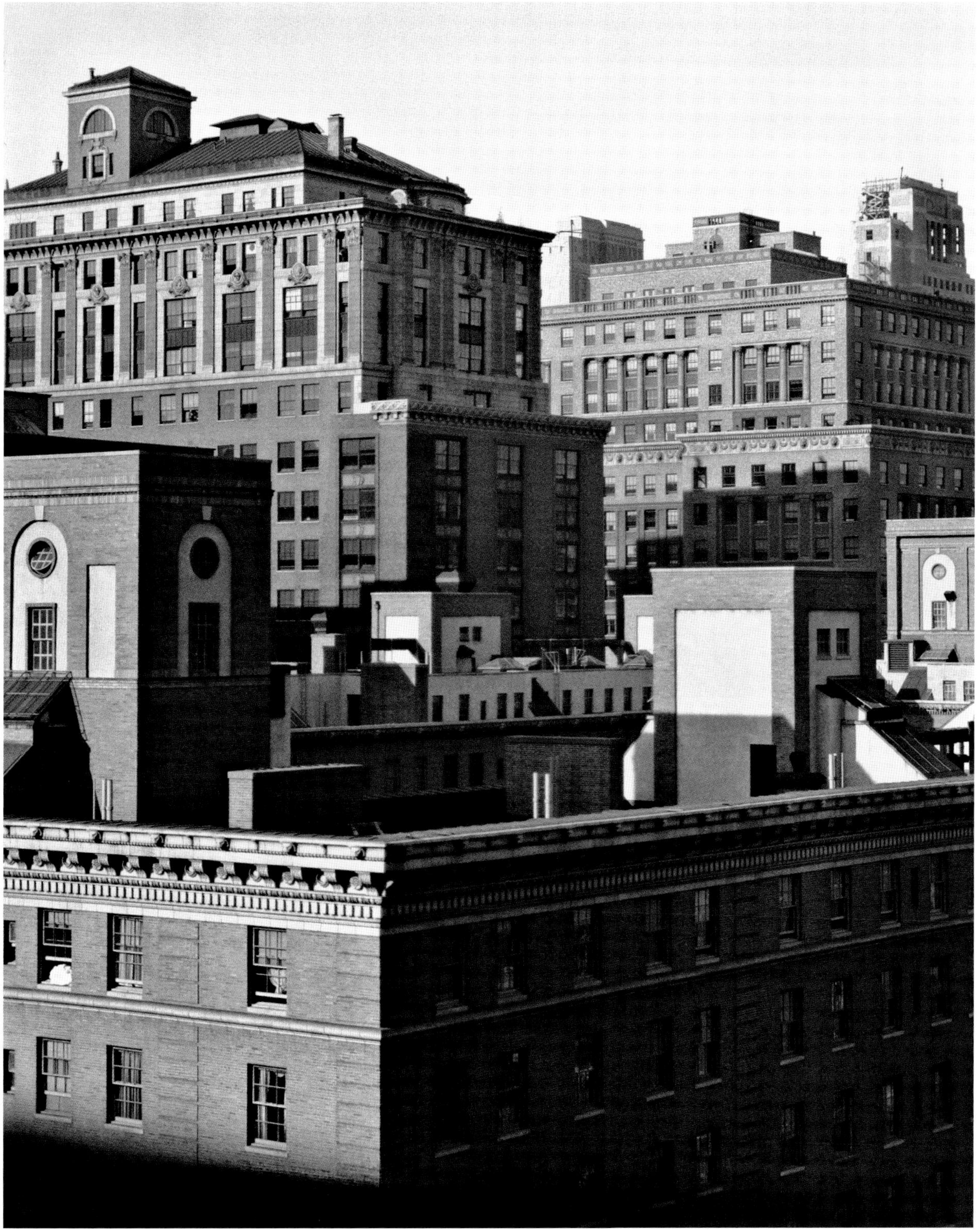

New York City Rooftops from Shelton Hotel, 1925

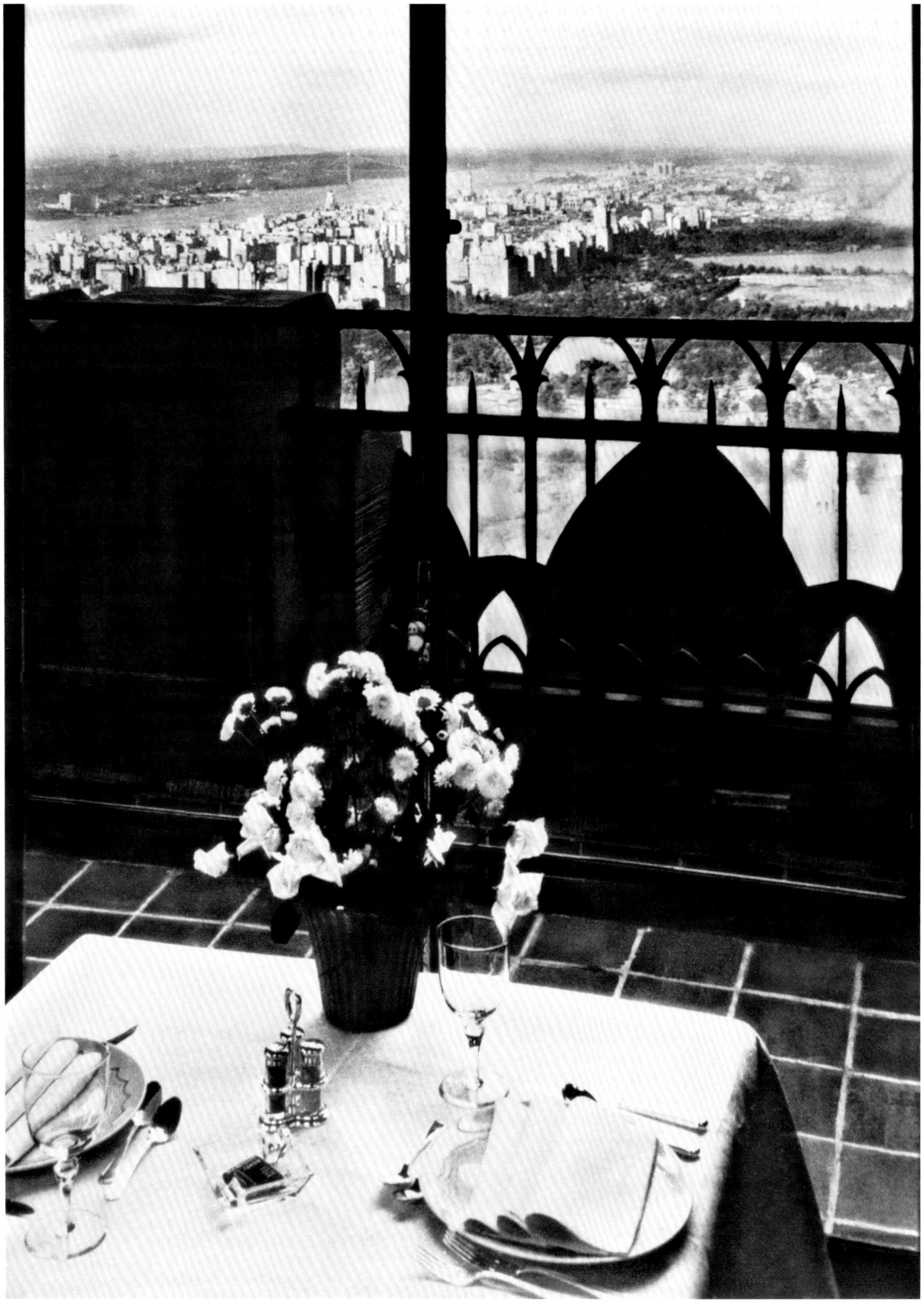

View from Restaurant, Rockefeller Building, New York City, 1926

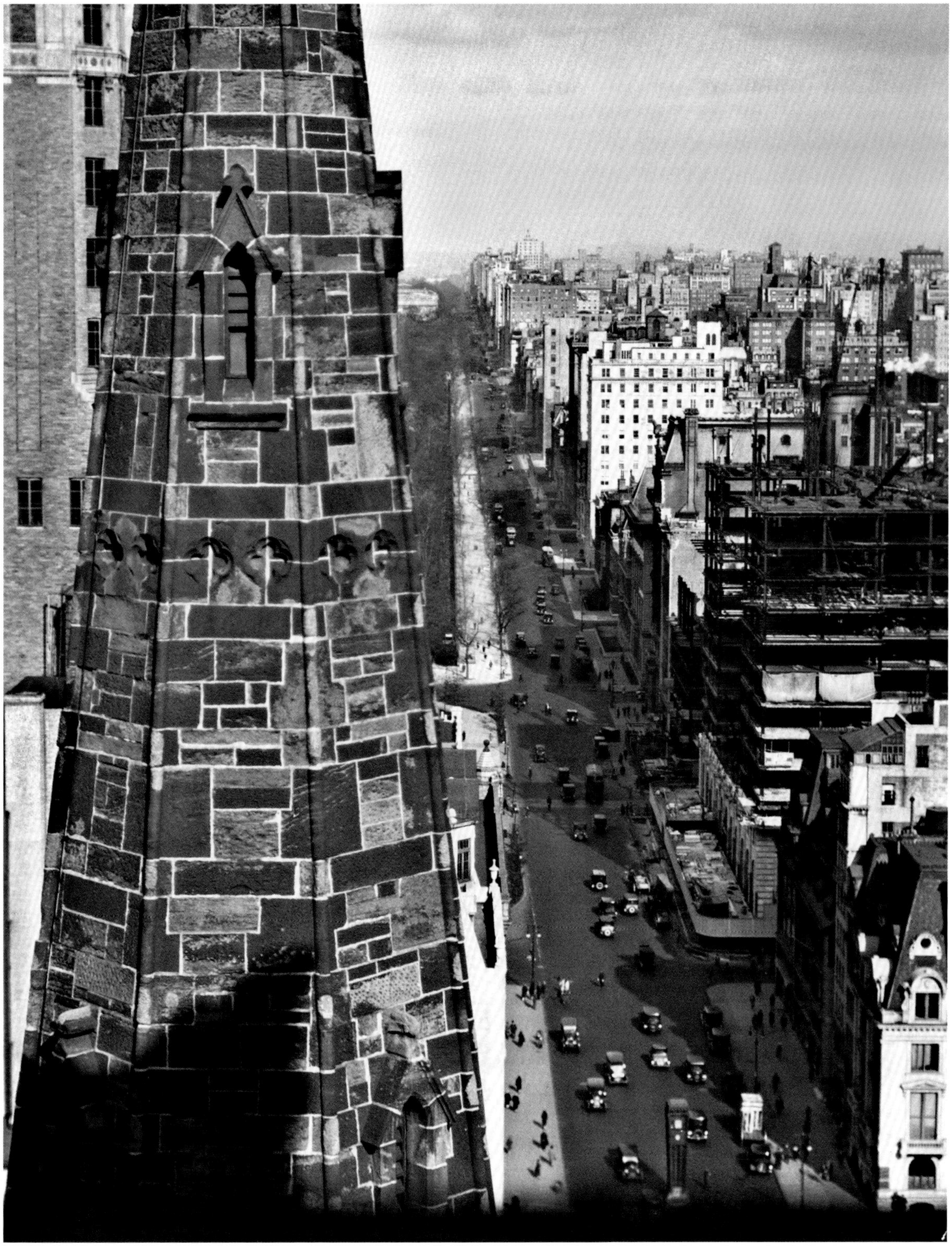

Fifth Avenue, New York City, 1921

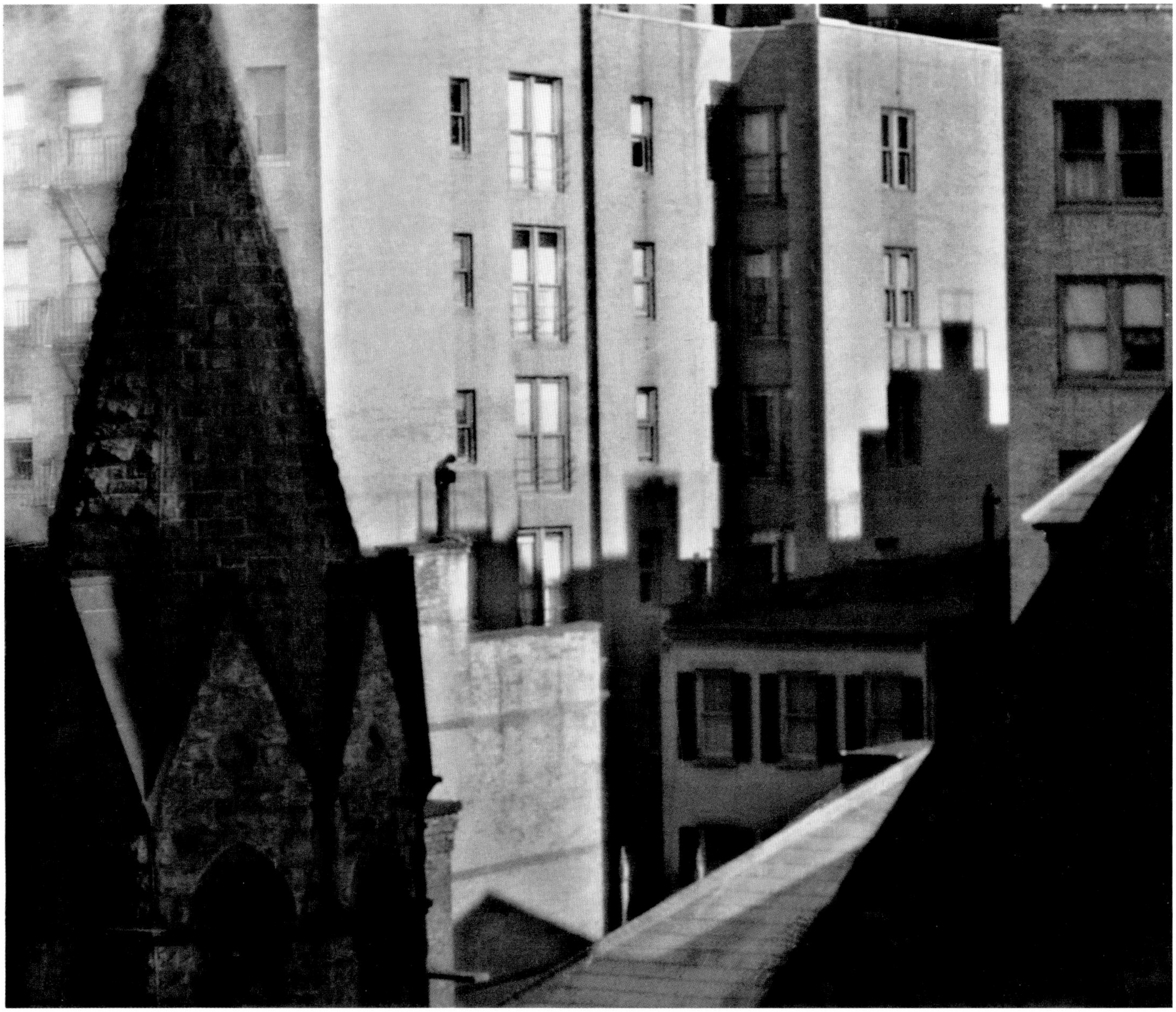

Rooftops, Apartments, New York City (view from E.O. Hoppé's studio on West 57th Street), 1921

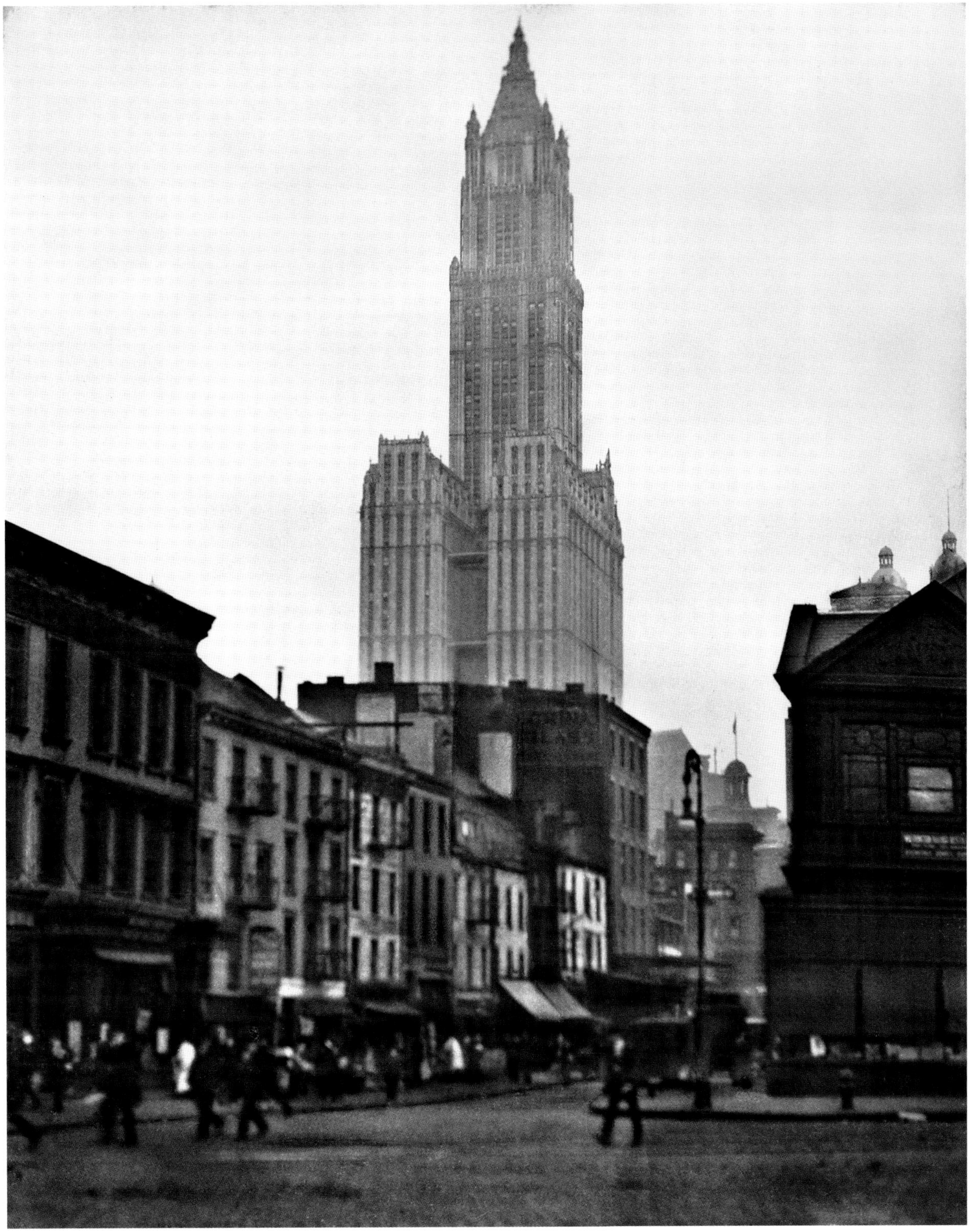

Woolworth Building, New York City, 1921

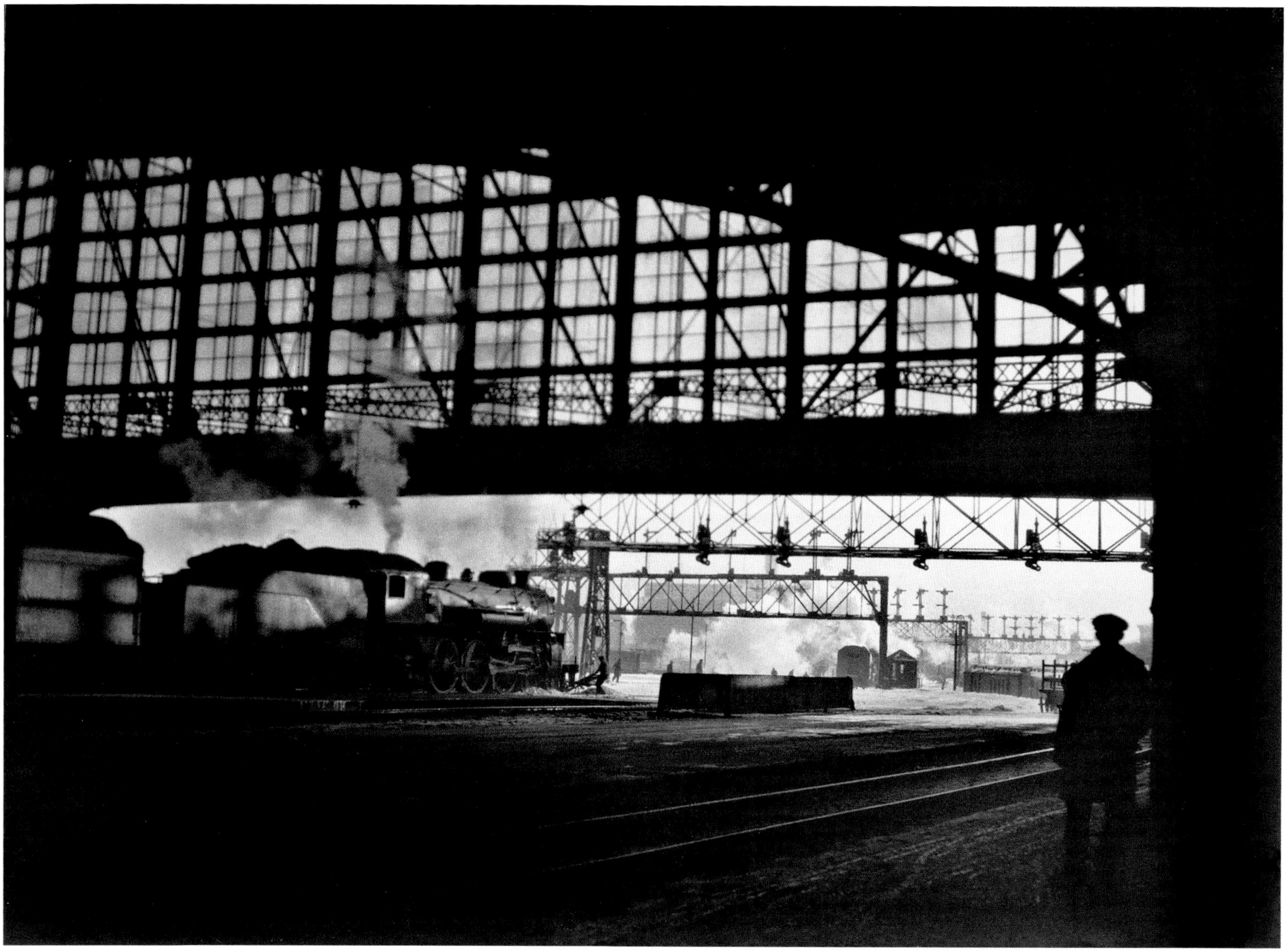

Boston Railway Station, Massachusetts, 1926

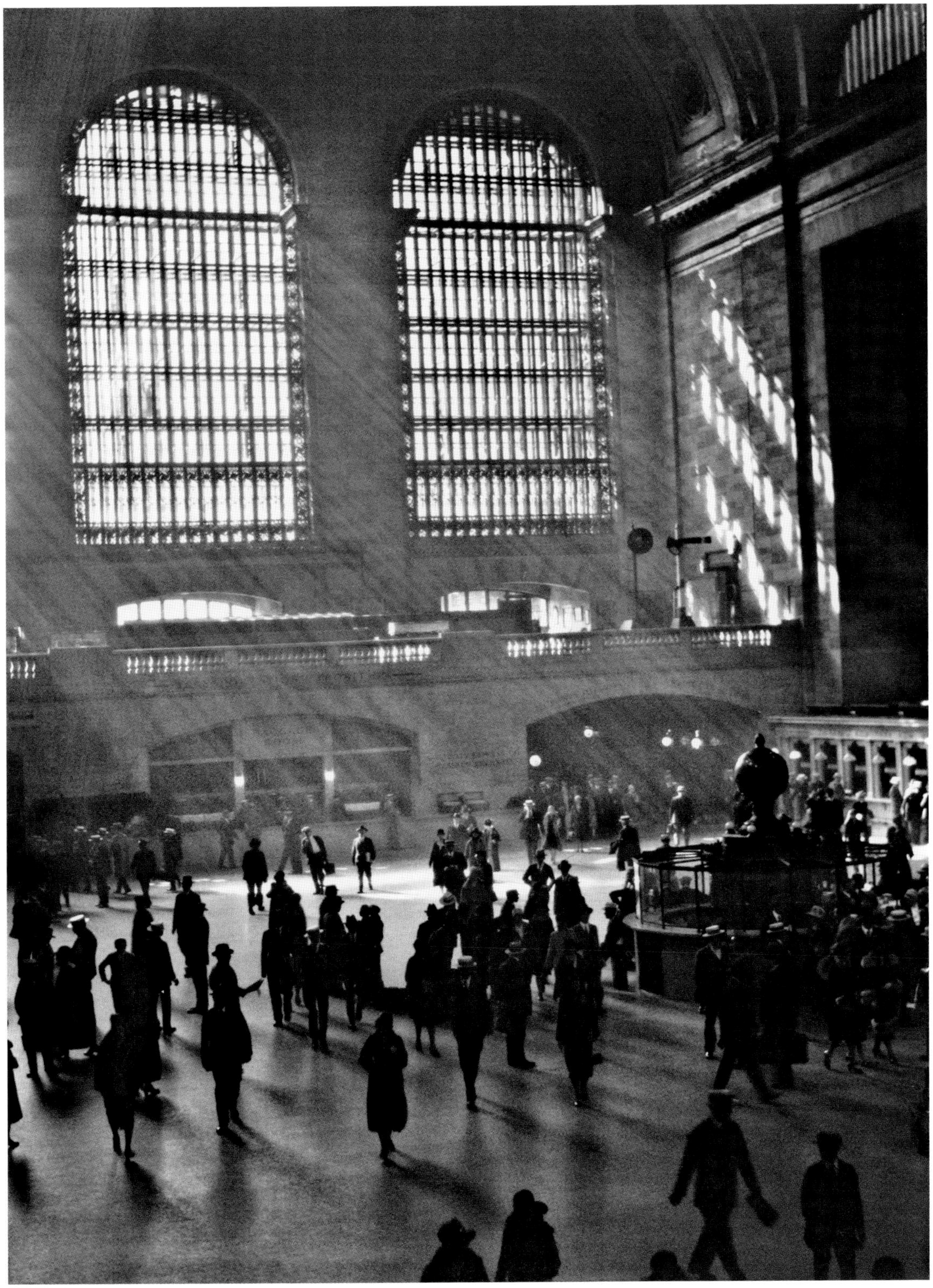

Grand Central Station, New York City, 1921

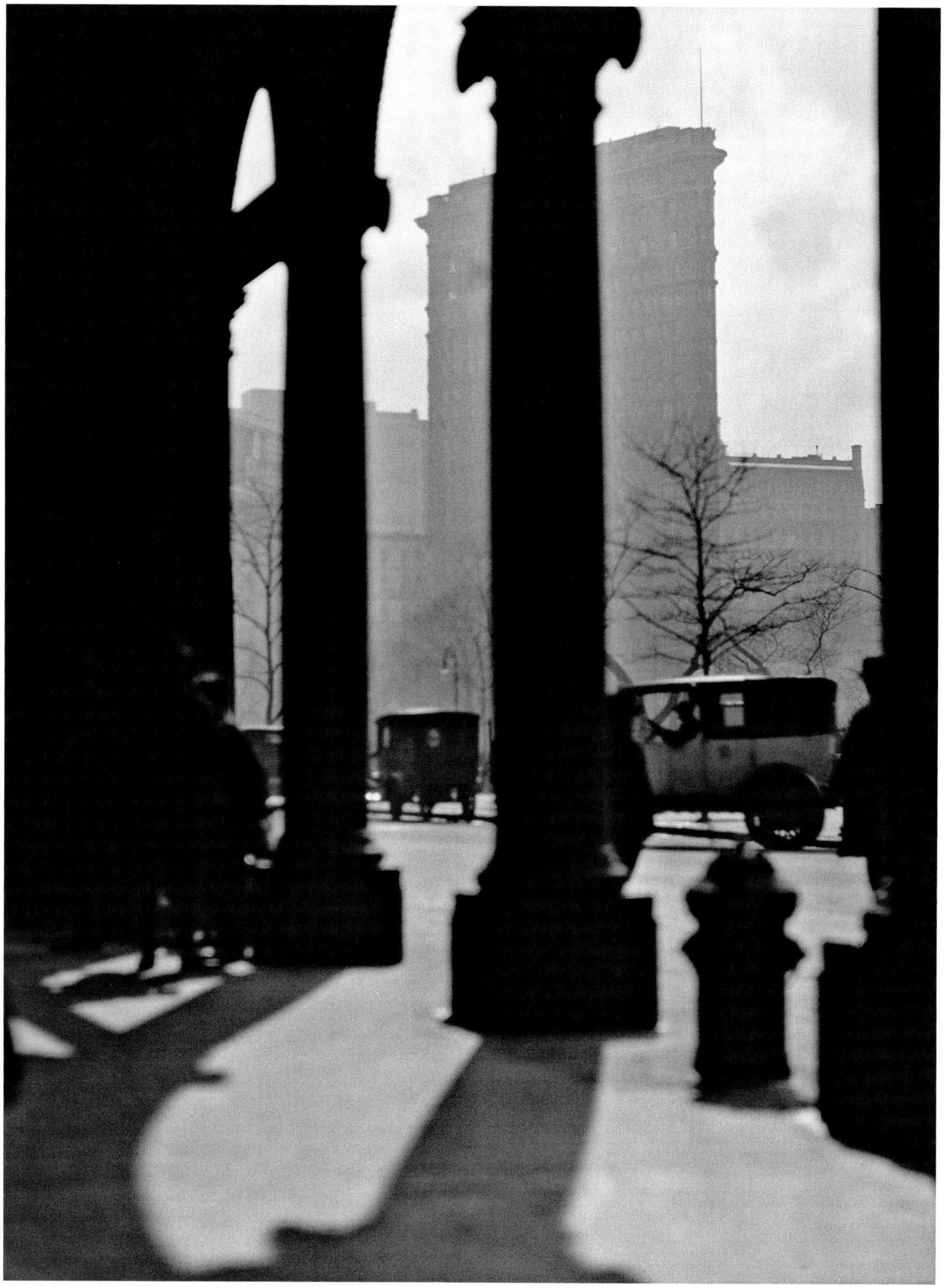

The Flatiron Building, New York City, 1925

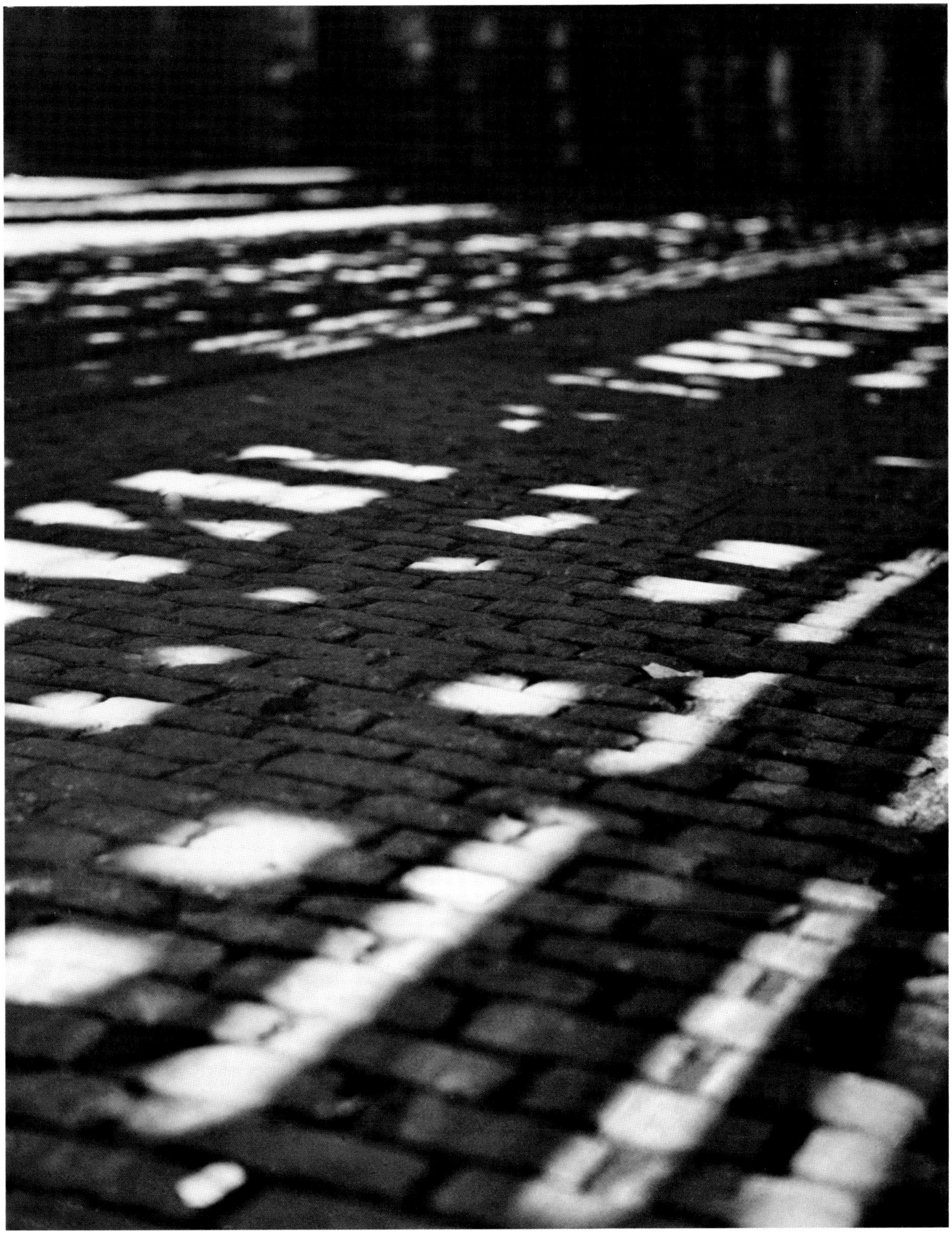

Cobblestone Road, New York City, 1921

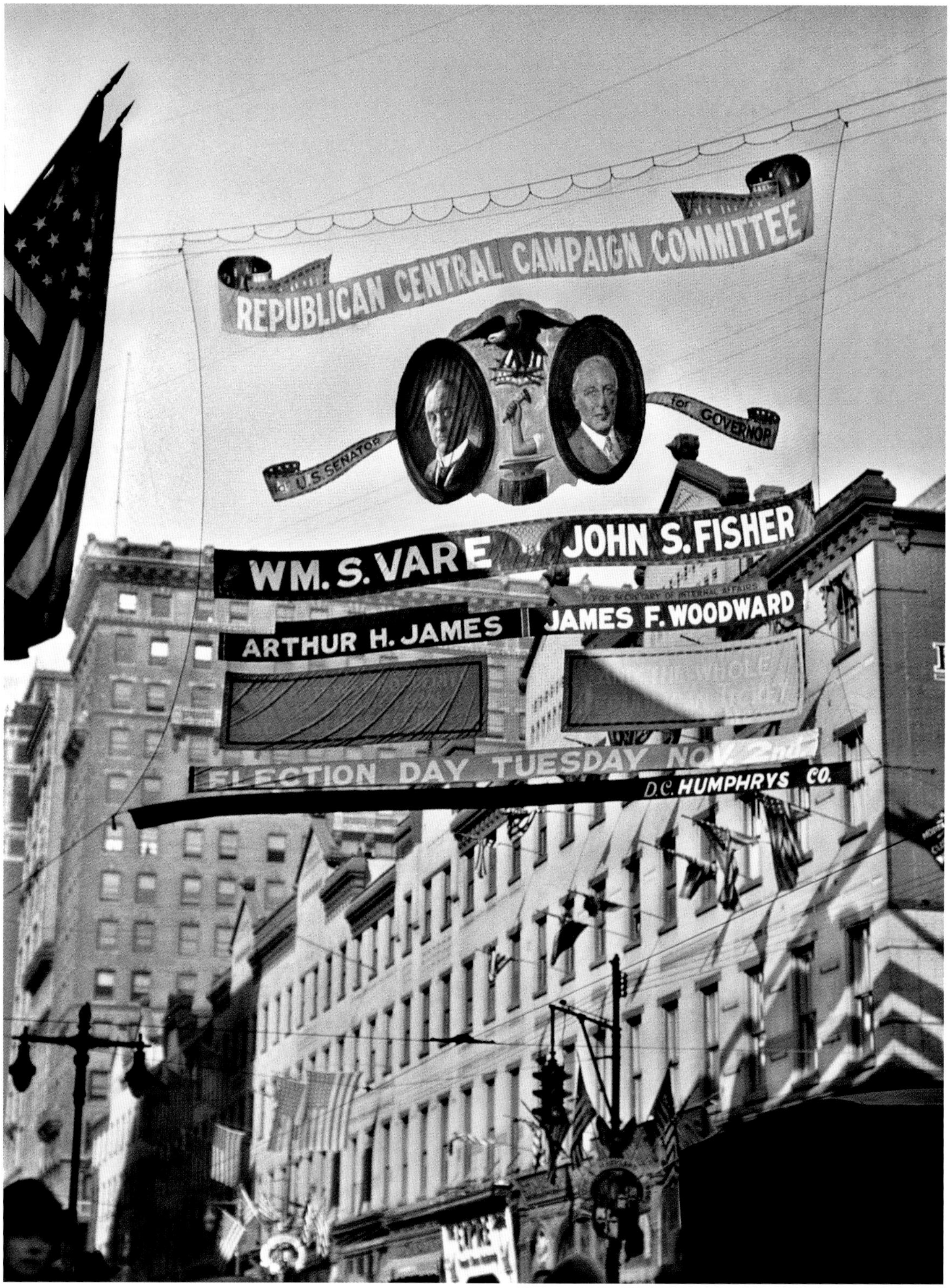

Election Signs, Philadelphia, Pennsylvania, 1926

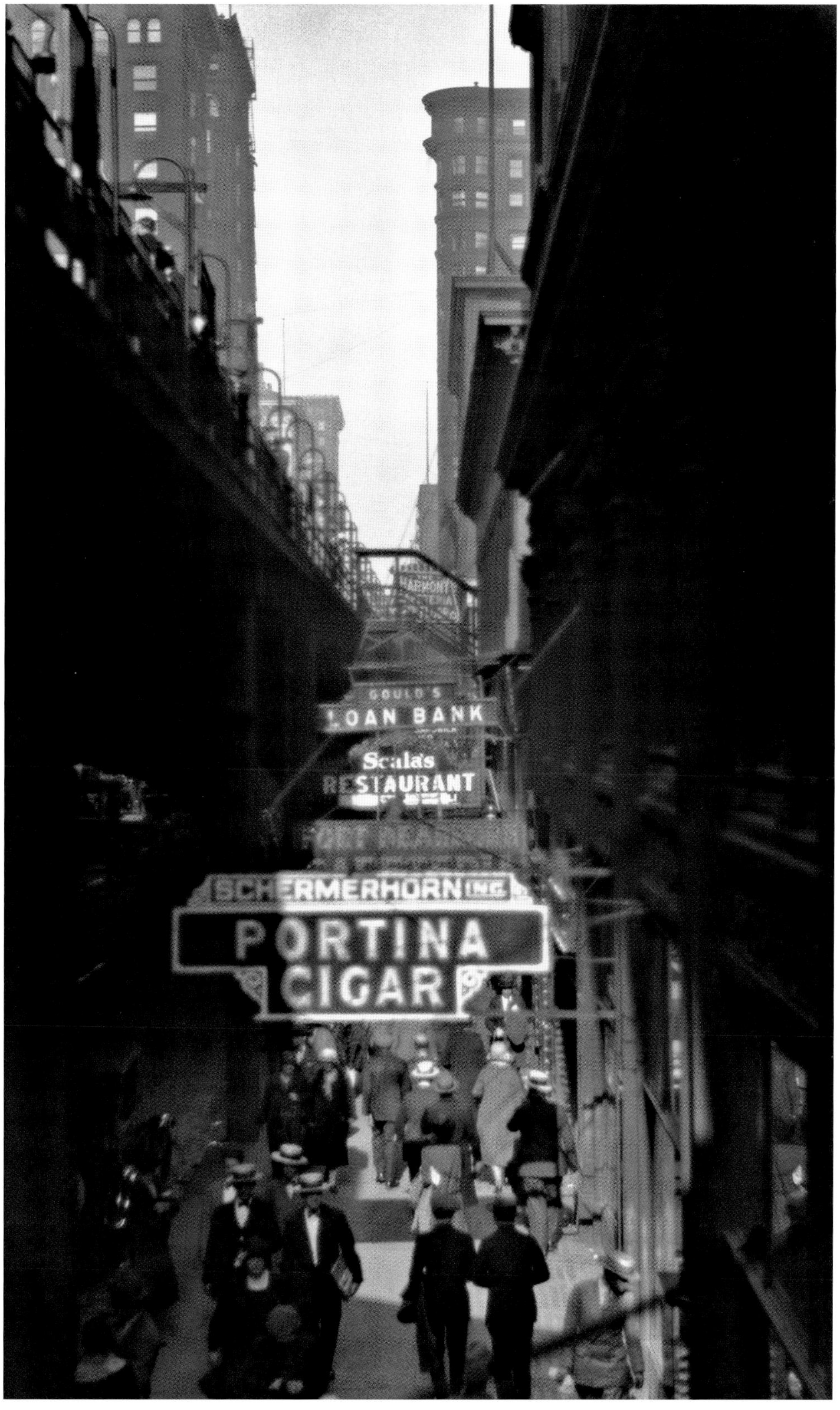

Jeweler's Building, Chicago, Illinois, 1926

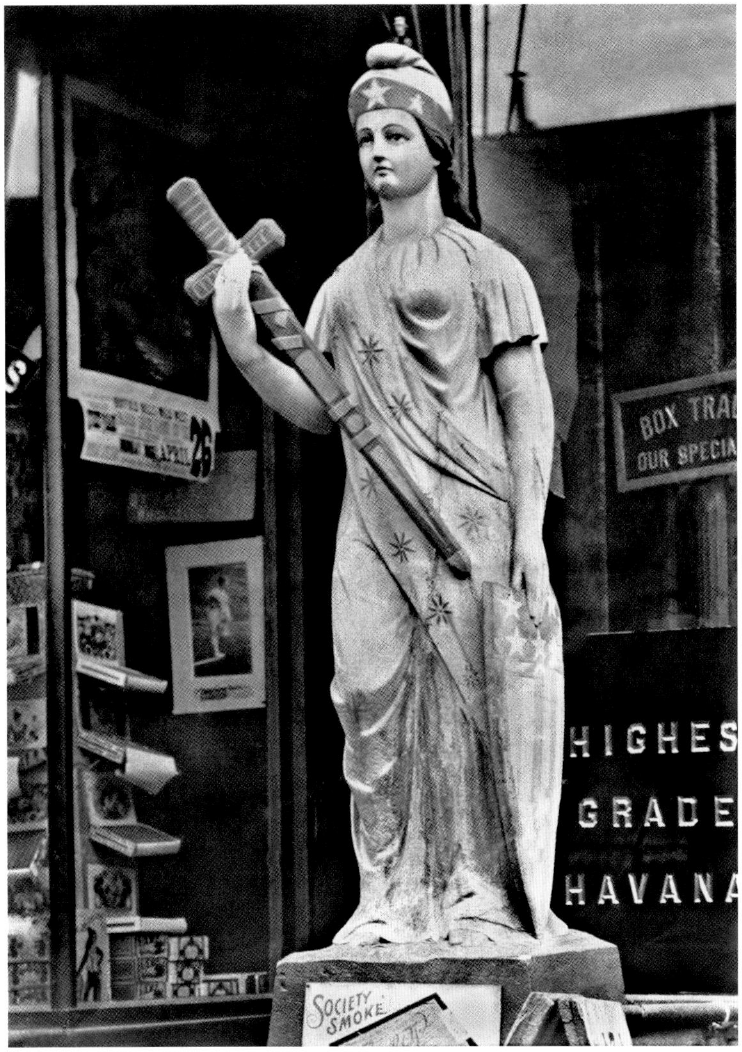

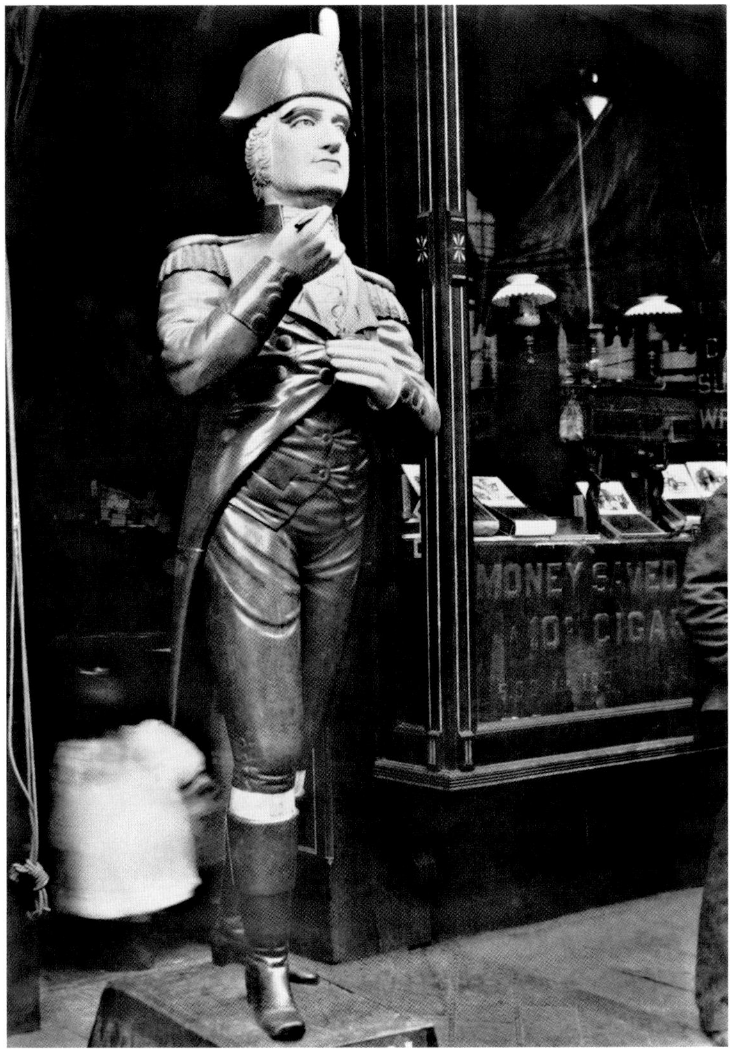

Cigar Store Figure, 1926 Cigar Store Figure, 1926

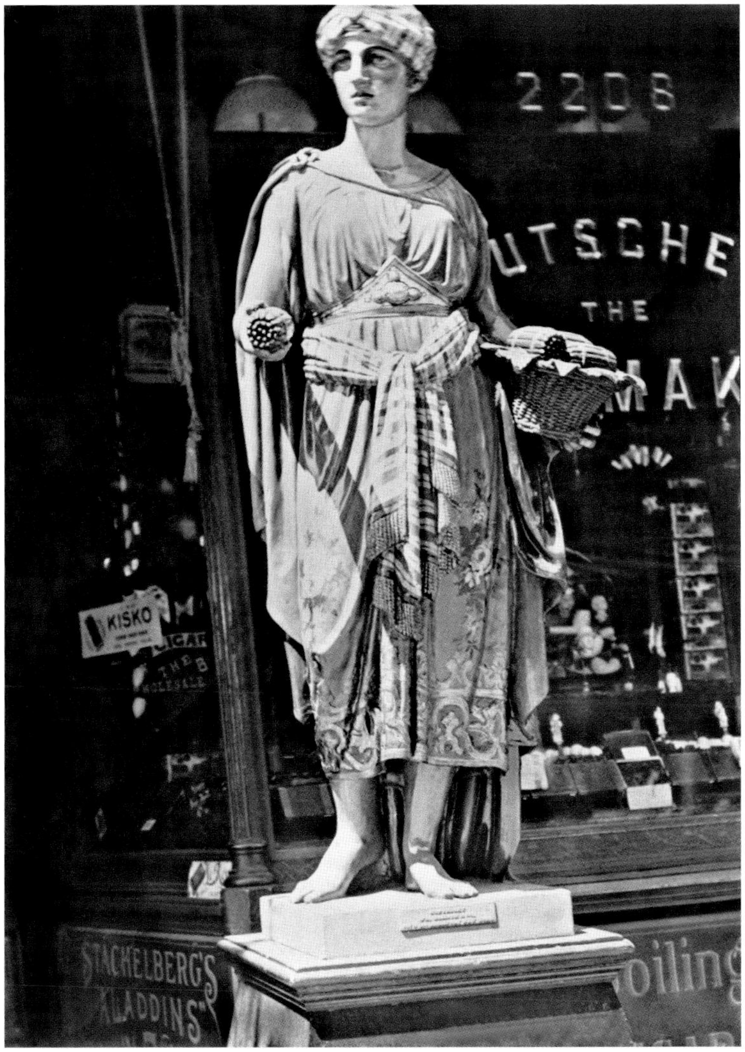

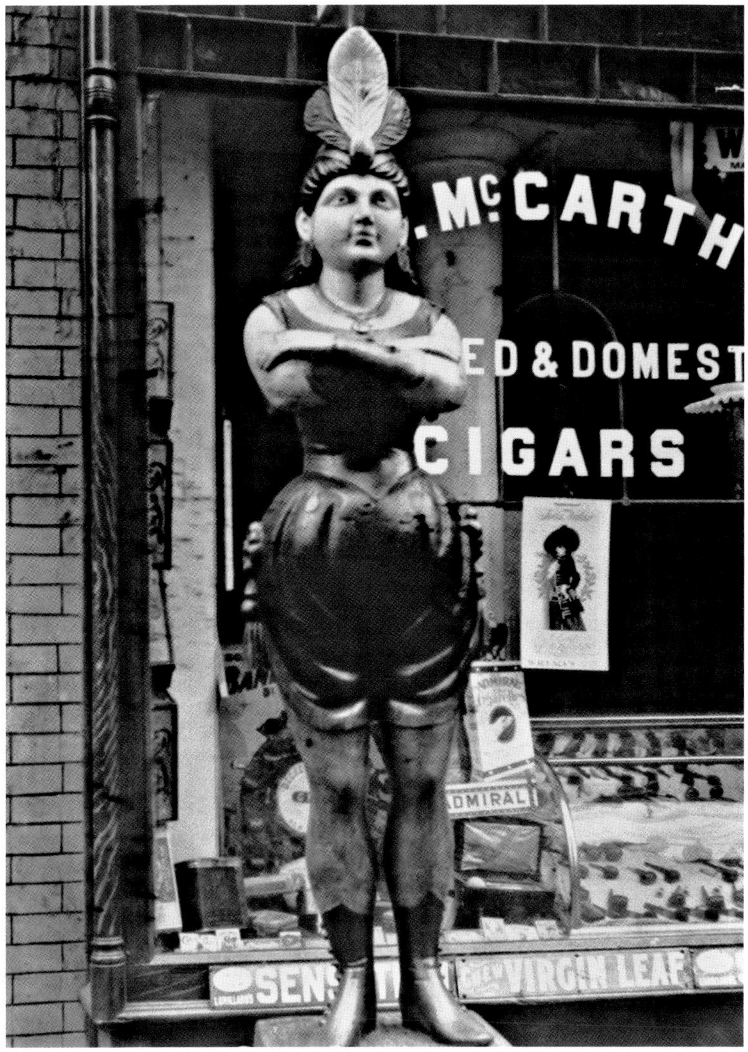

Cigar Store Figure, 1926   Cigar Store Figure, 1926

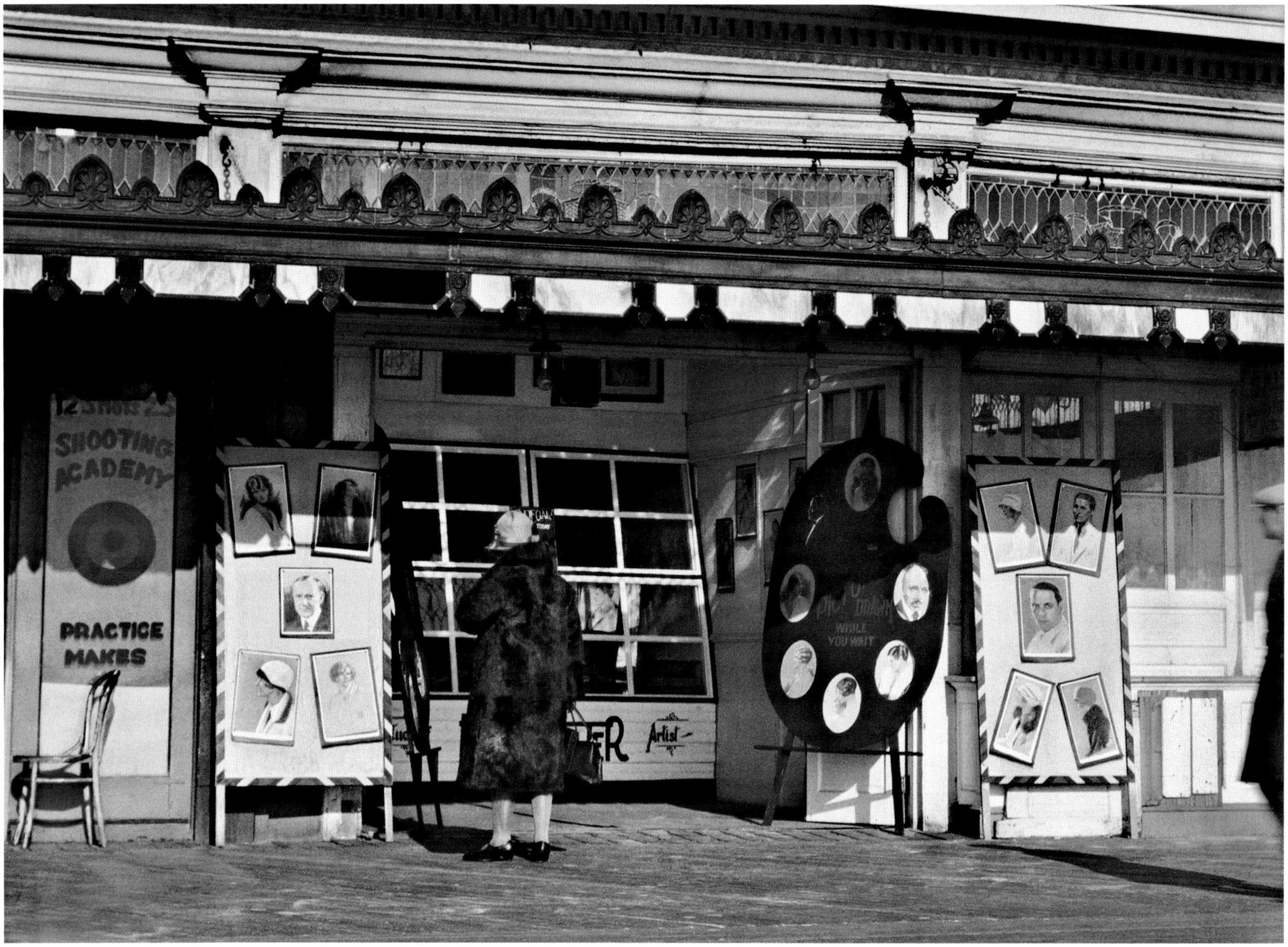

Artist's Storefront on the Boardwalk, Atlantic City, New Jersey, 1926

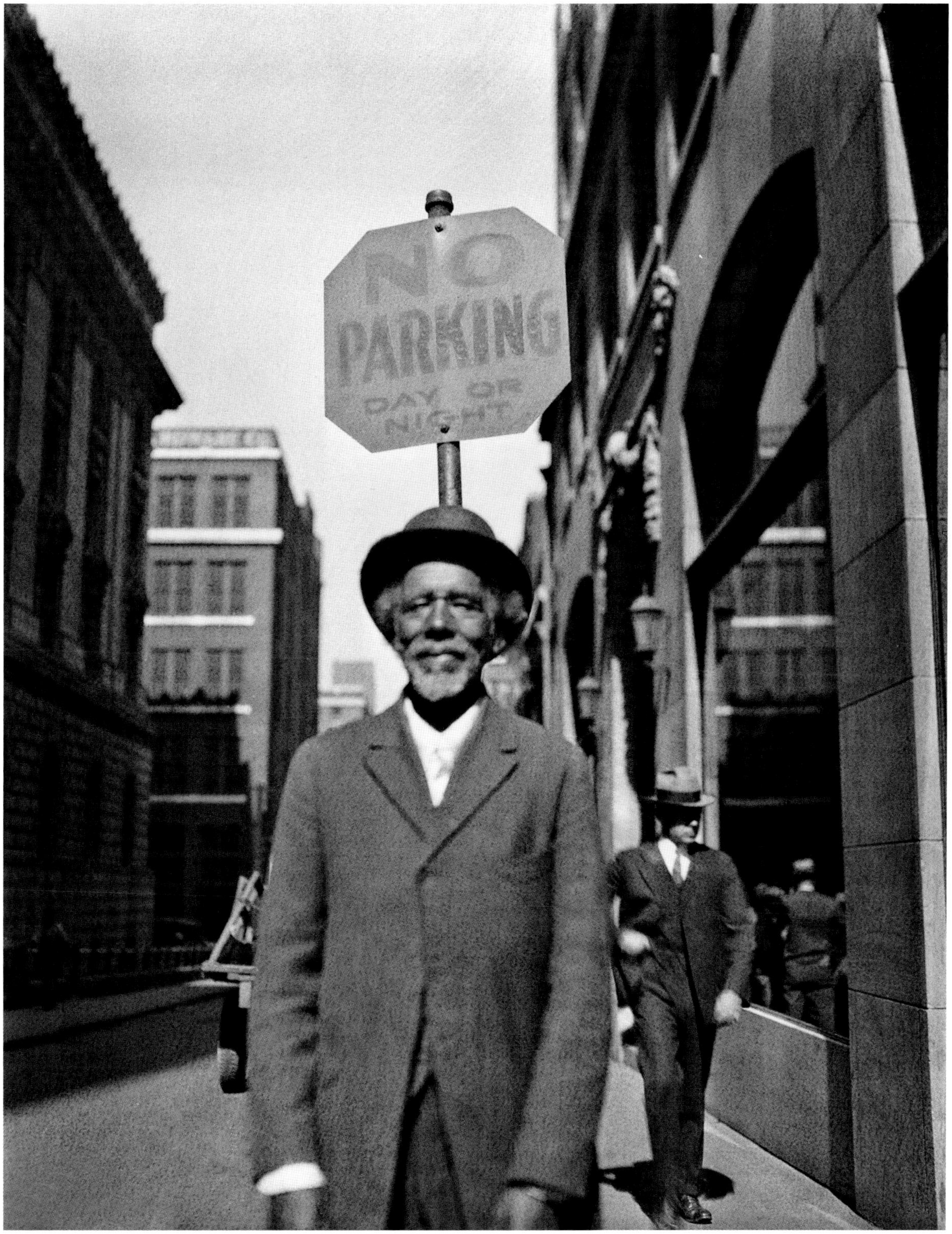

Black Man in Hat, Atlanta, Georgia, 1926

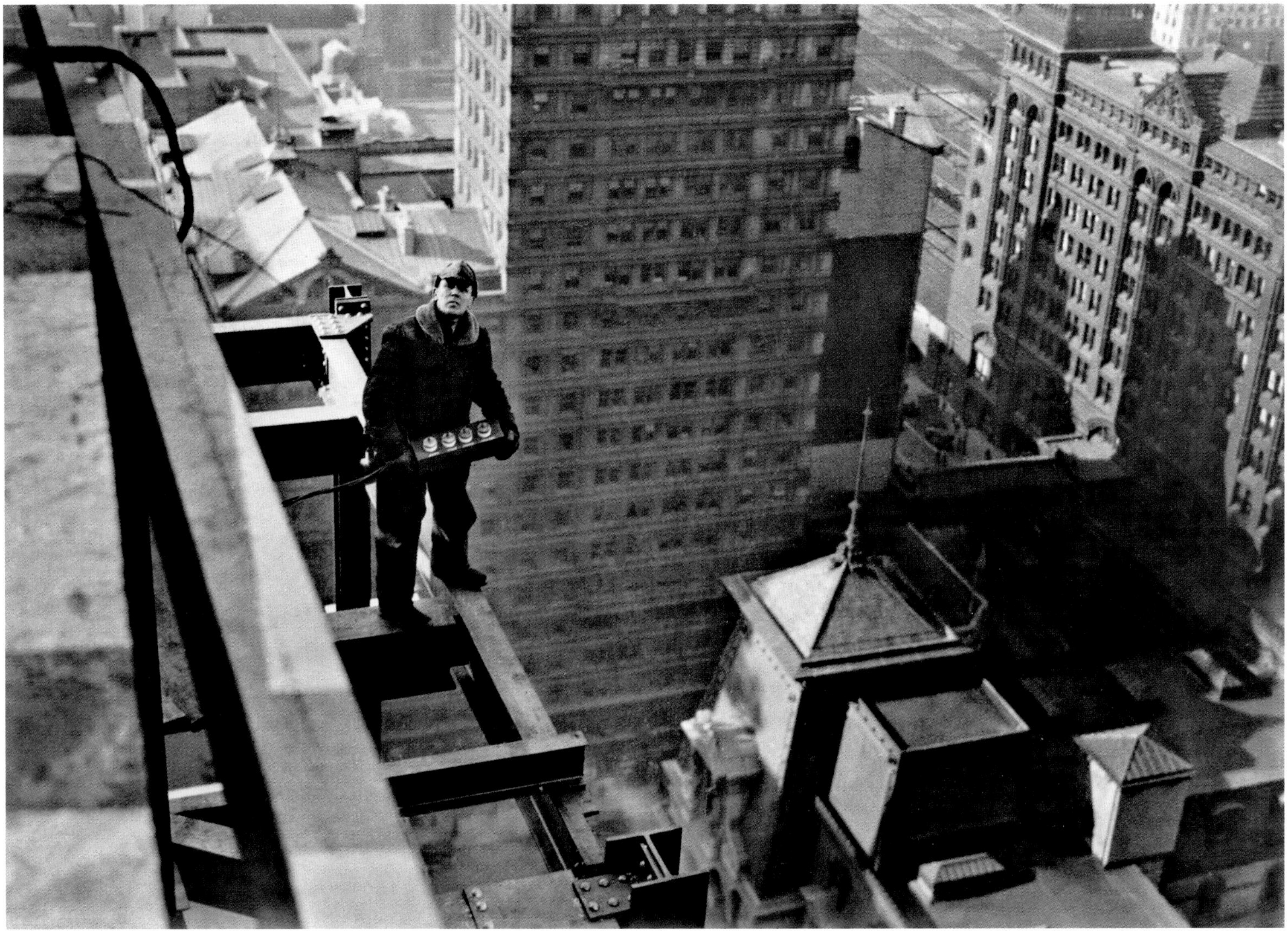

Steelworkers, Lincoln Liberty Building, Philadelphia, Pennsylvania, 1926

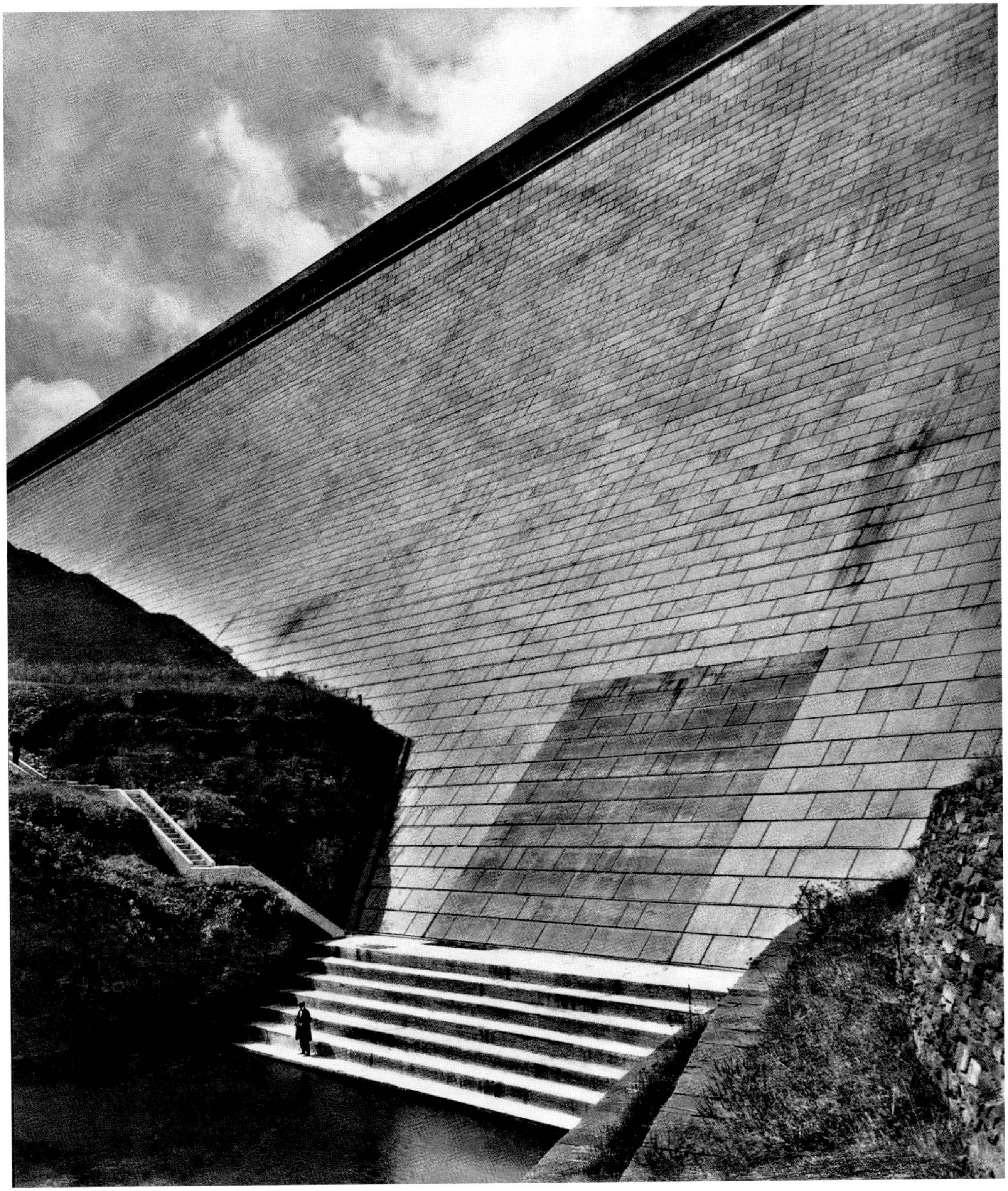

Reservoir, New York, 1926

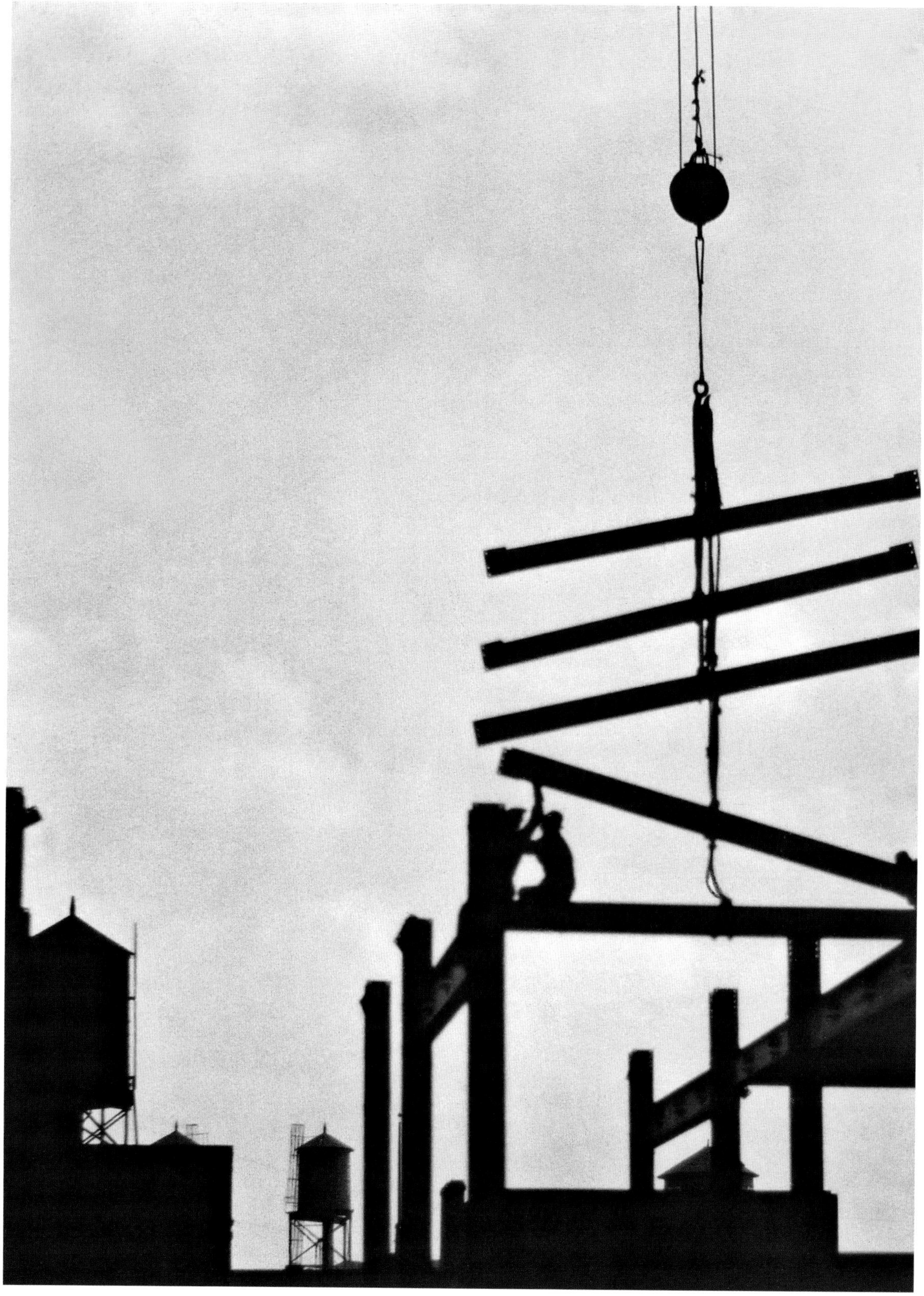

Steel Construction, Philadelphia, Pennsylvania, 1926

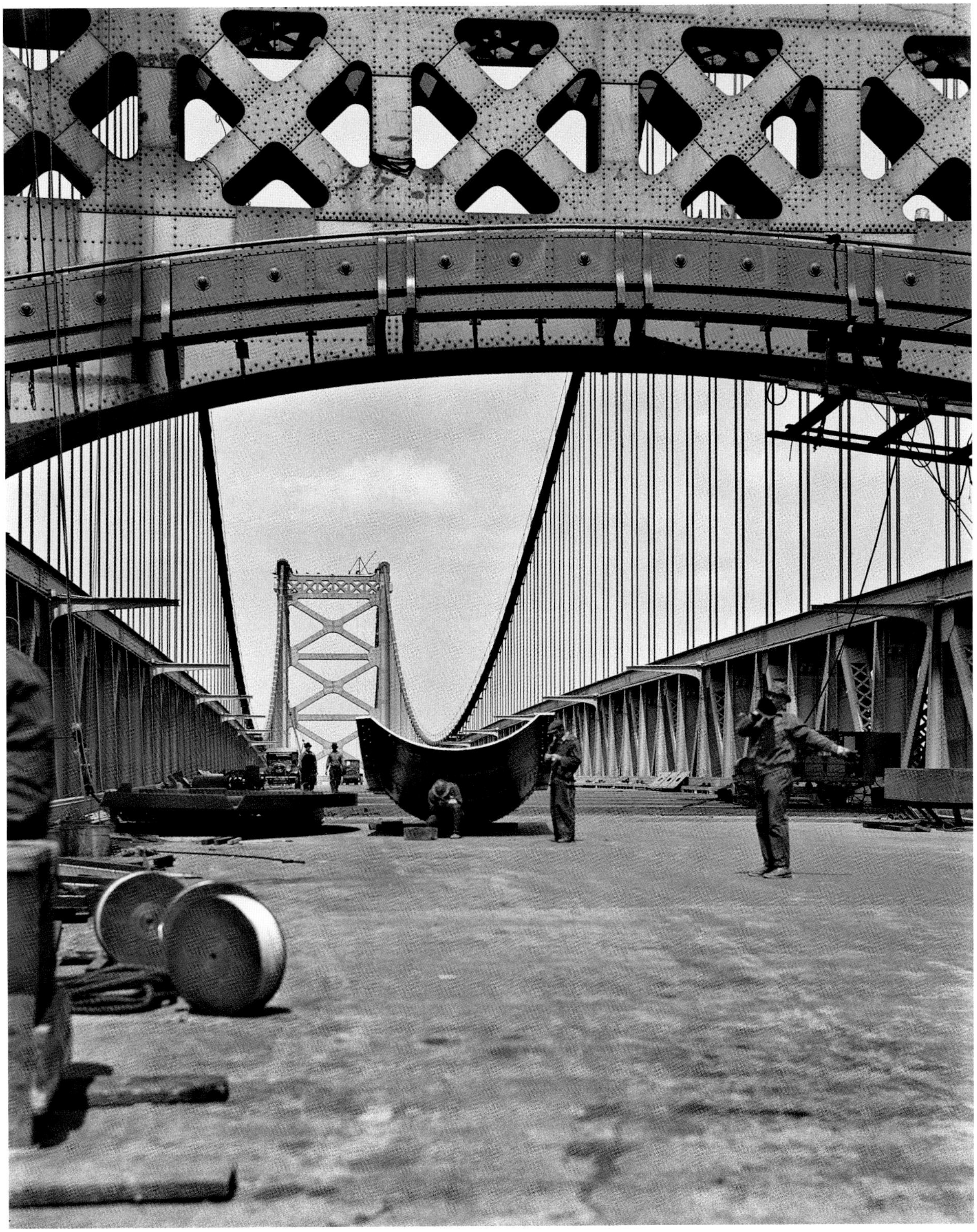

Construction, Delaware Bridge, Wilmington, 1926

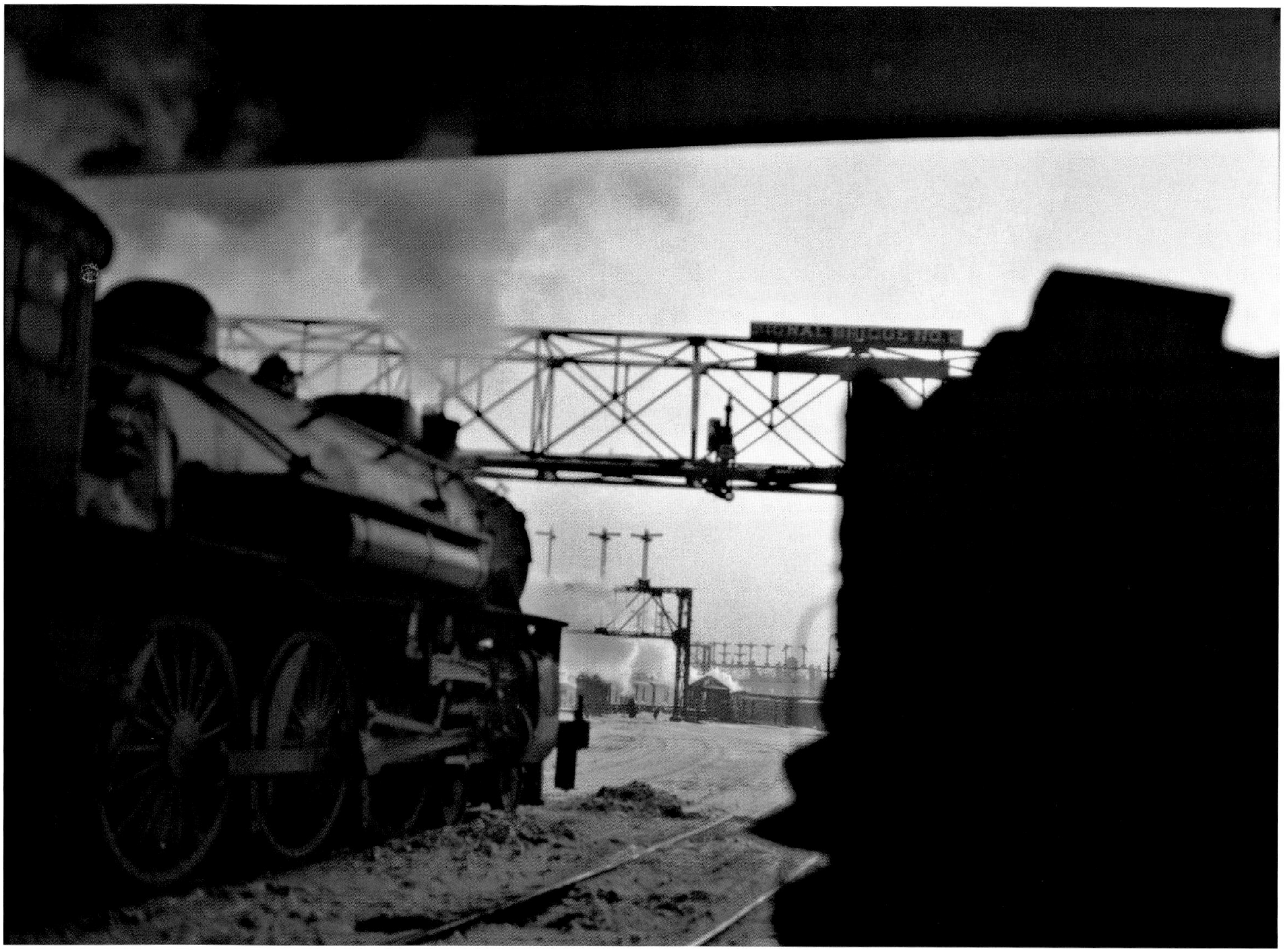

Locomotive, Boston Railway Station, Massachusetts, 1926

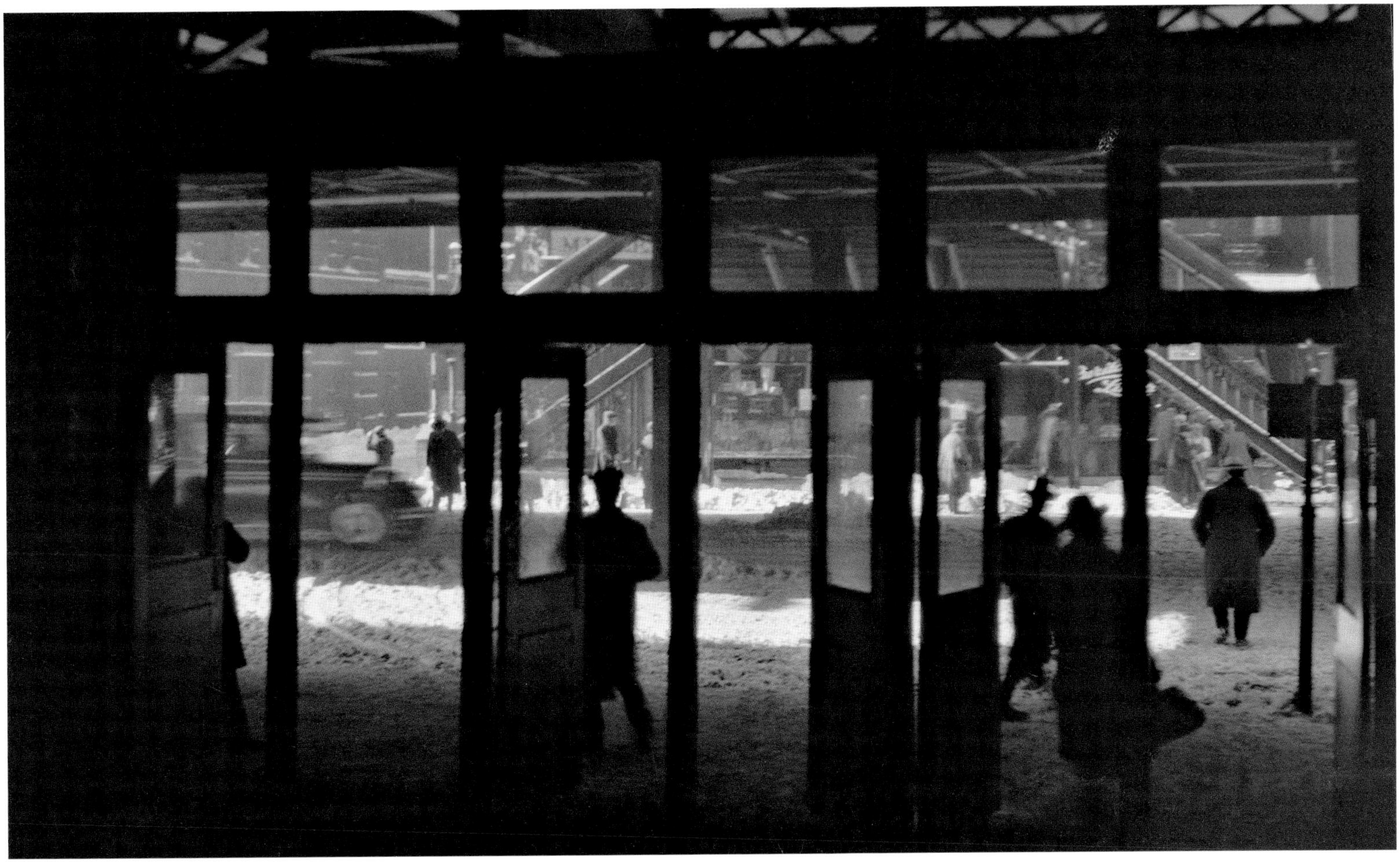

Snow at Boston Railway Station, Massachusetts, 1926

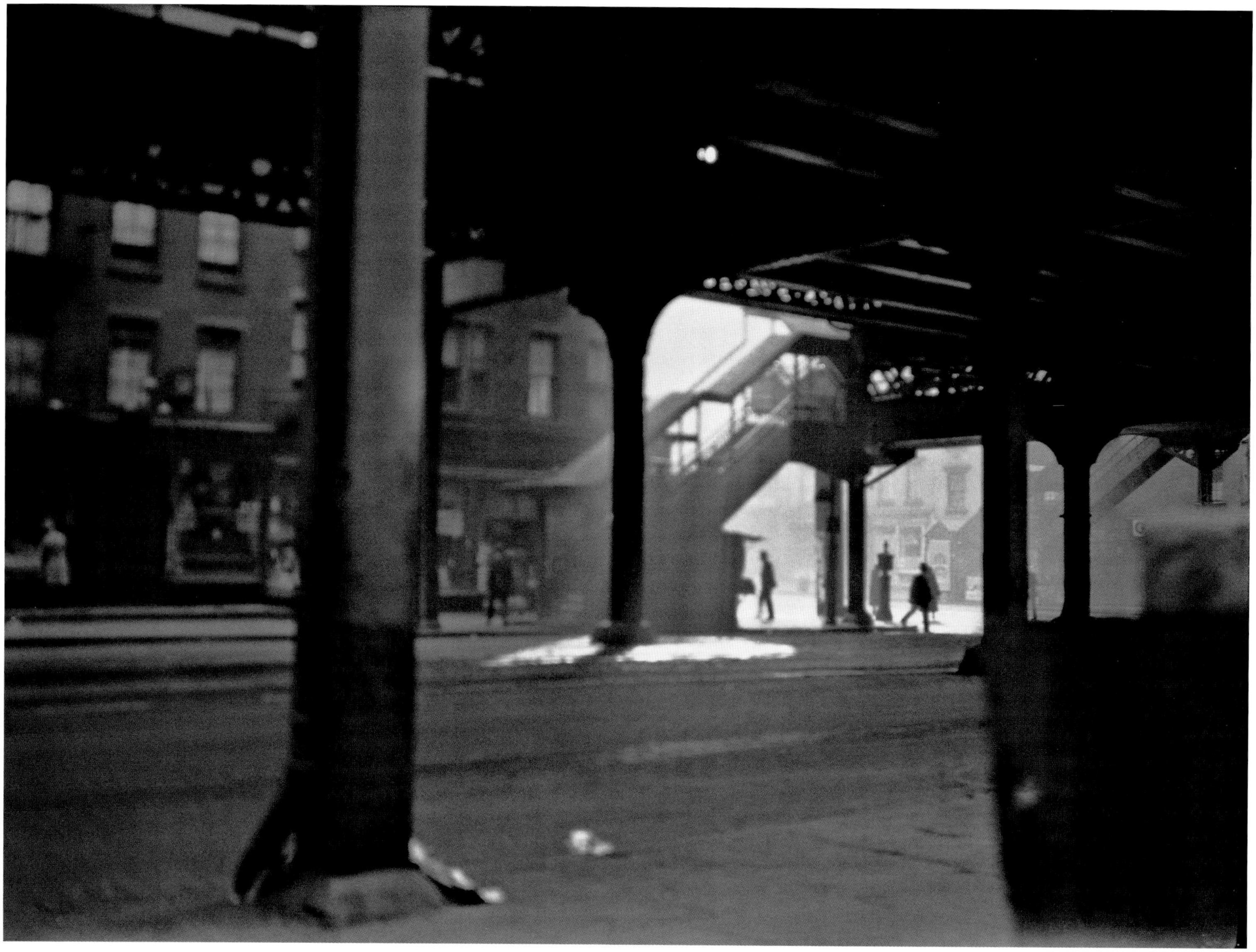

The El at Third Avenue and 42nd Street, New York City, 1921

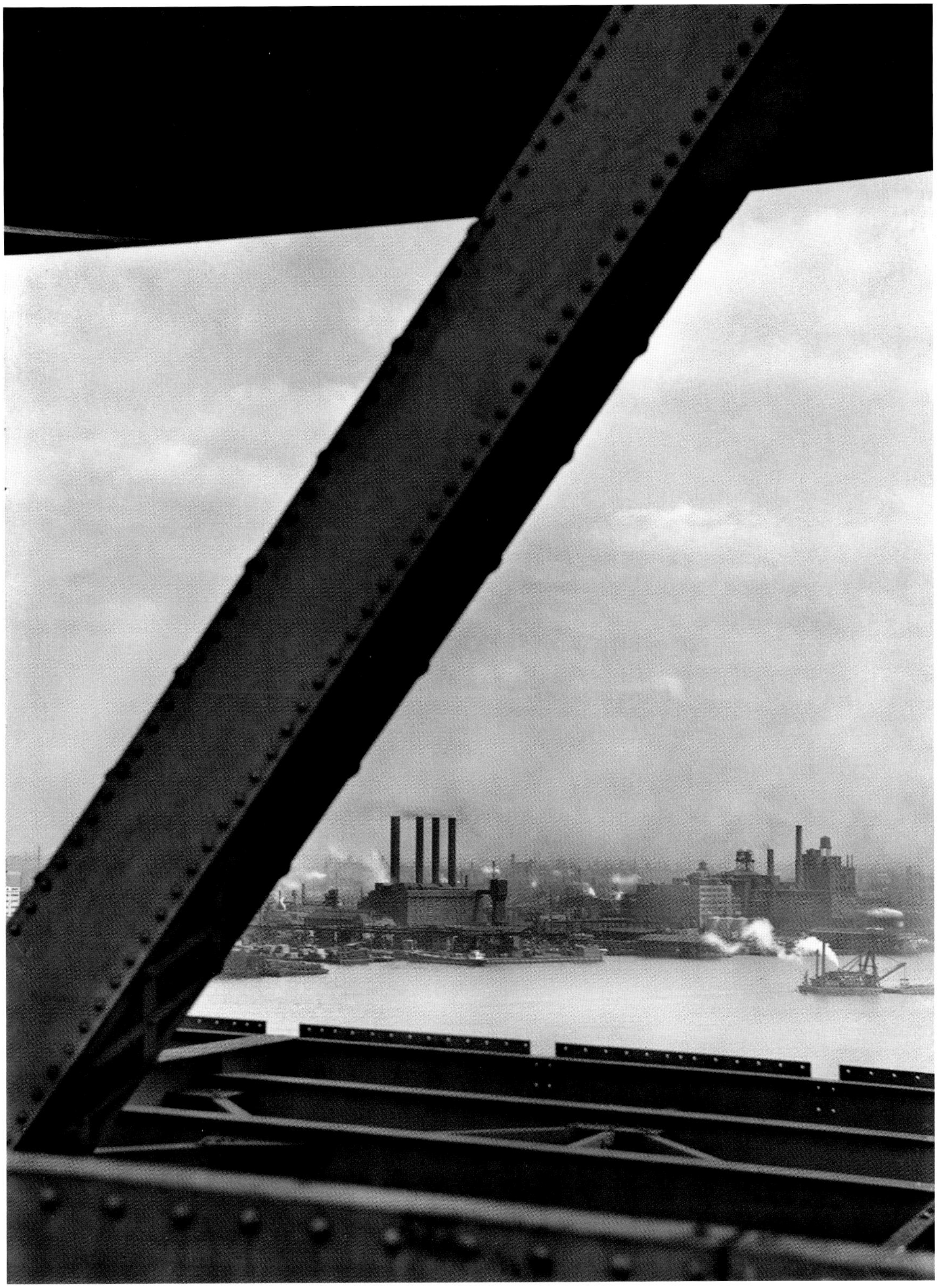

View from the Delaware Bridge, Wilmington, 1926

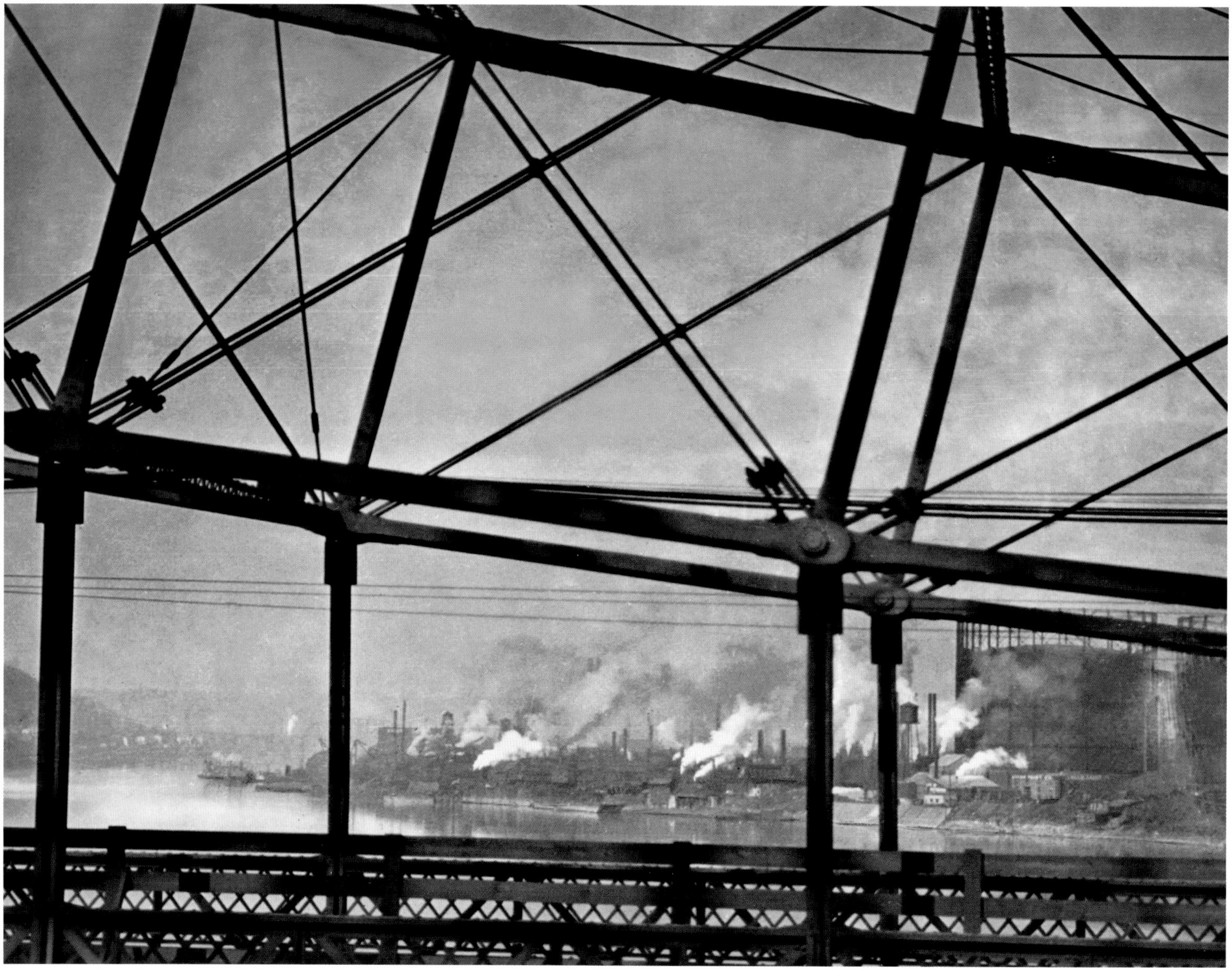

Industrial View through Bridge, Pittsburgh, Pennsylvania, 1926

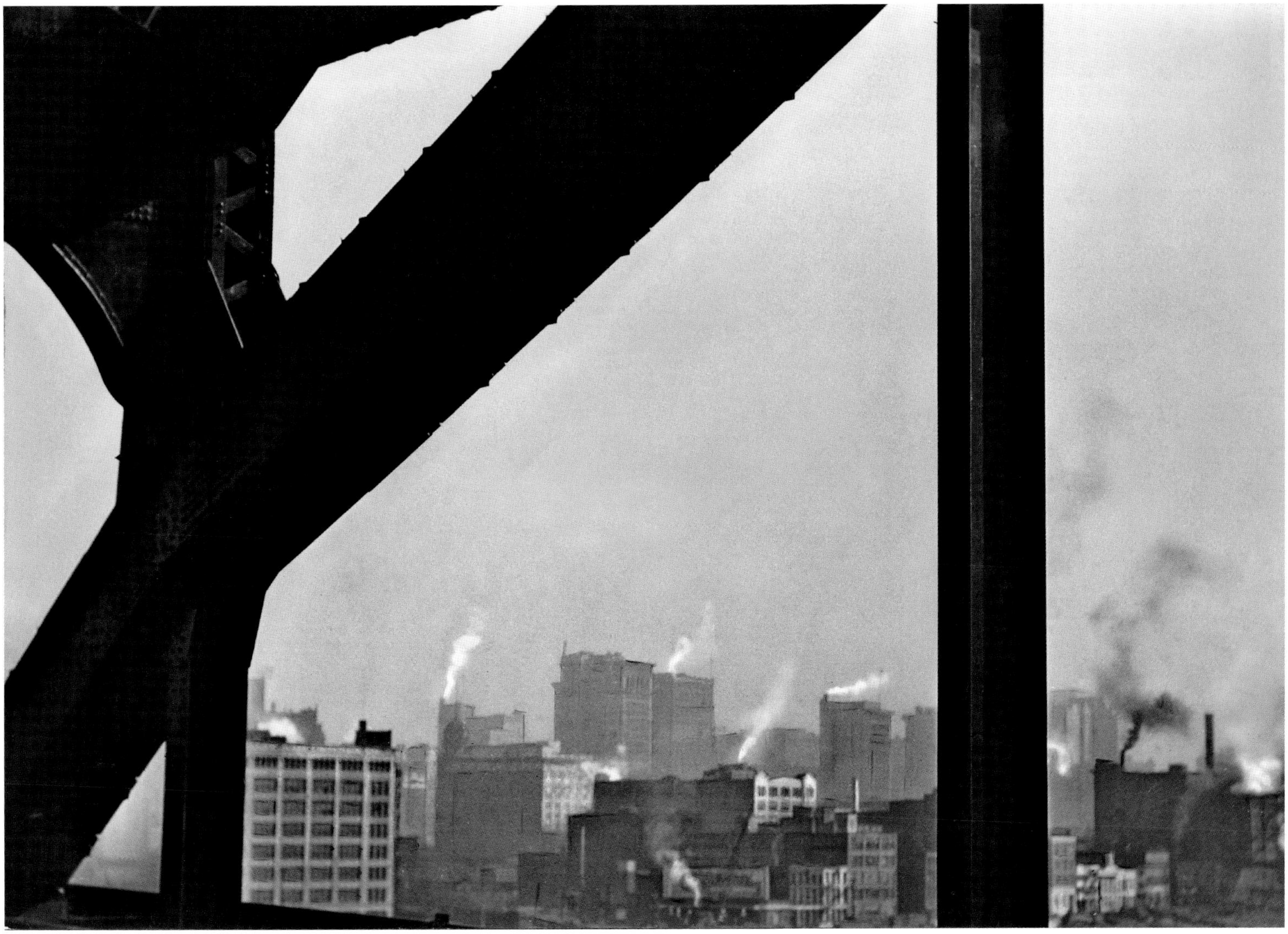

View of Pittsburgh through Bridge, Pennsylvania, 1926

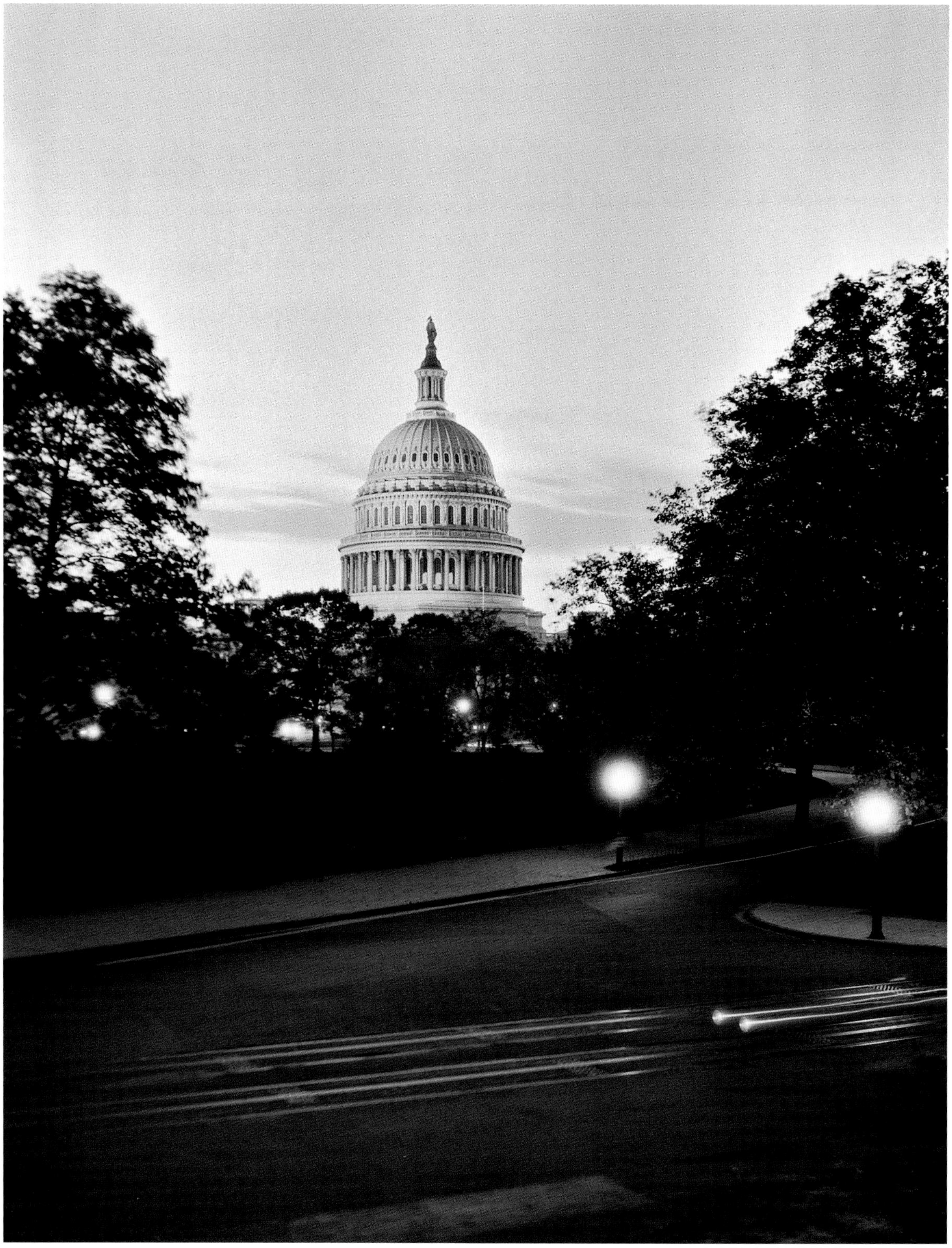

Capitol Building, Washington, D.C., 1926

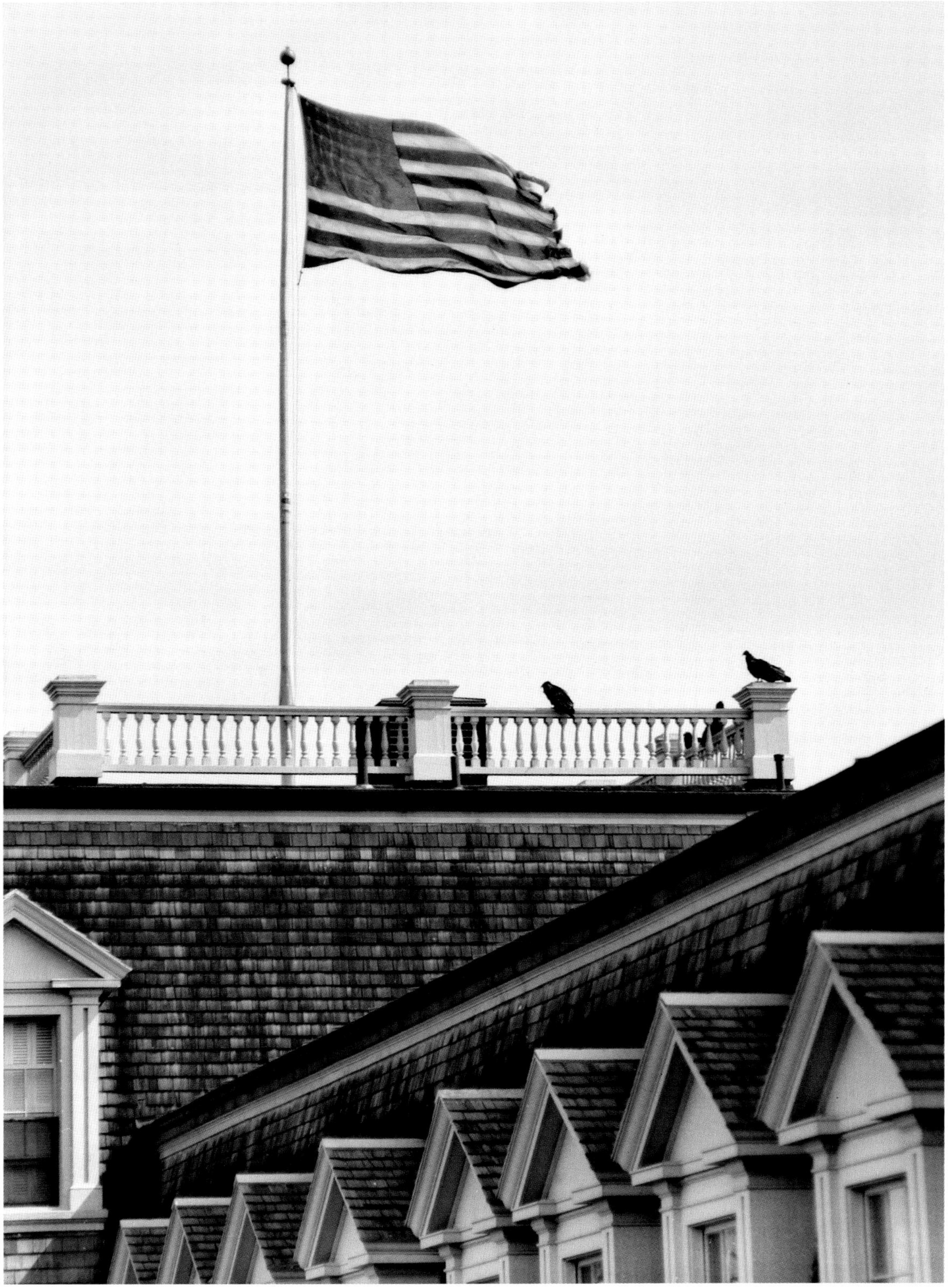

Star-Spangled Banner, Royal Palm Hotel, Miami, Florida, 1926

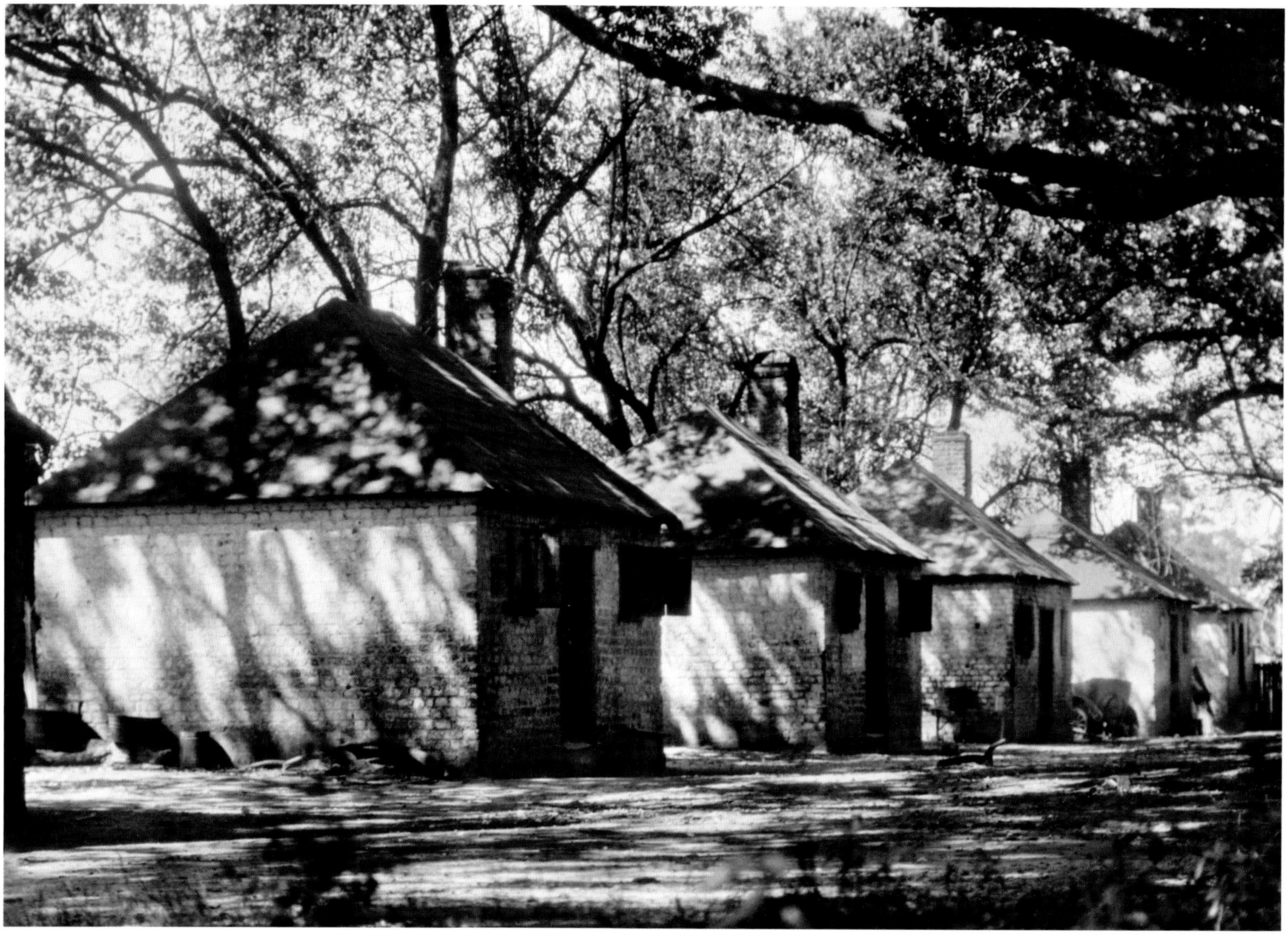

Slave Quarters, Old Plantation, Savannah, Georgia, 1926

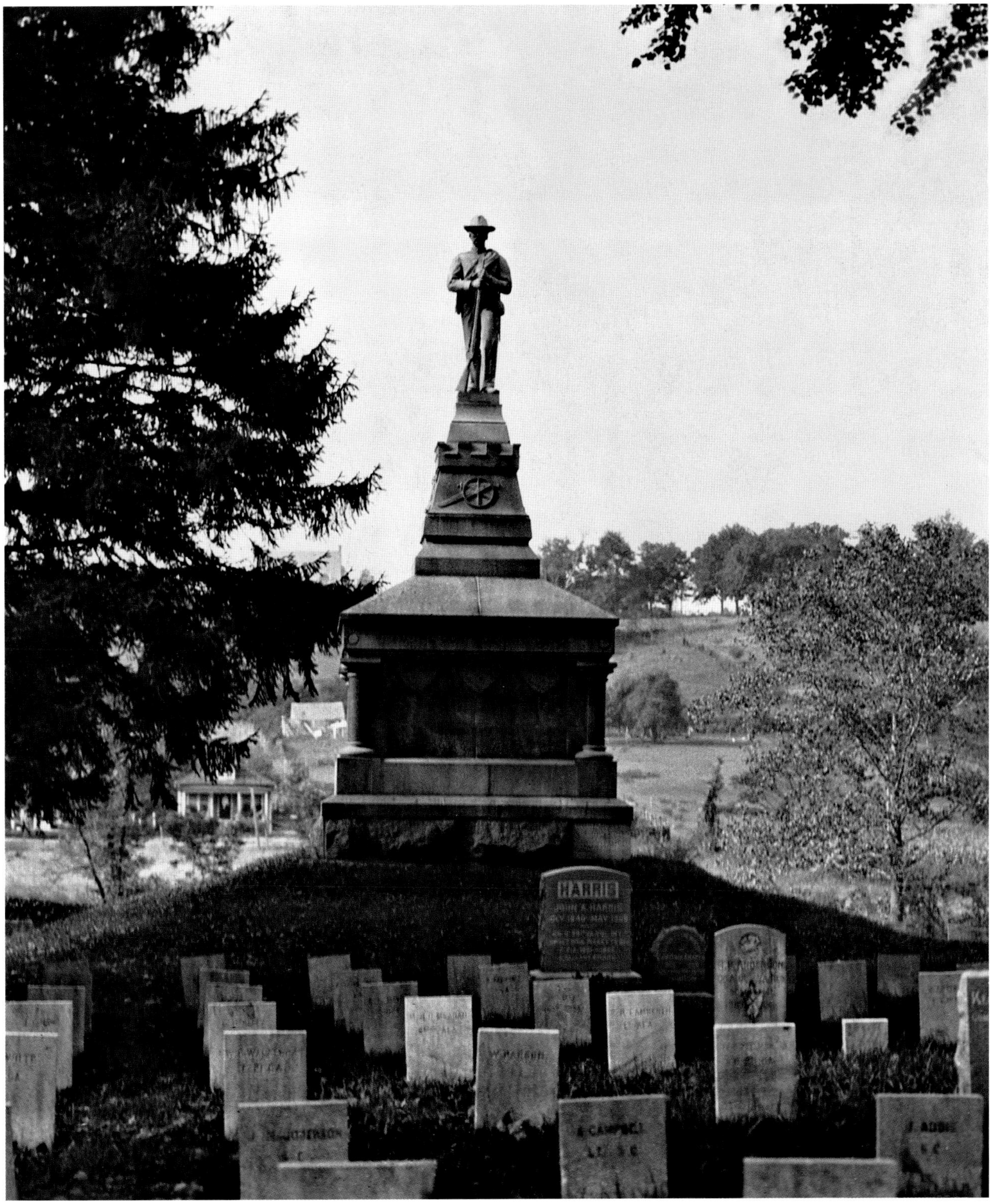

Cemetery, Fredericksburg, Virginia, 1926

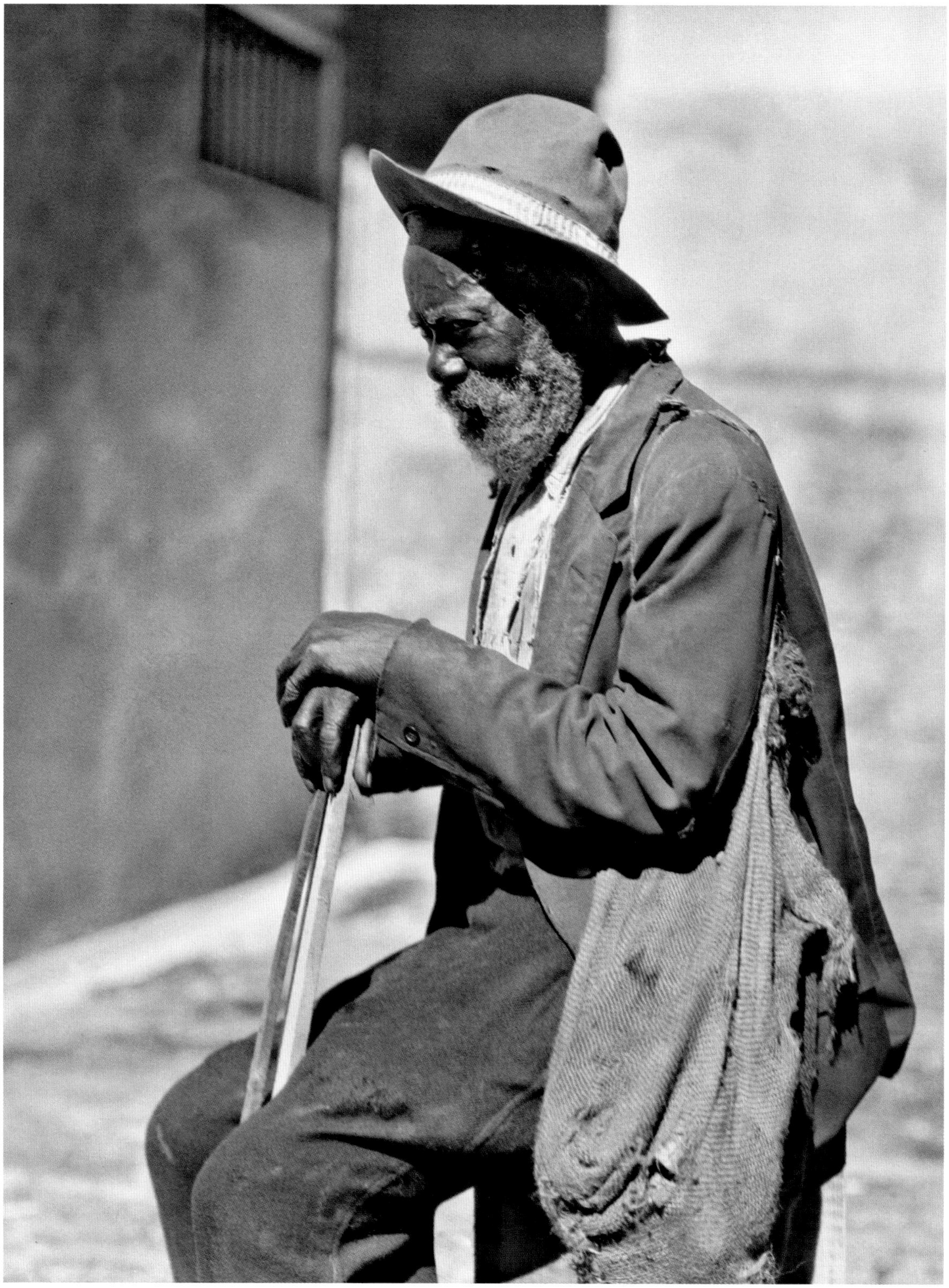

Tennessee, 1926

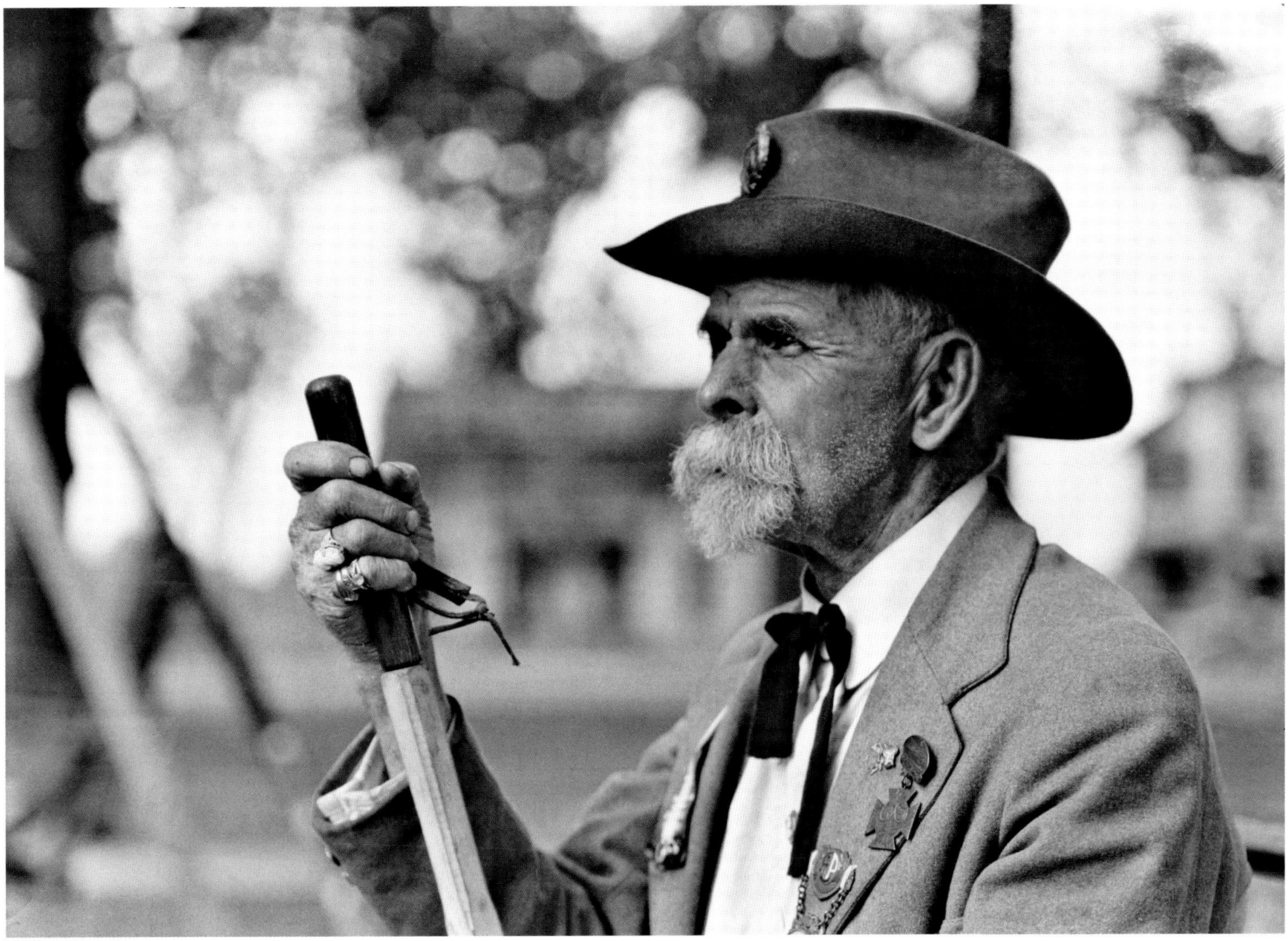

War Veteran, Texas, 1926

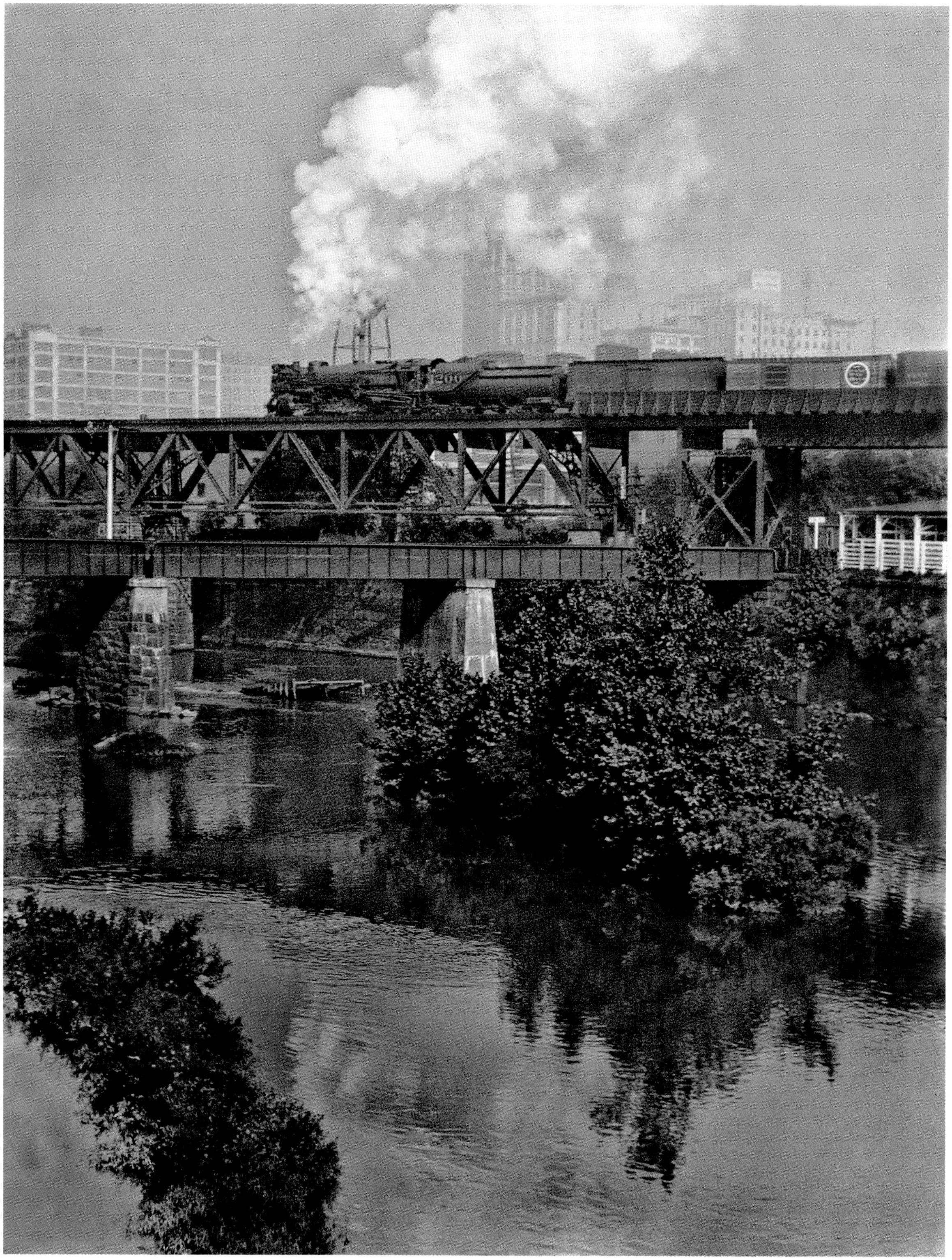

Train Crossing the James River, Richmond, Virginia, 1926

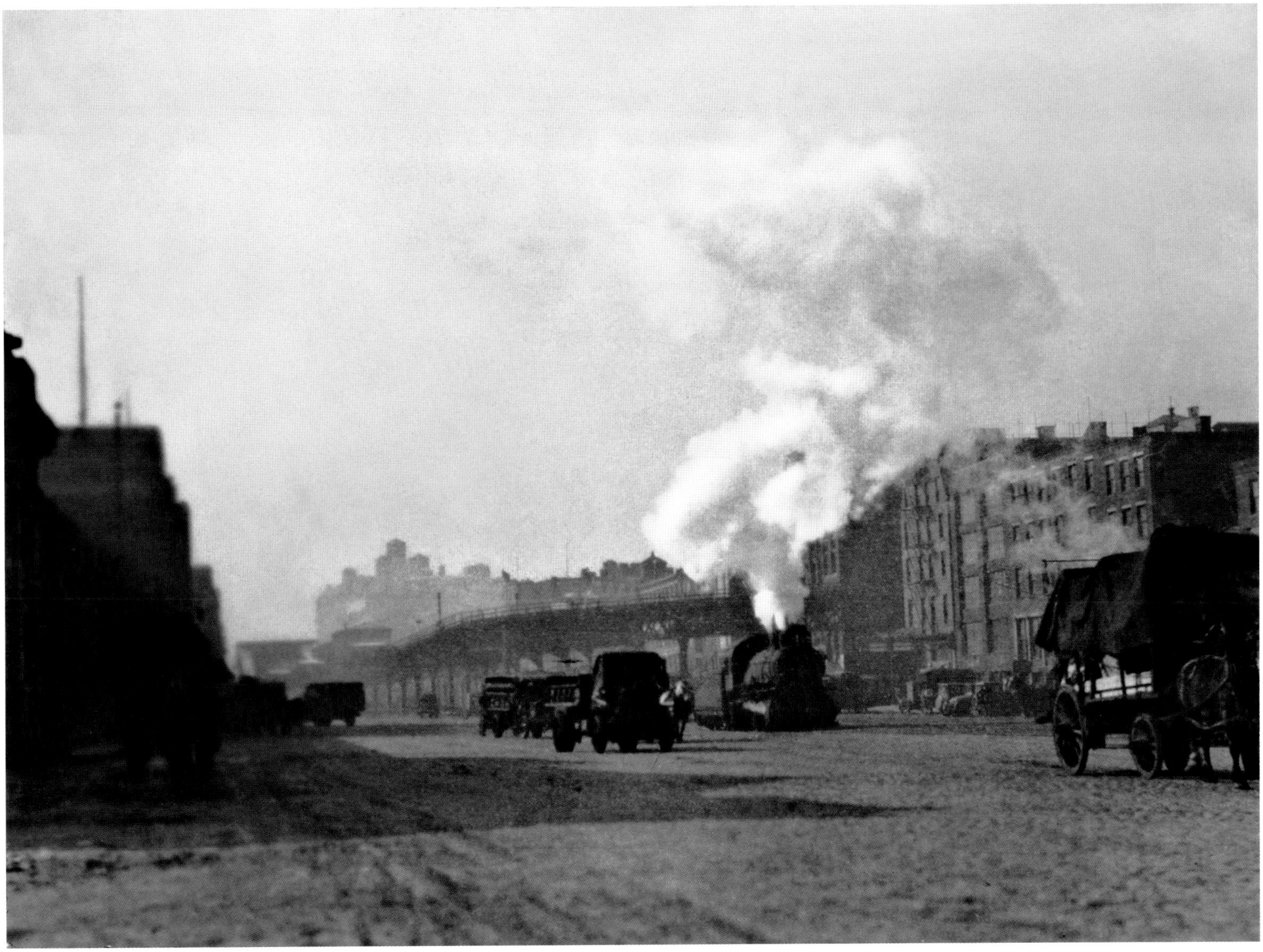

Philadelphia Railway Station, Pennsylvania, 1926

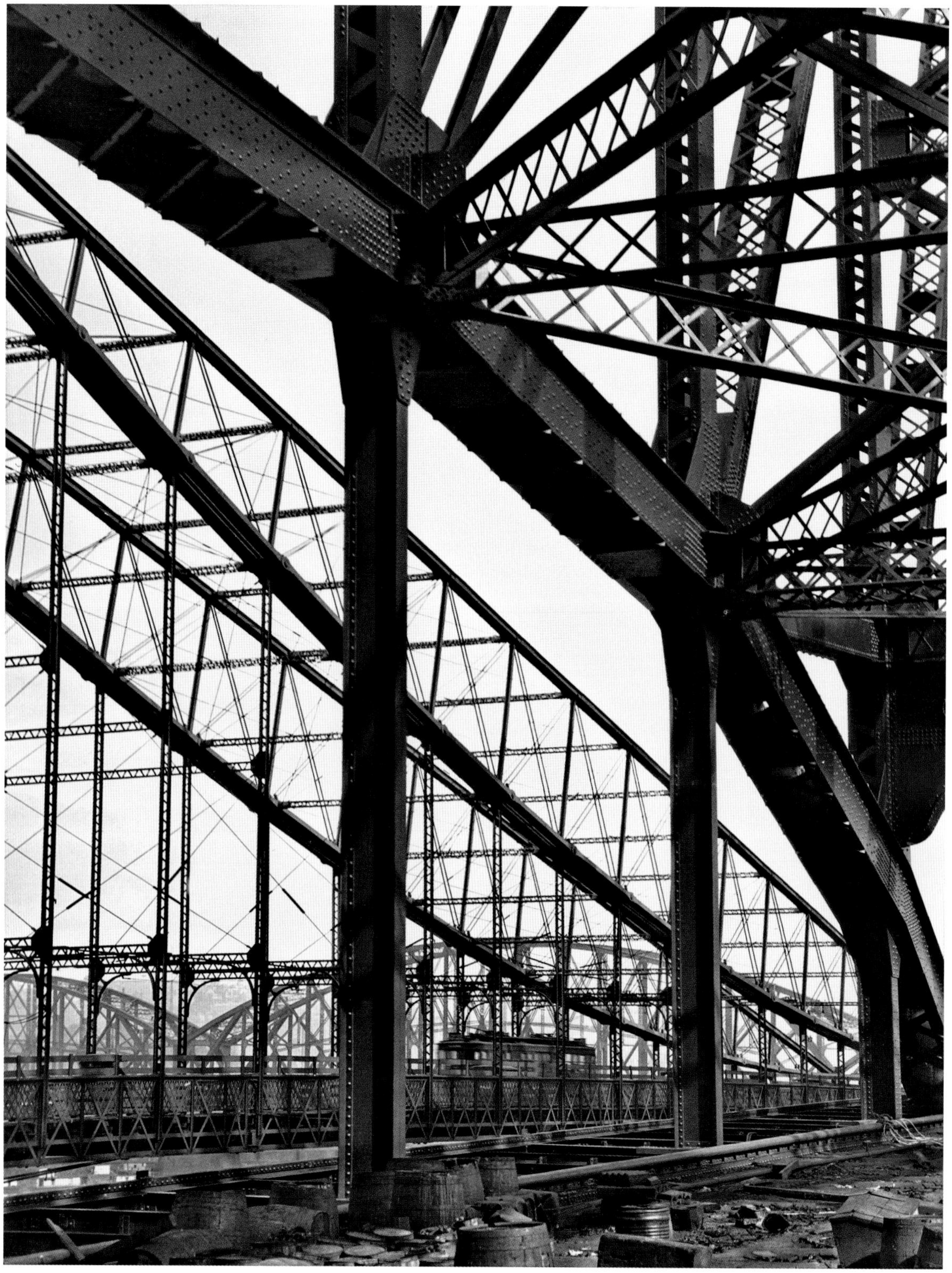

Steel Railway Bridge, Pittsburgh, Pennsylvania, 1926

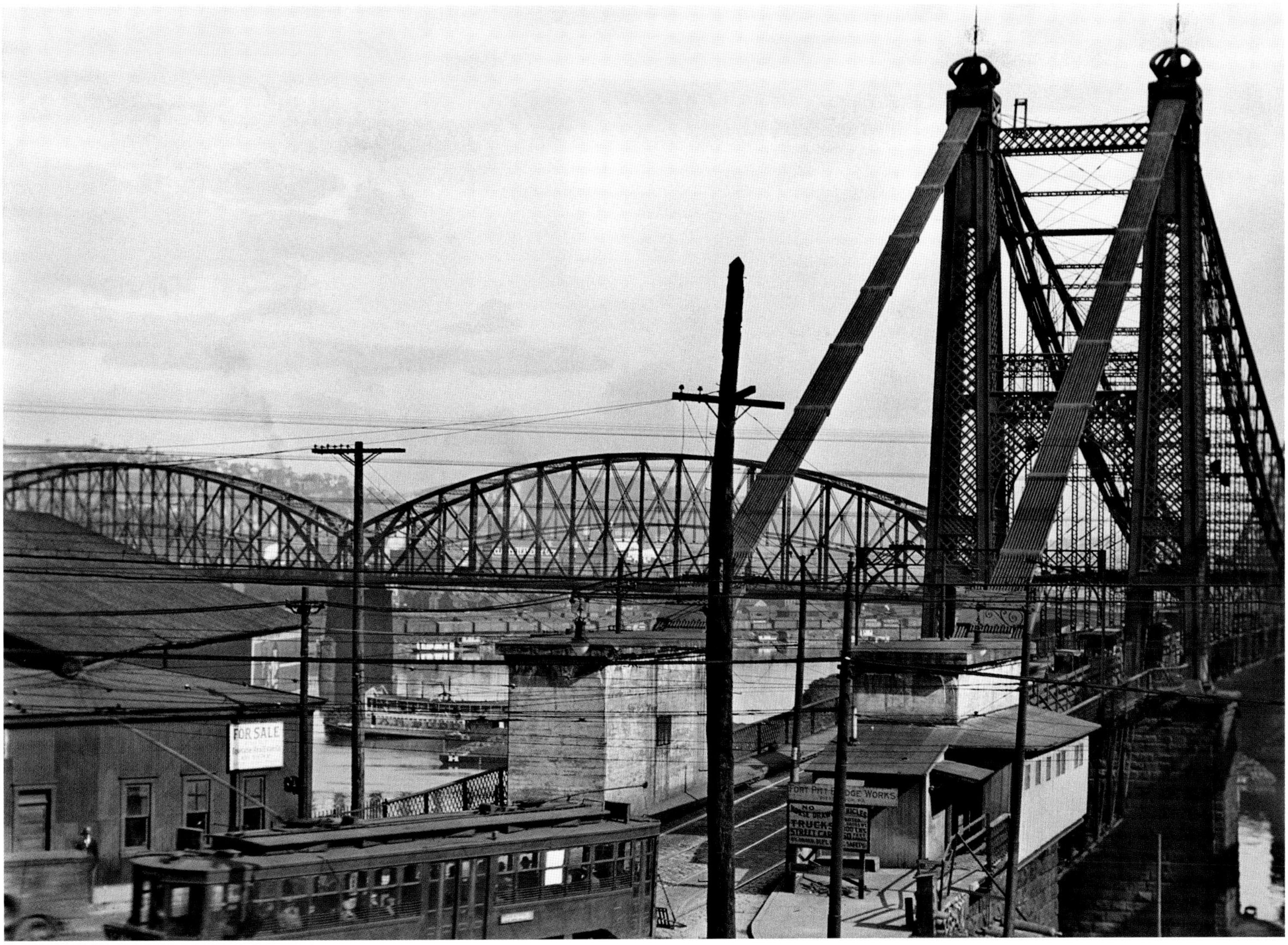

Waterfront Railway Bridge and Tram, Pittsburgh, Pennsylvania, 1926

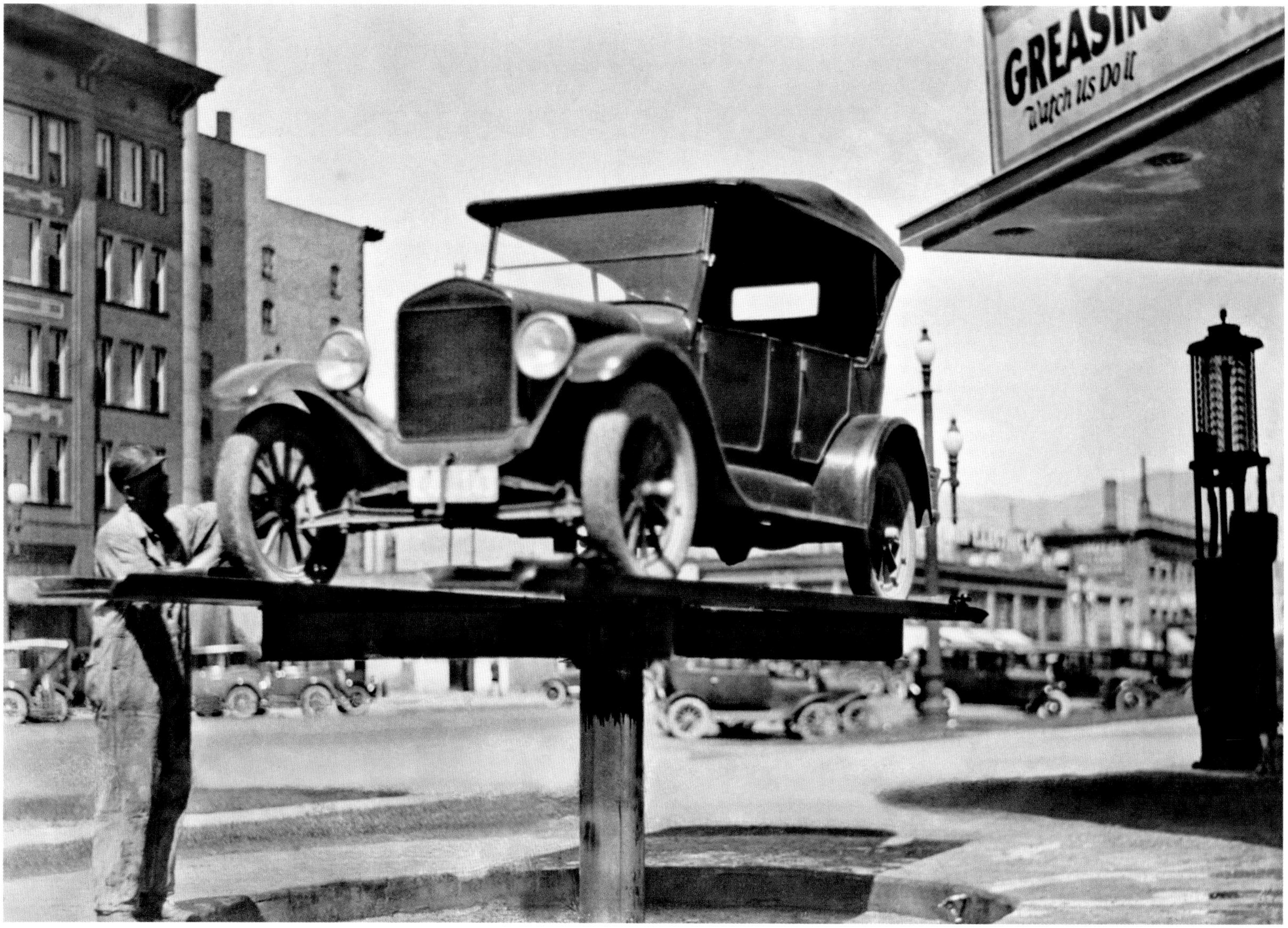

Auto Shop, Los Angeles, California, 1926

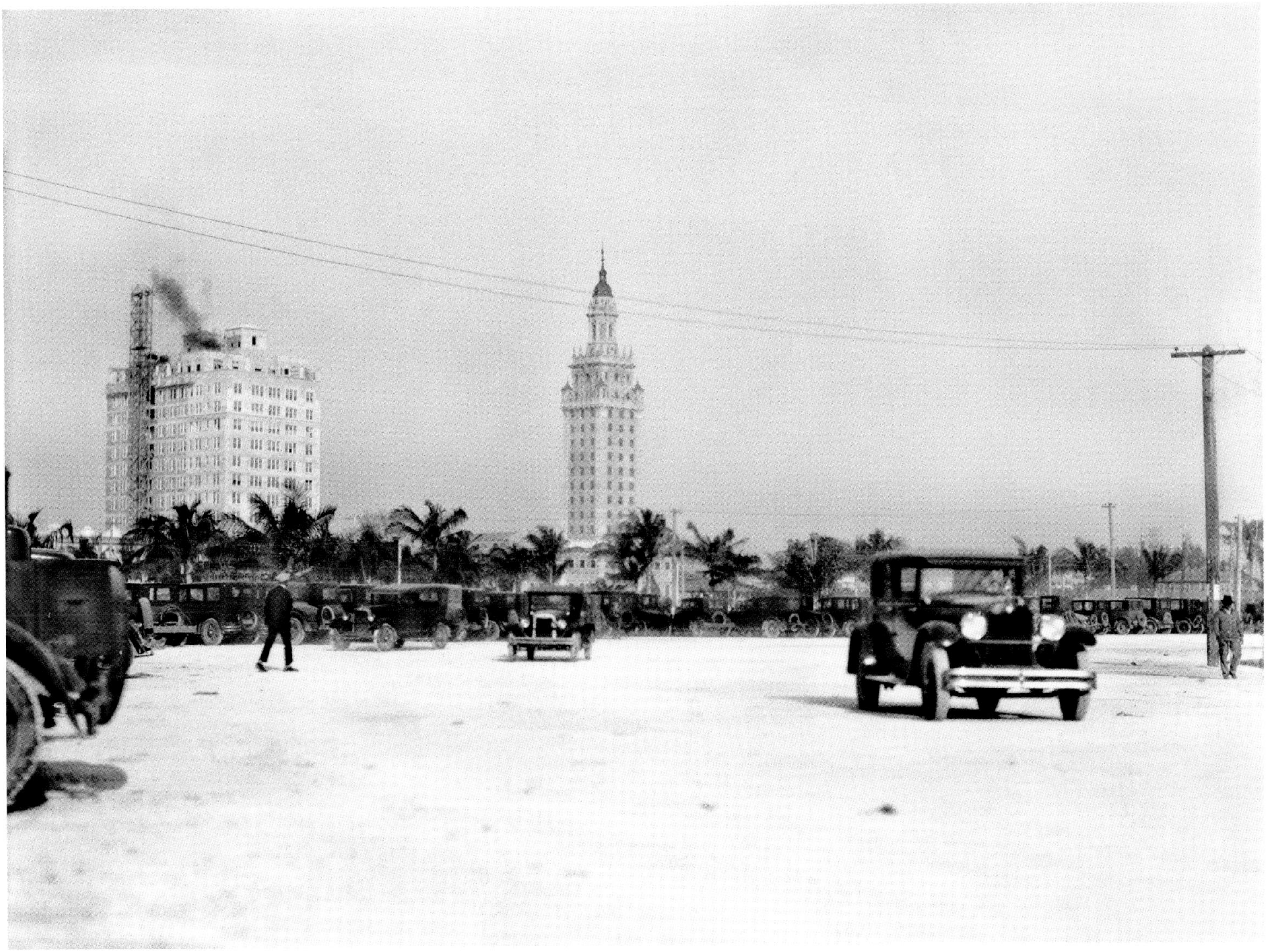

Cars, Miami, Florida, 1926

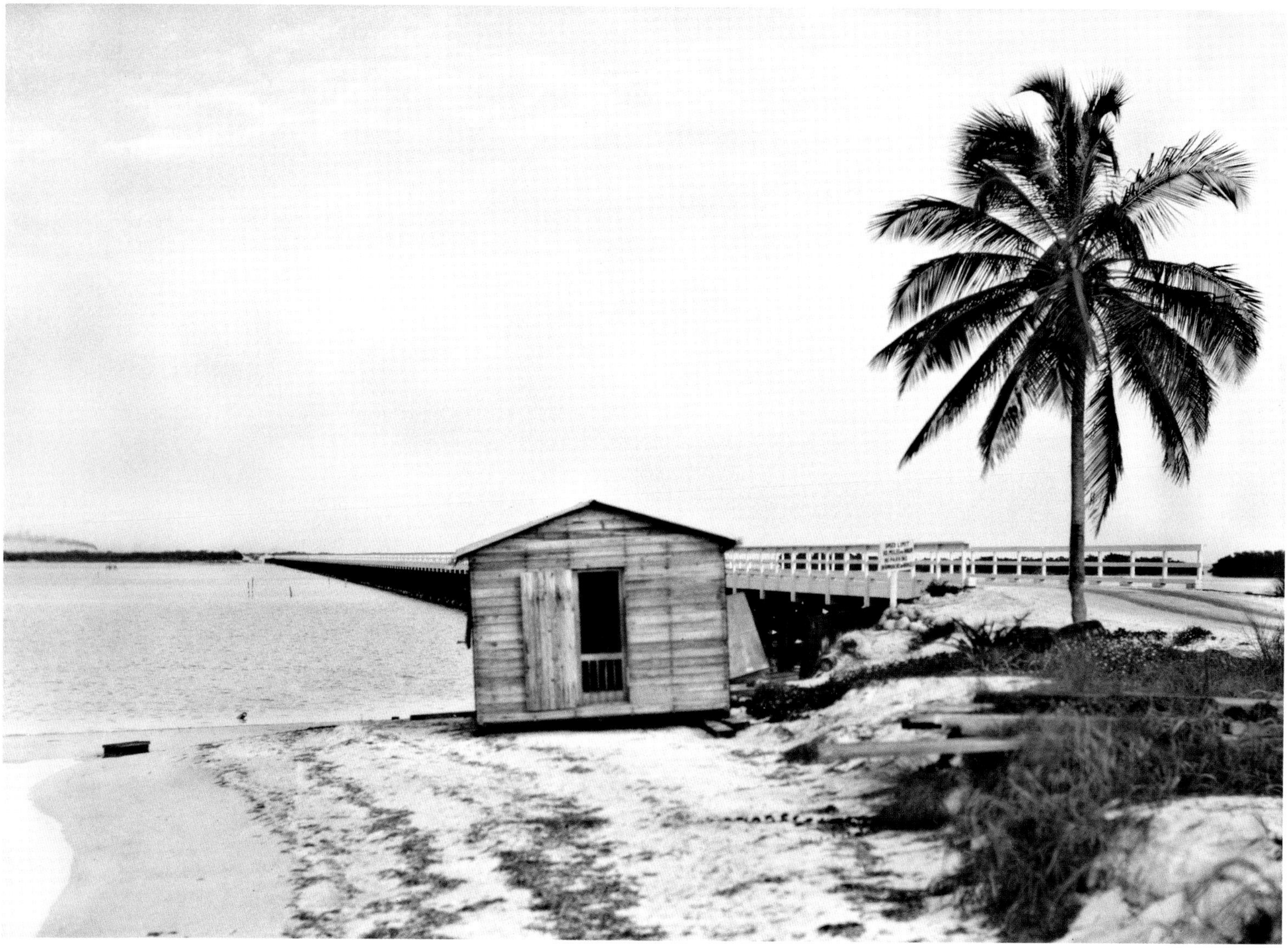

Causeway, Key West, Florida, 1926

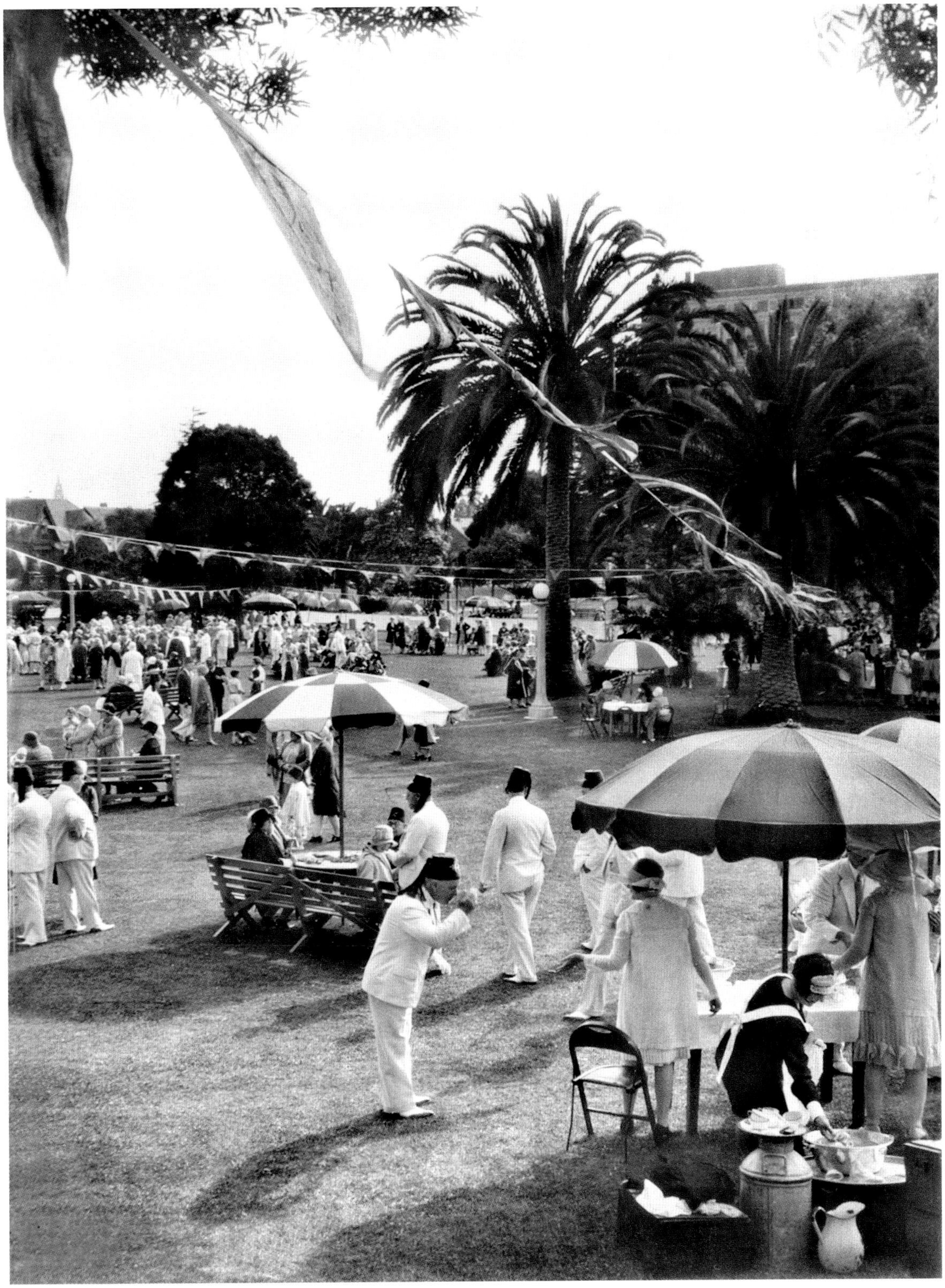

Shriners' Picnic, Lafayette Park, Los Angeles, California, 1926

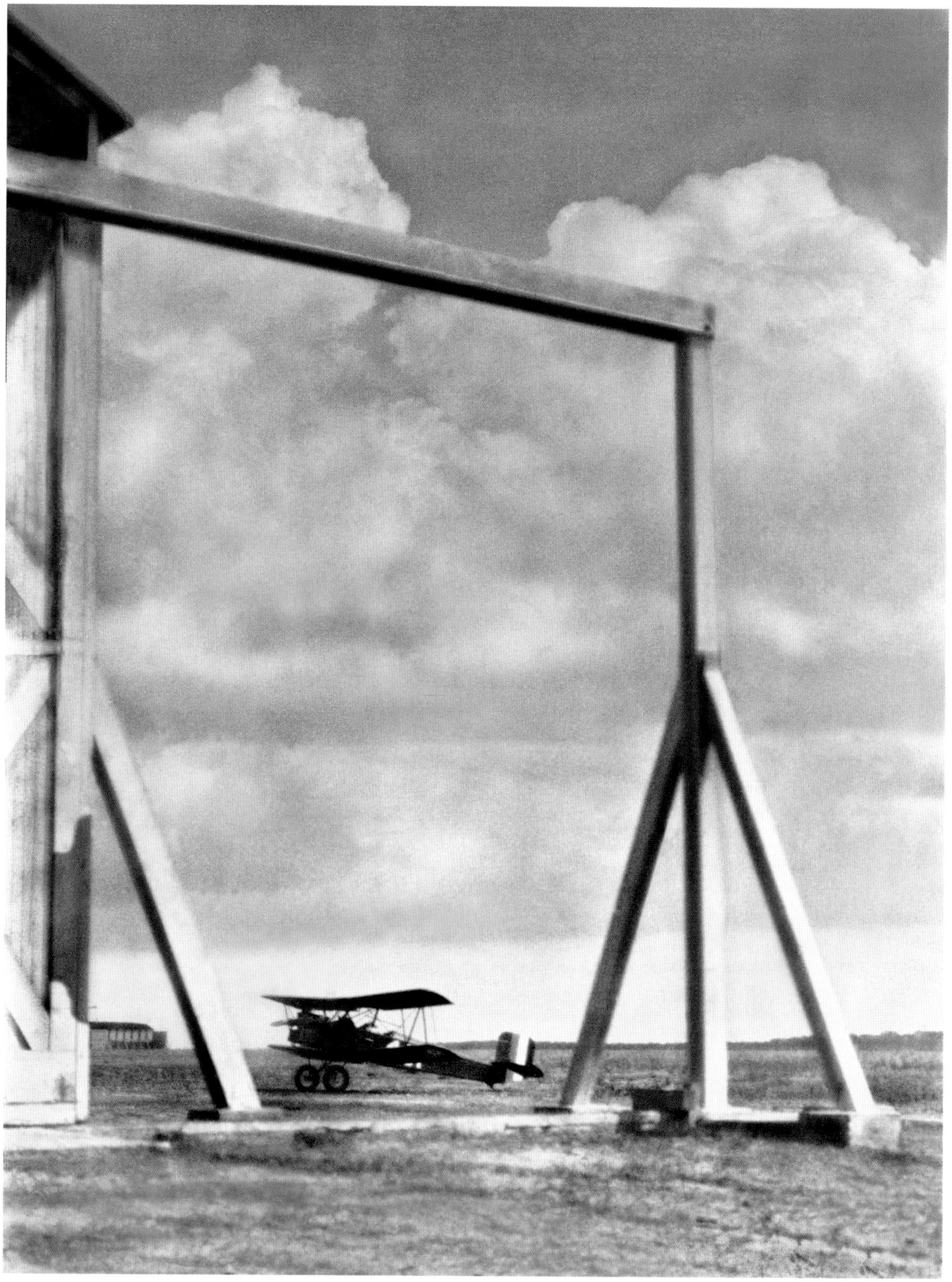

The U.S. Army Aviation Field, San Antonio, Texas, 1926

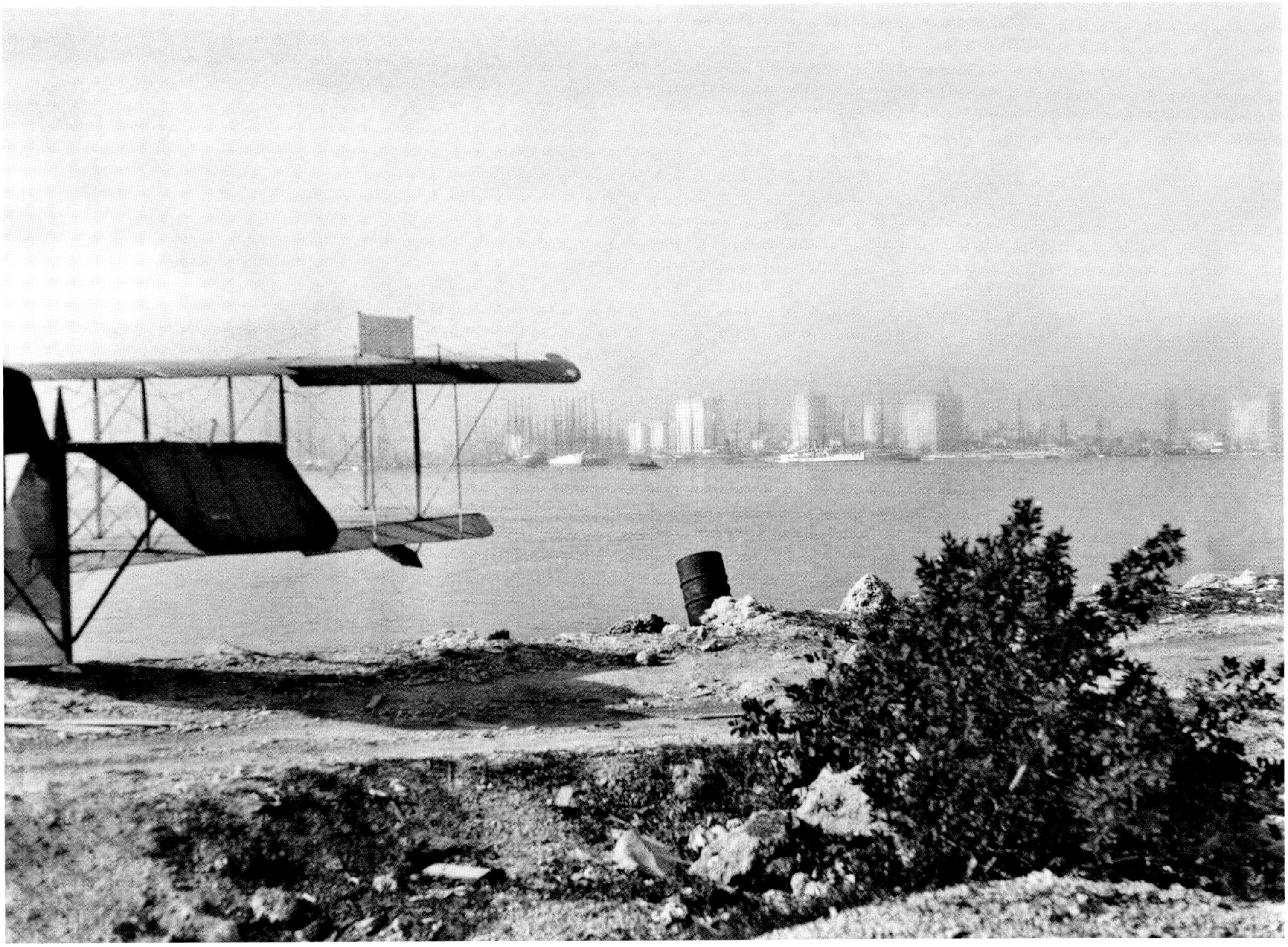

Waterfront View with Plane, Miami, Florida, 1926

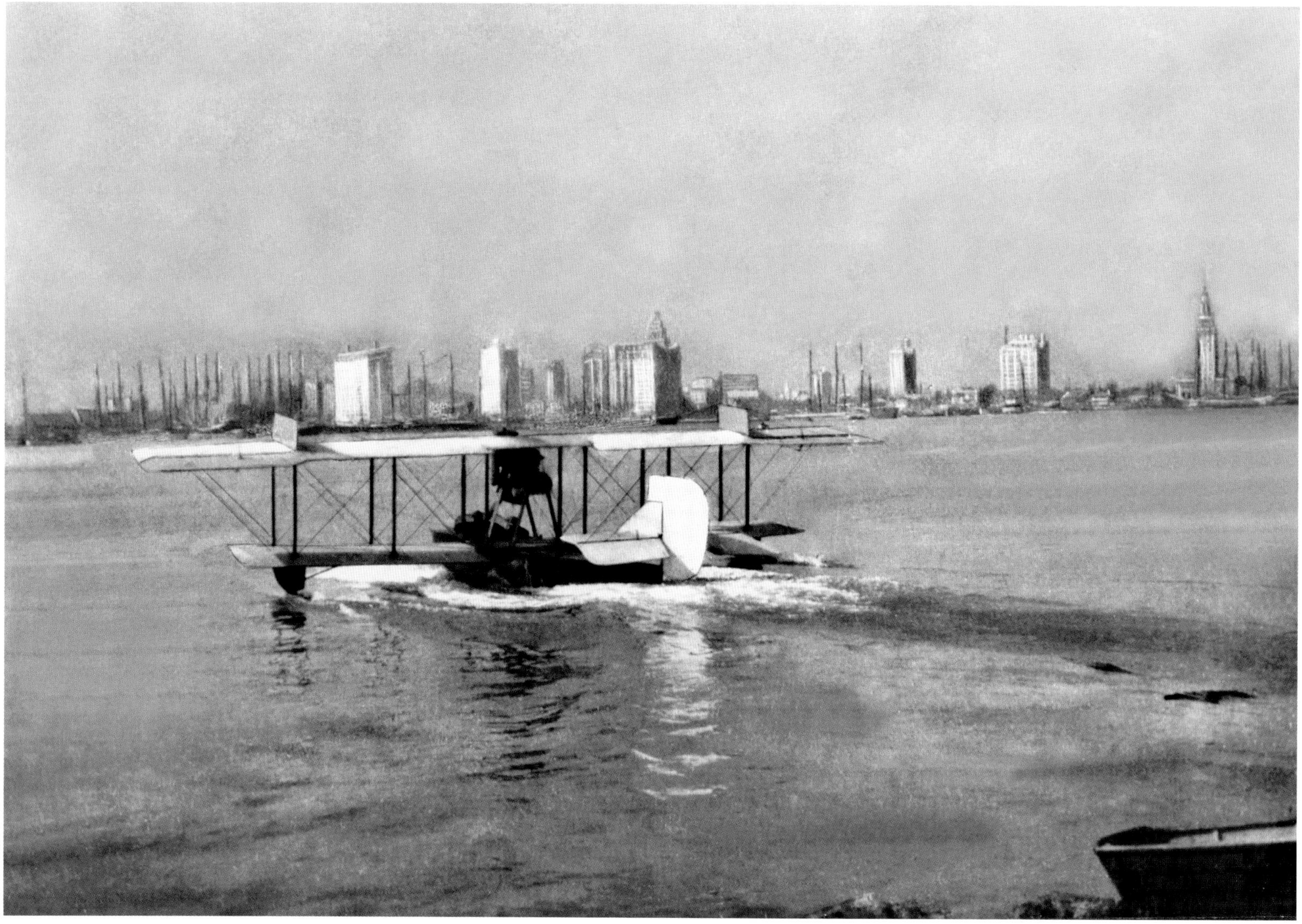

Seaplane, Miami, Florida, 1926

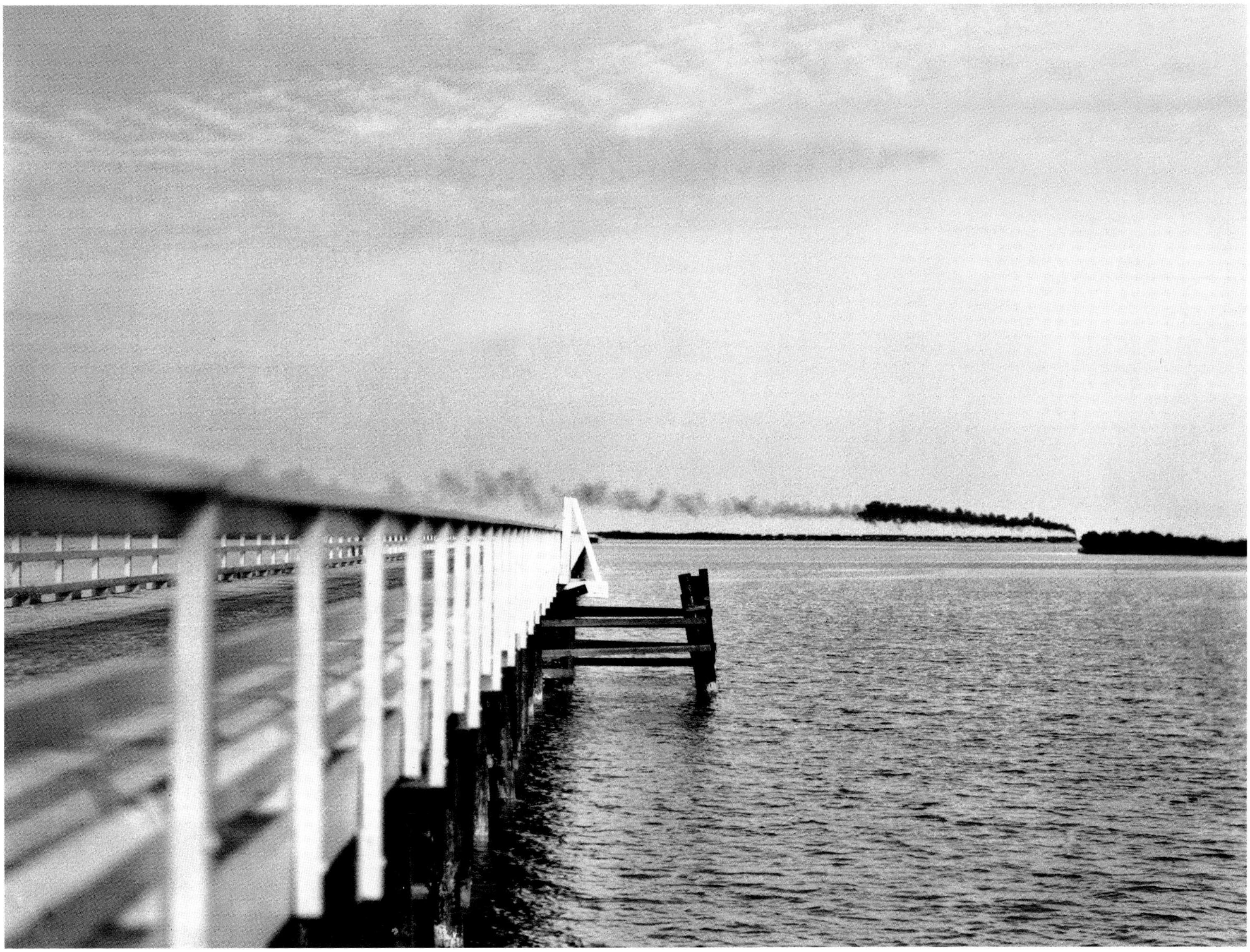

Bridge and Smoke Trail, Key West, Florida, 1926

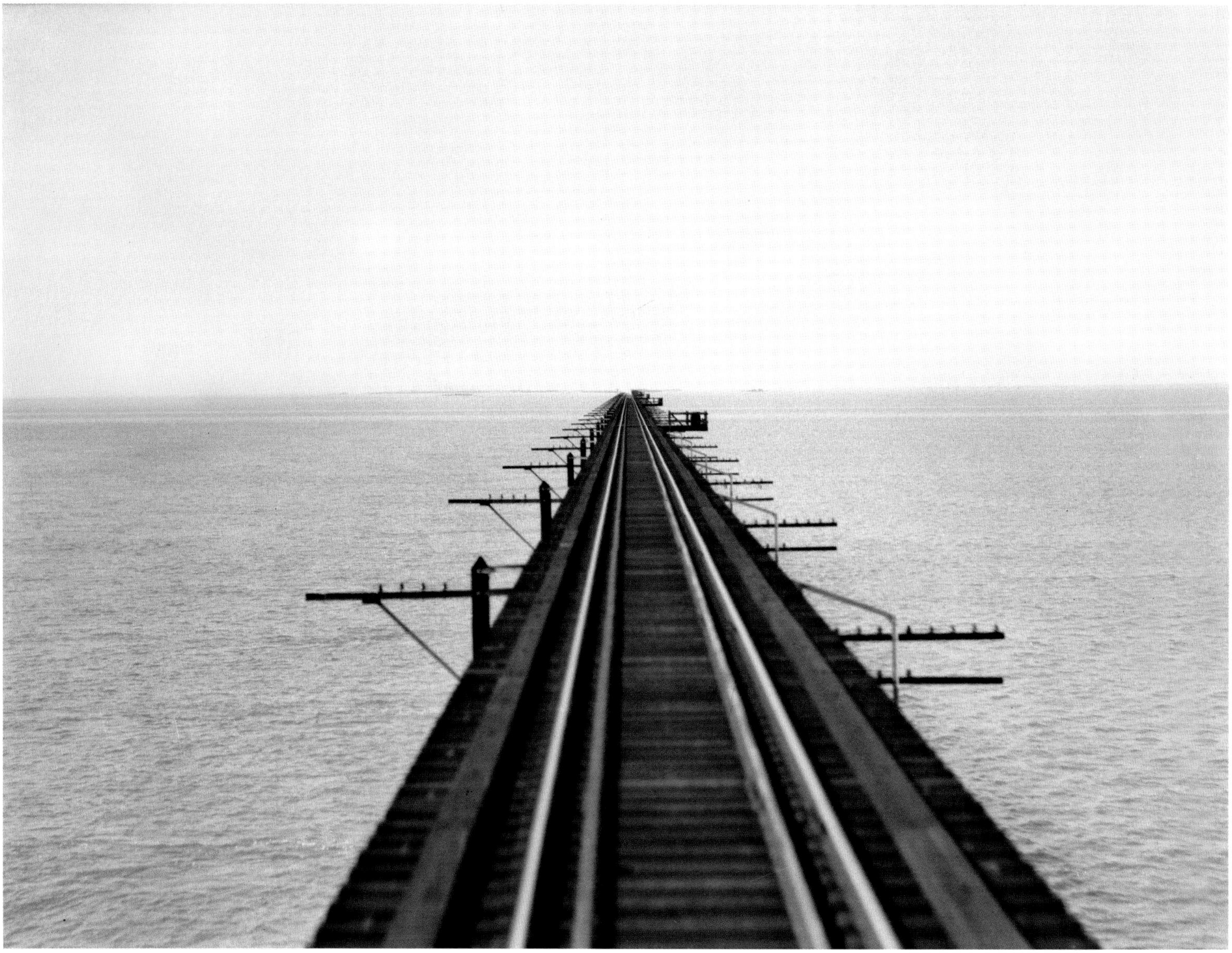

On the Railway, Key West, Florida, 1926

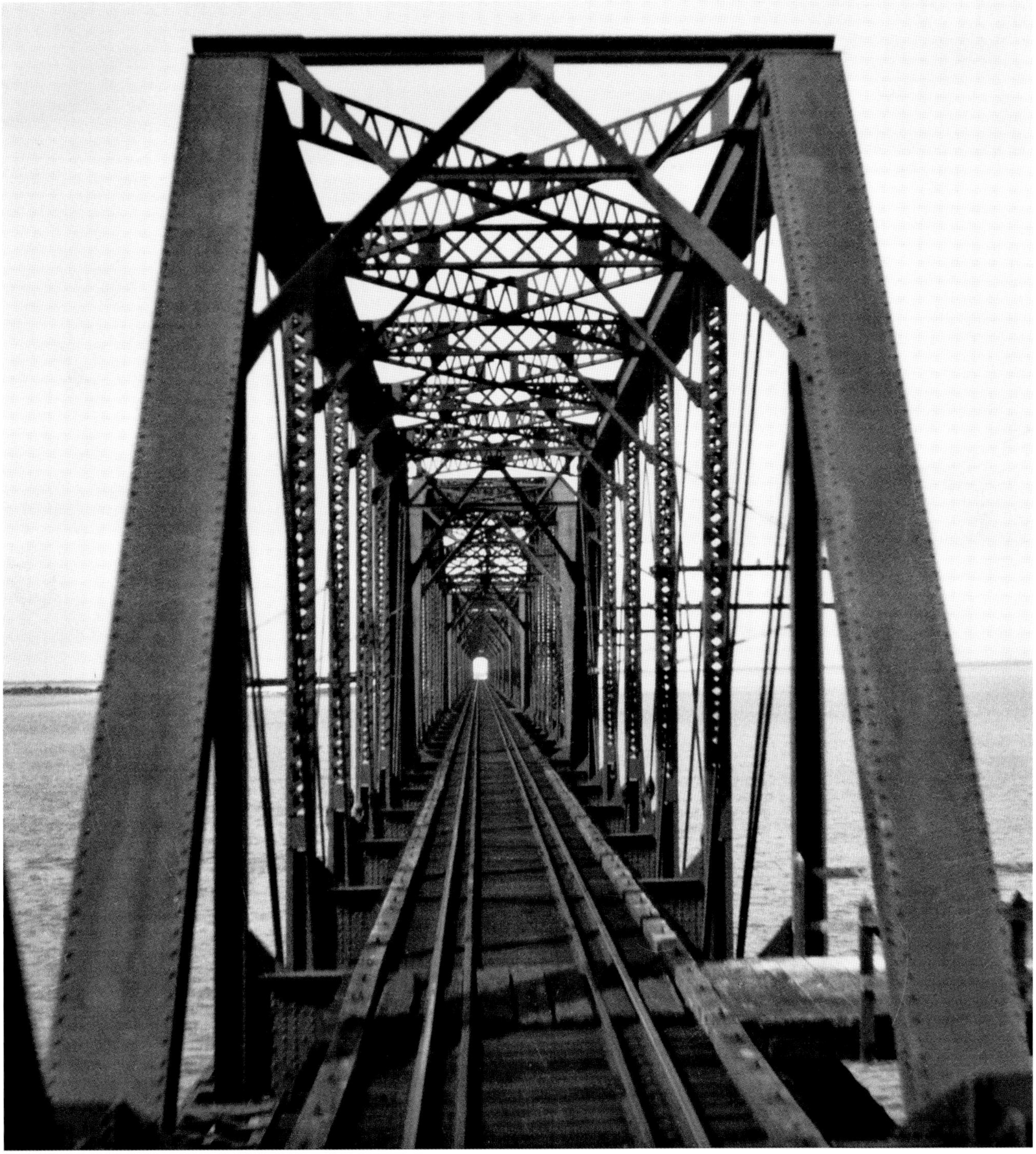

Railroad Bridge, Key West, Florida, 1926

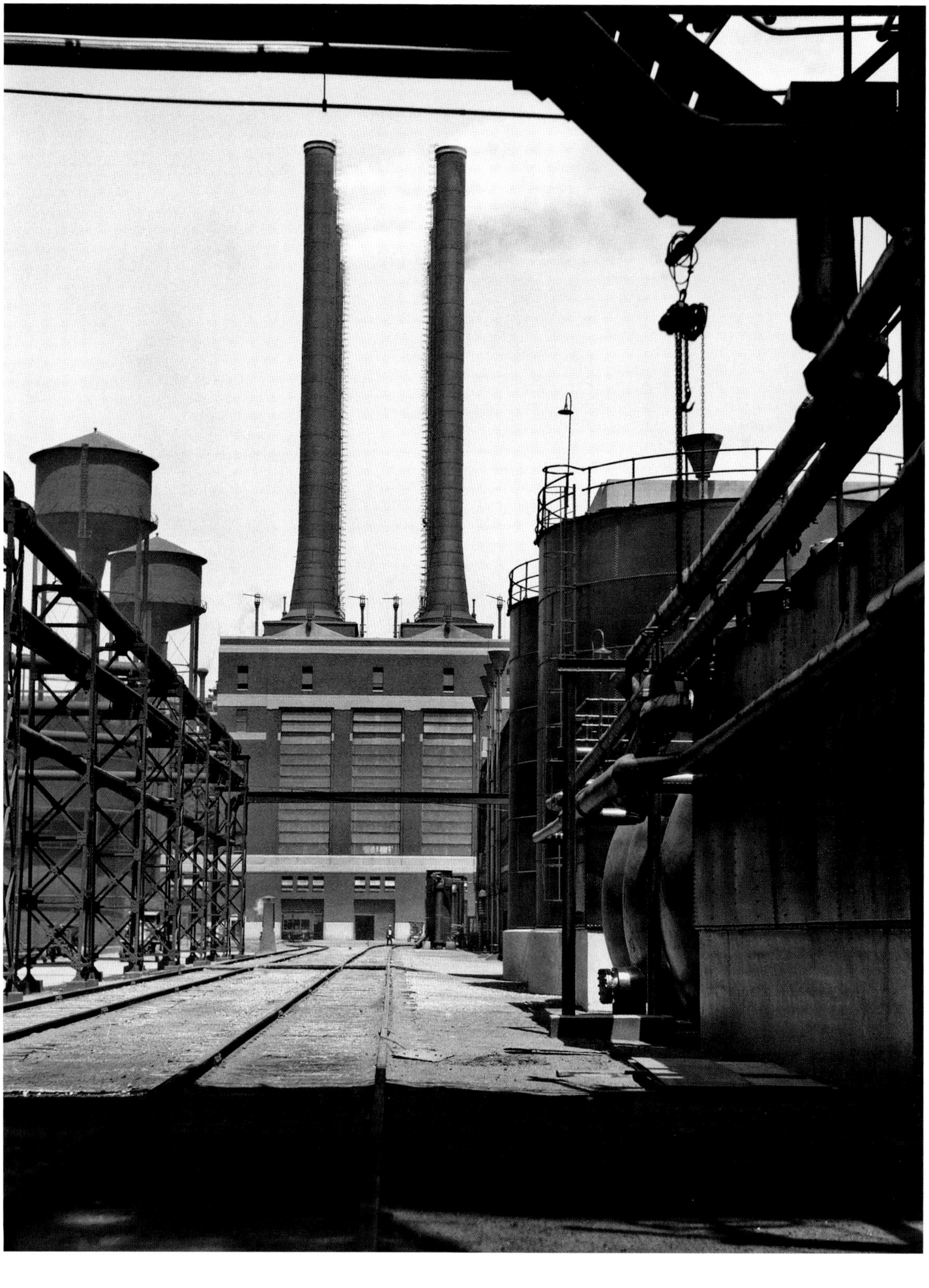

Two Smokestacks, Ford Factory, Detroit, Michigan, 1926

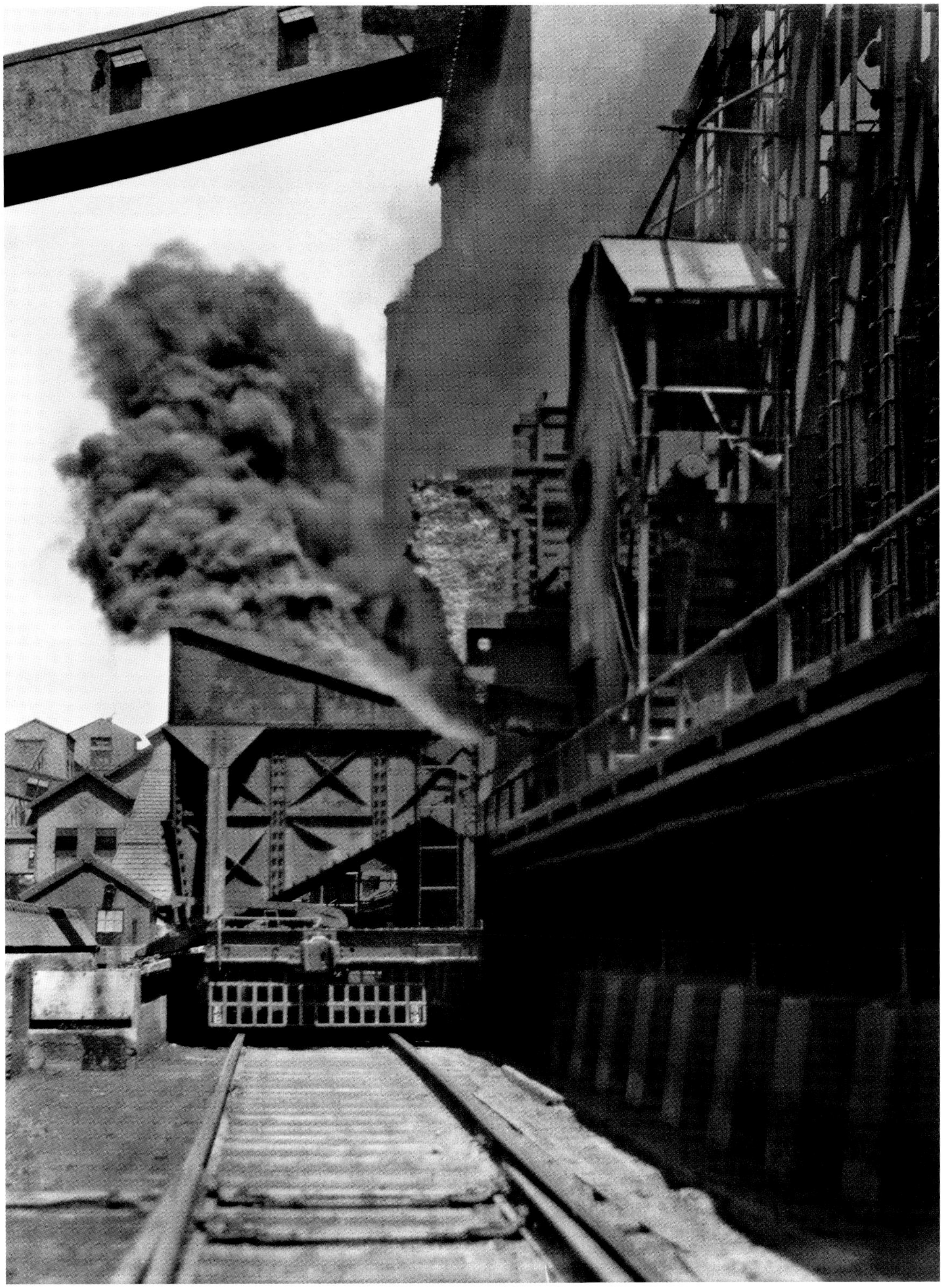

Coal Loading, Ford Factory, Detroit, Michigan, 1926

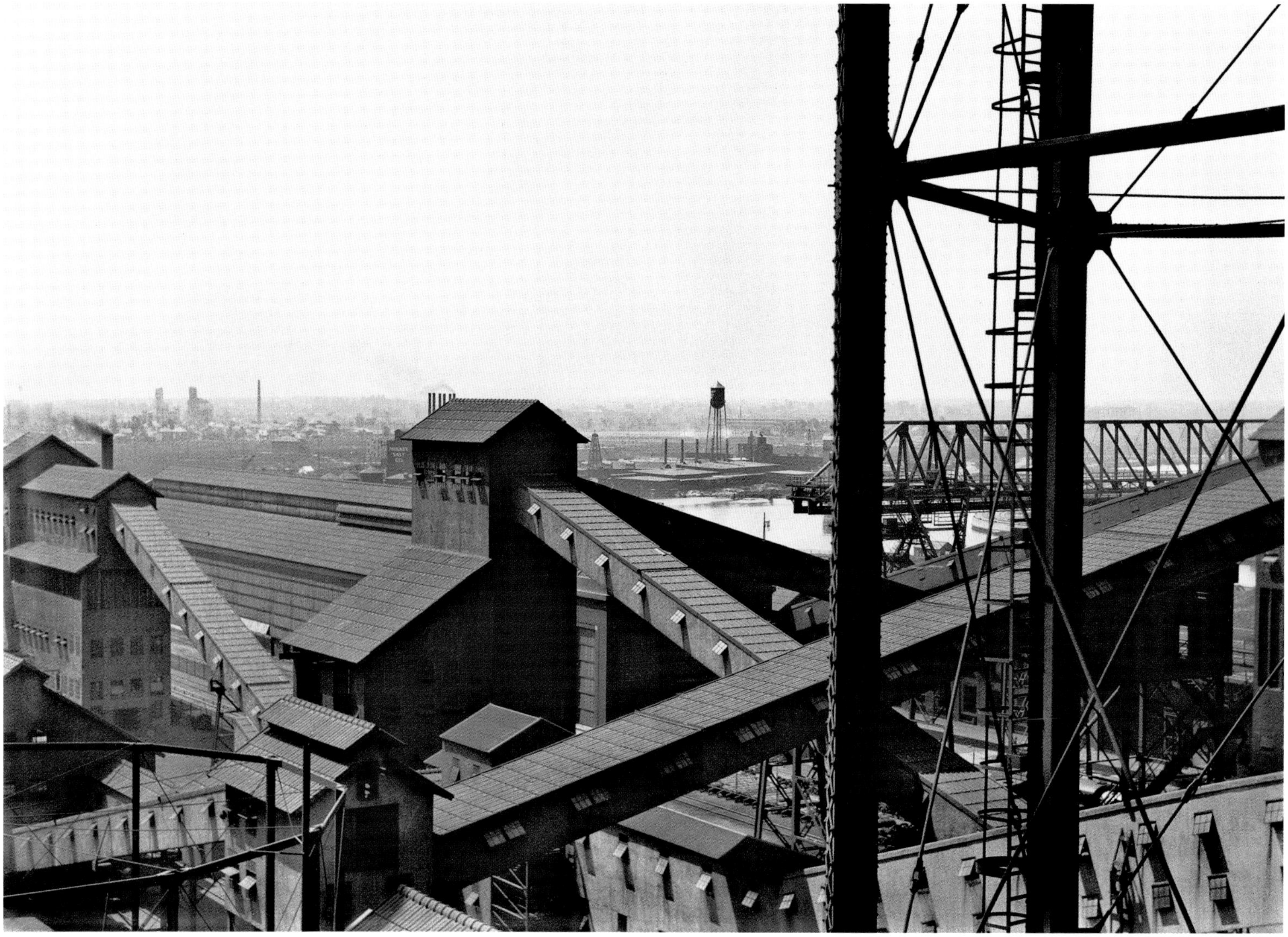

Crossed Conveyers, Ford Factory, Detroit, Michigan, 1926

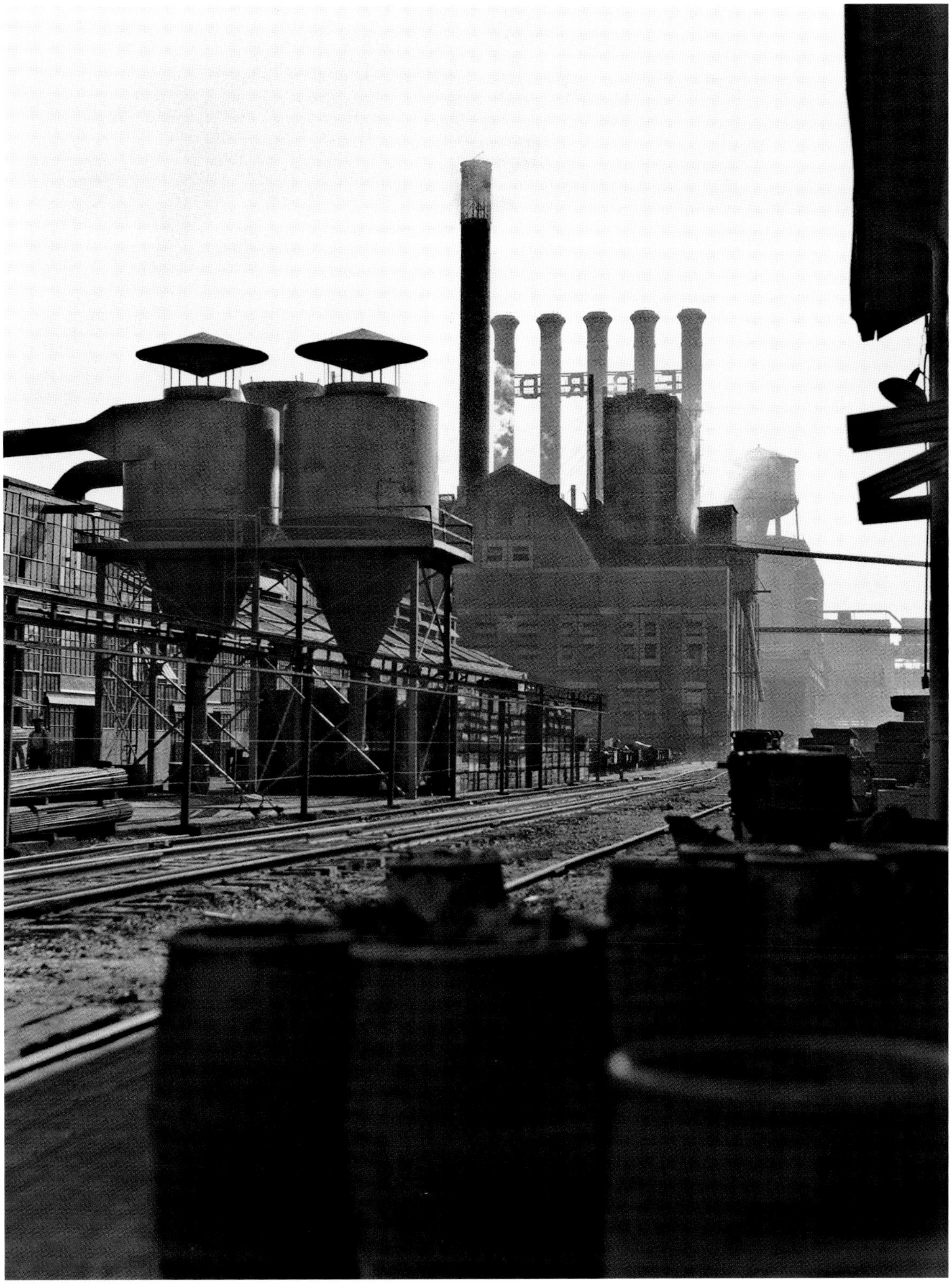

Barrels, Ford Factory, Detroit, Michigan, 1926

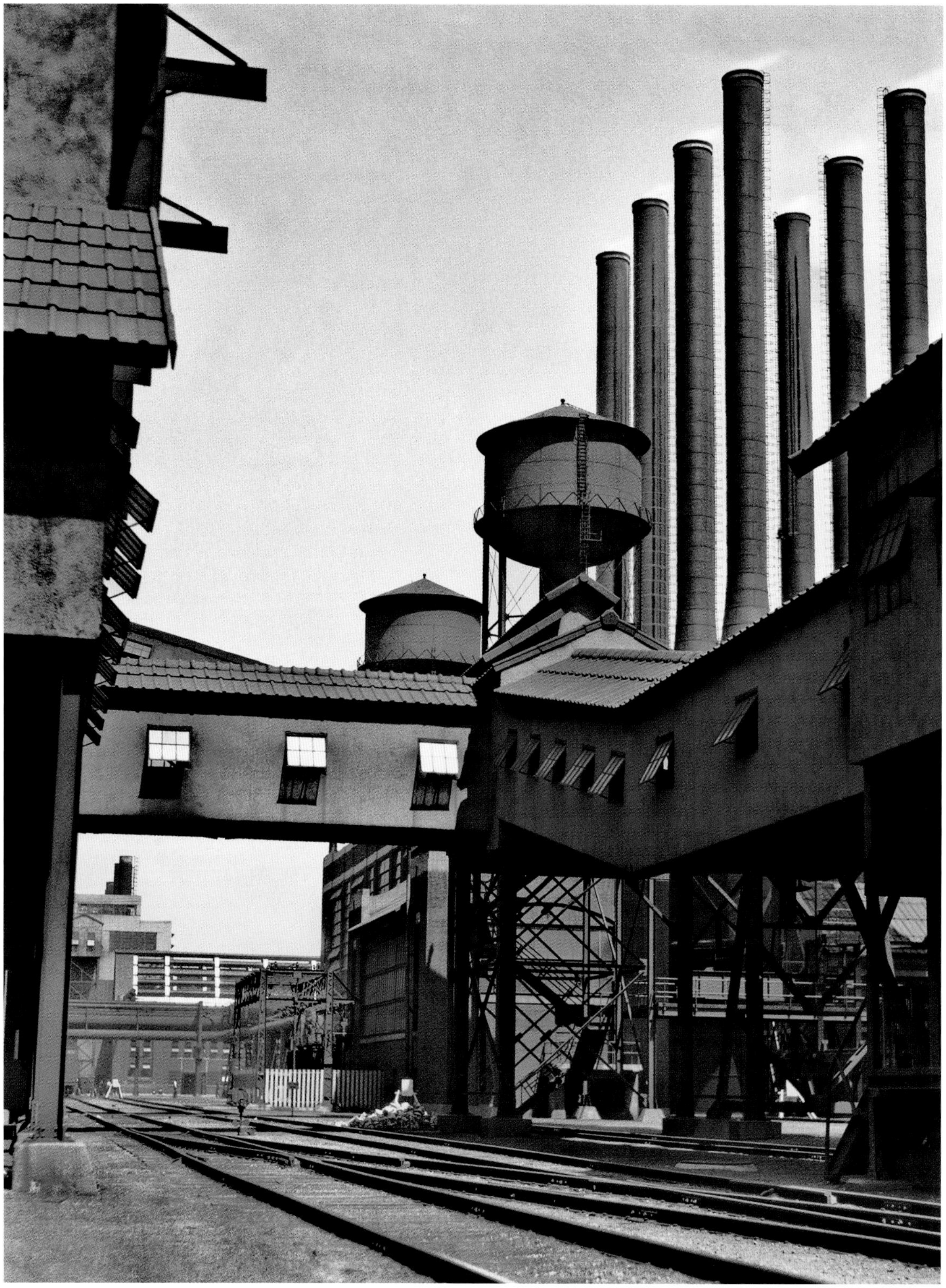

Ford Factory, Detroit, Michigan, 1926

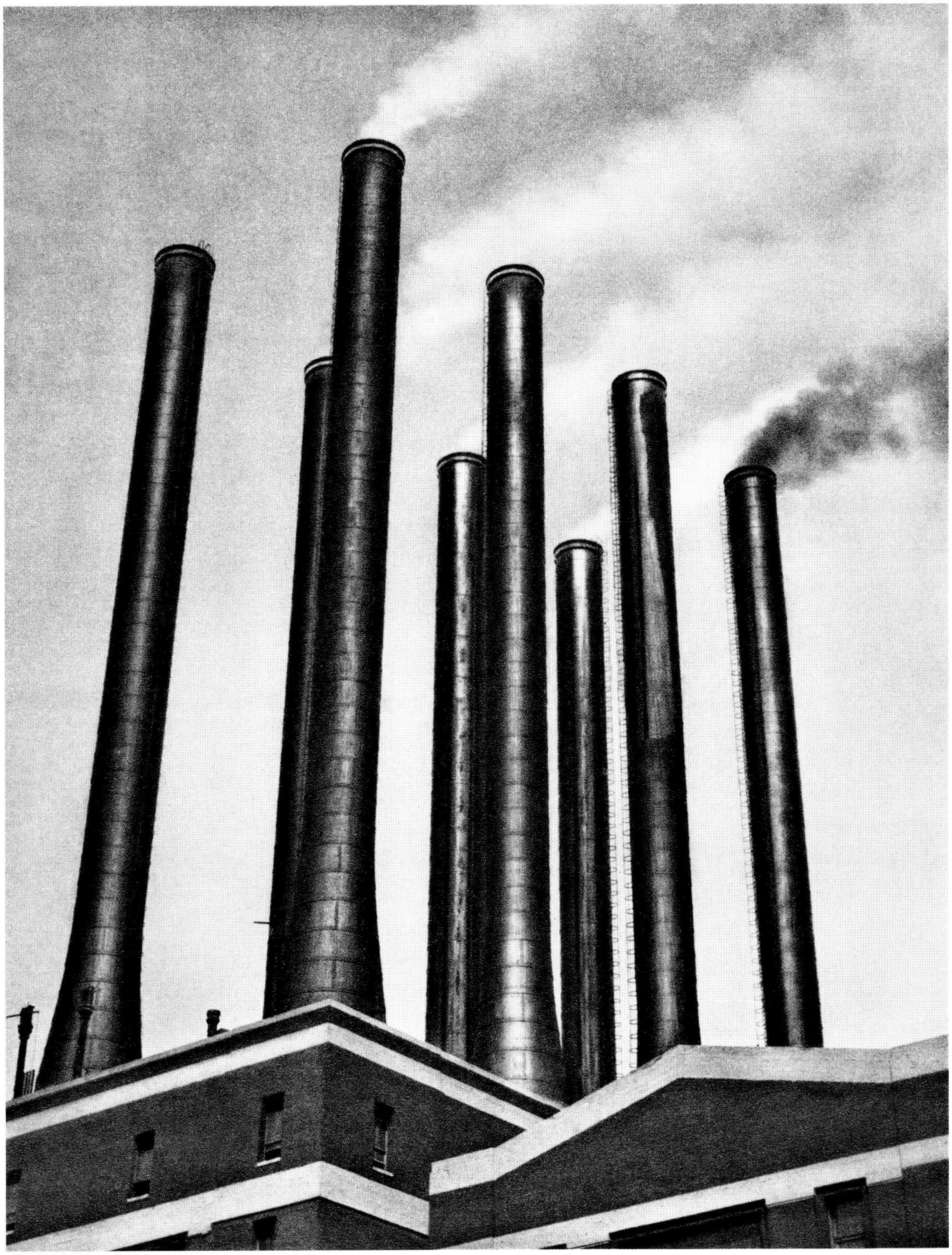

Smokestacks, Ford Factory, Detroit, Michigan, 1926

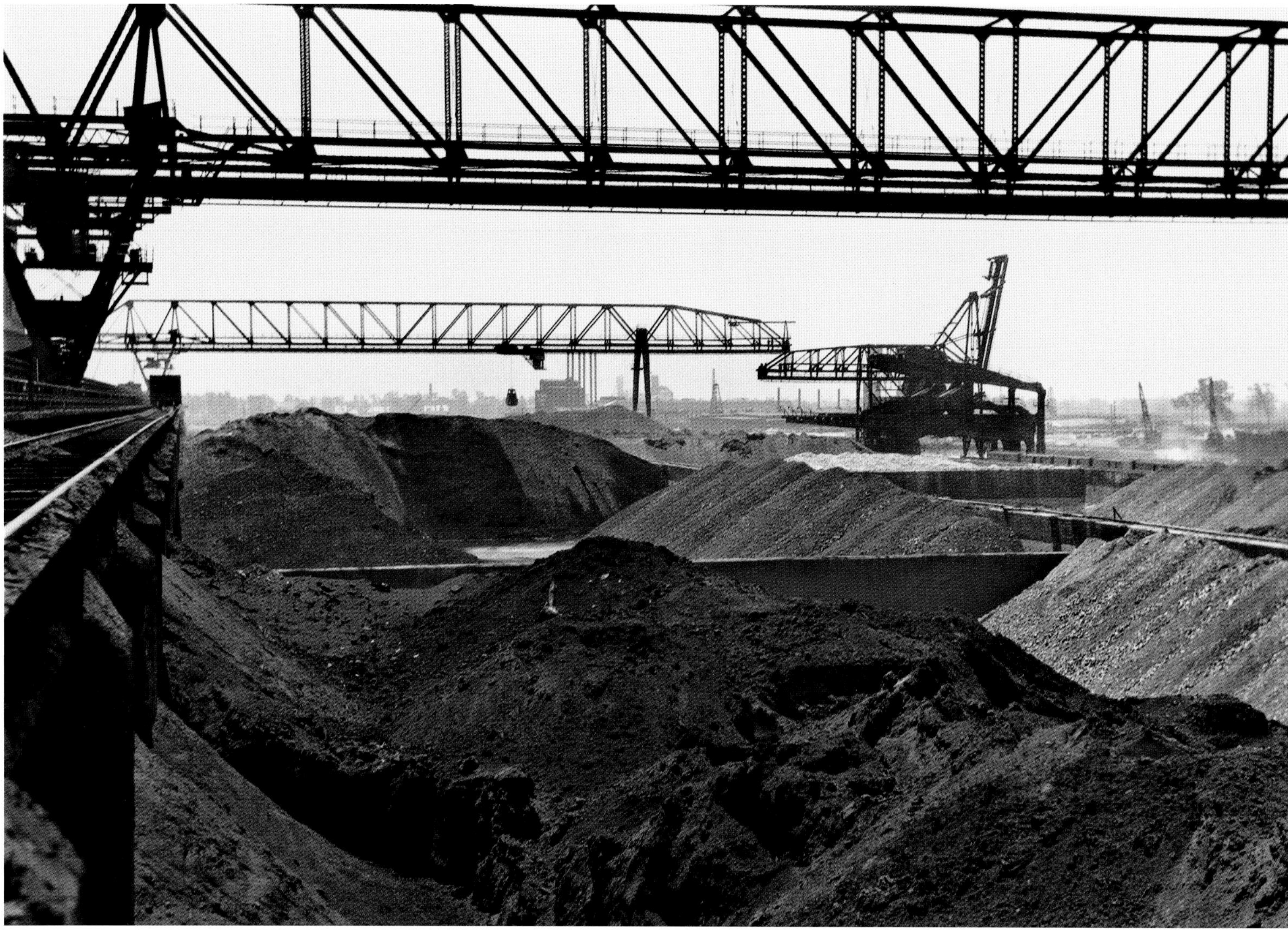

Gorges of Iron Ore, Ford Factory, Detroit, Michigan, 1926

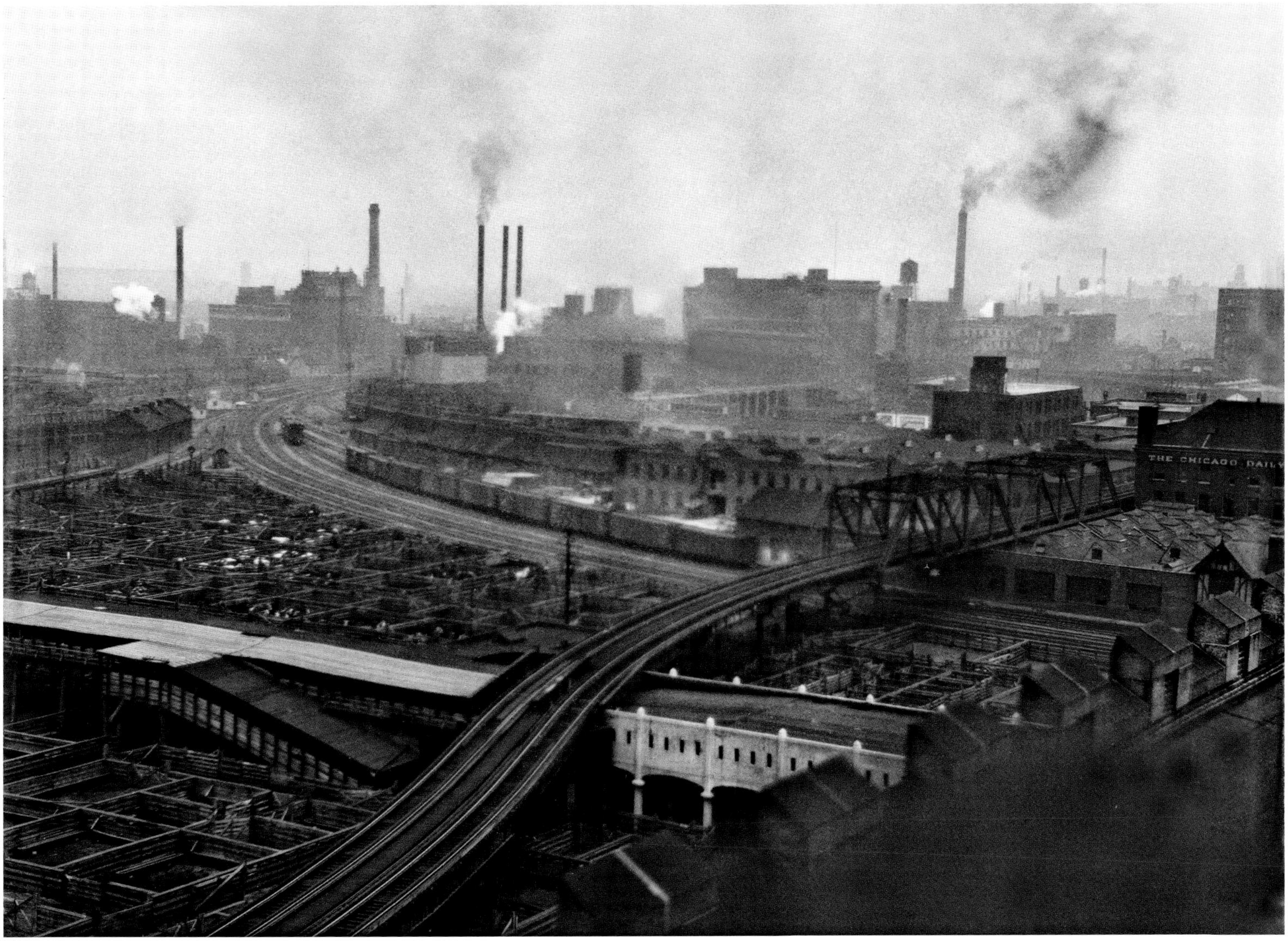

Stockyards and Railway, Chicago, Illinois, 1926

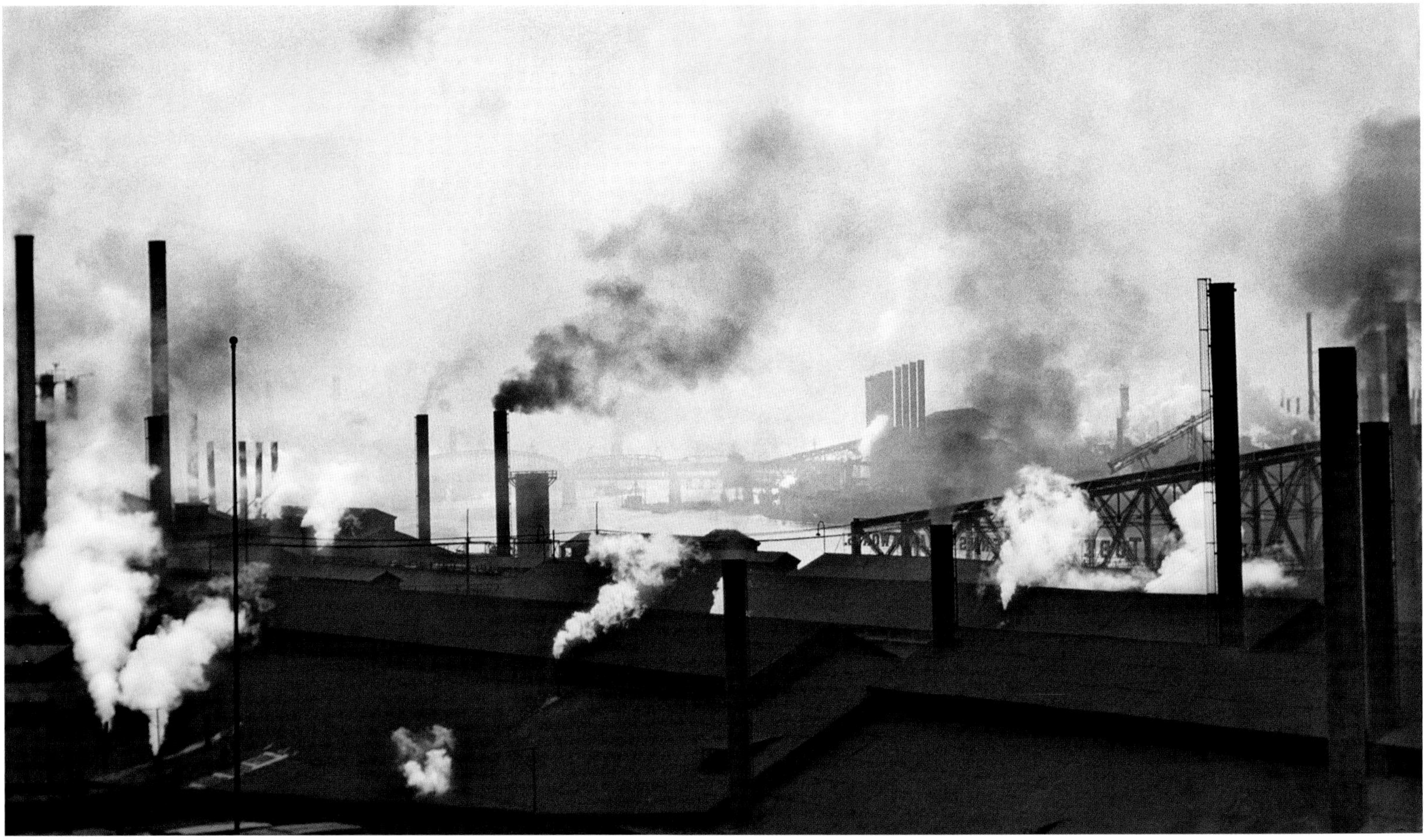

Rooftops and Smoking Chimneys, Pittsburgh, Pennsylvania, 1926

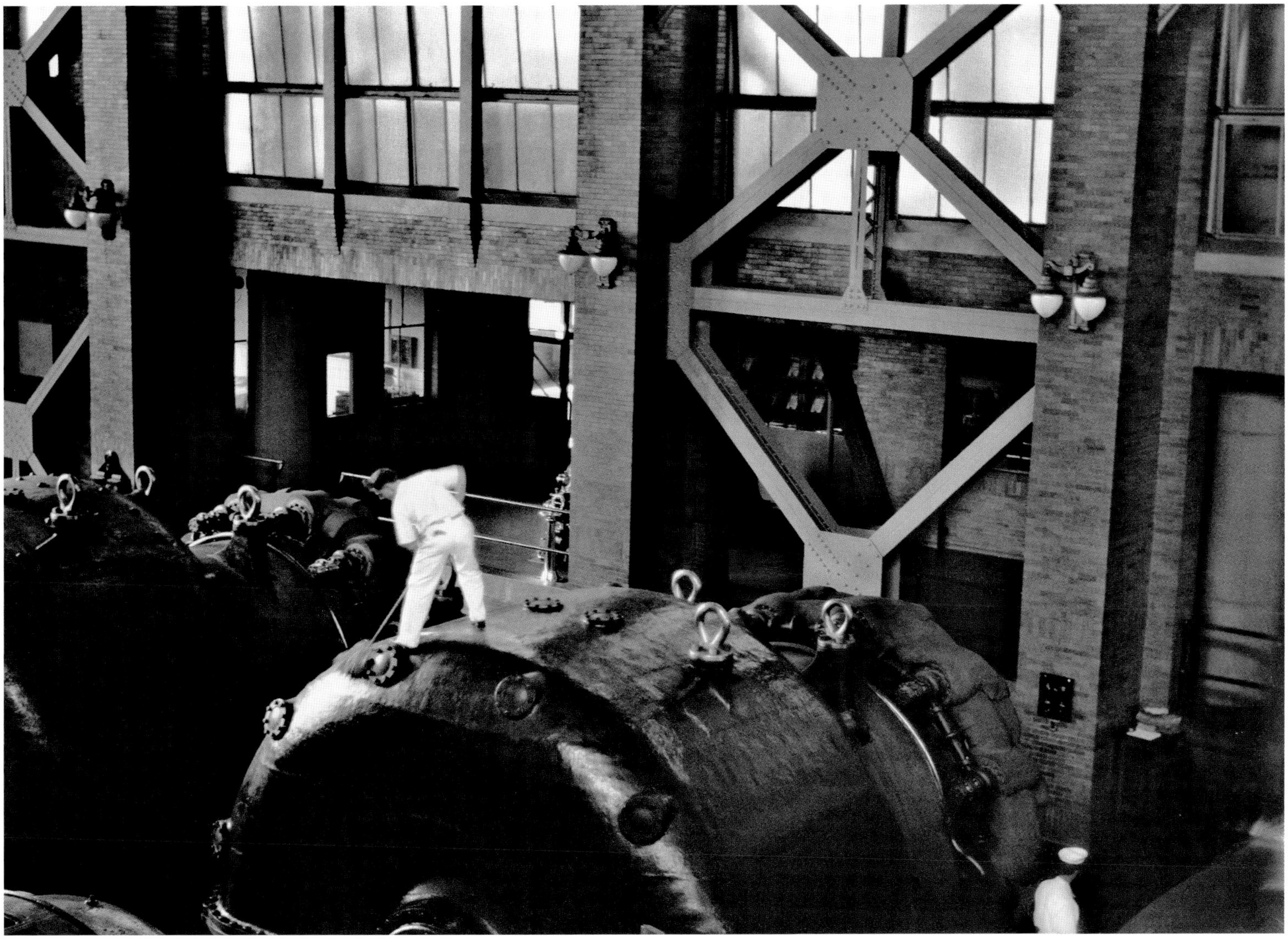

Worker at the Ford Factory, Detroit, Michigan, 1926

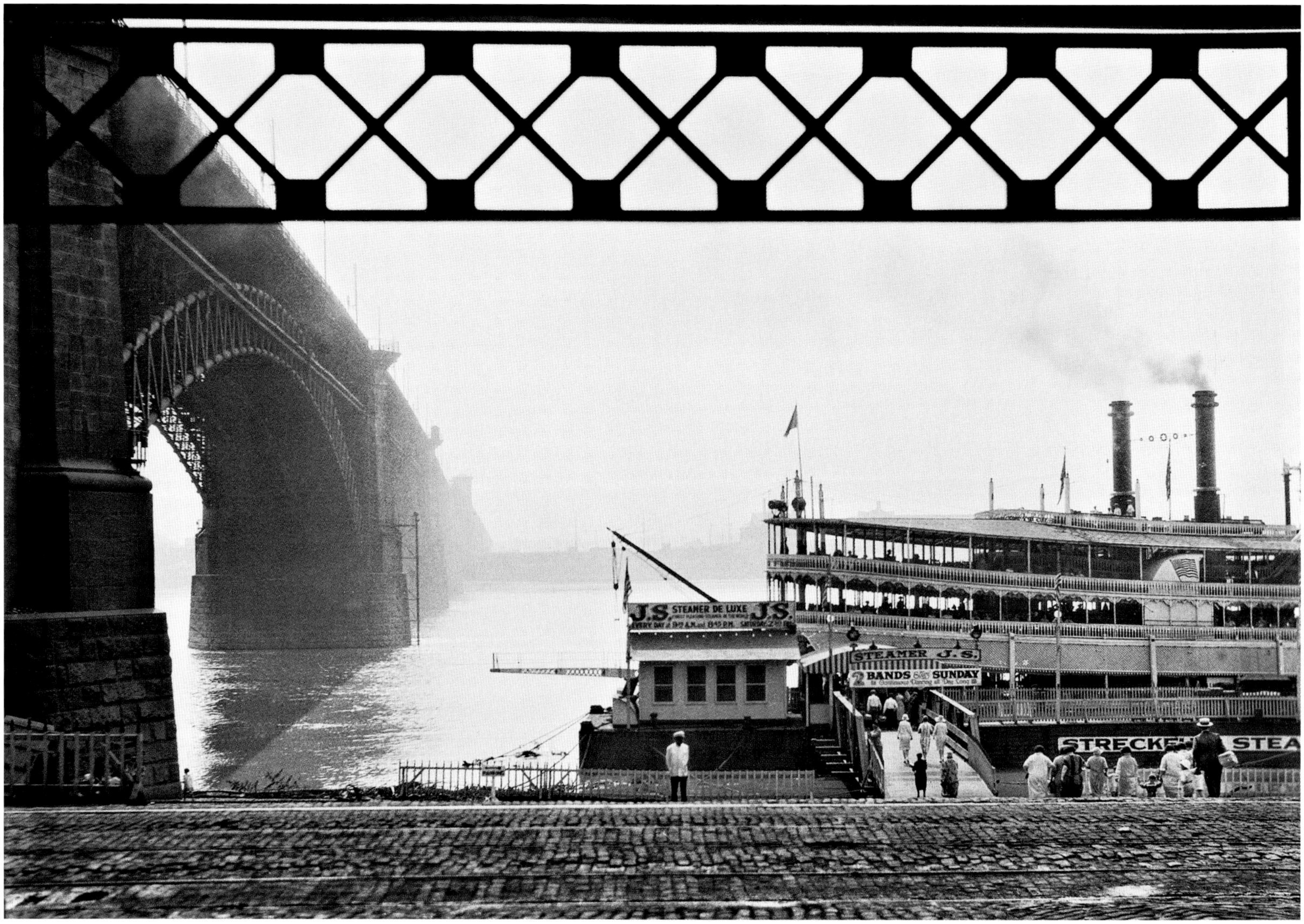

Paddle Steamer at Dock, St. Louis, Missouri, 1926

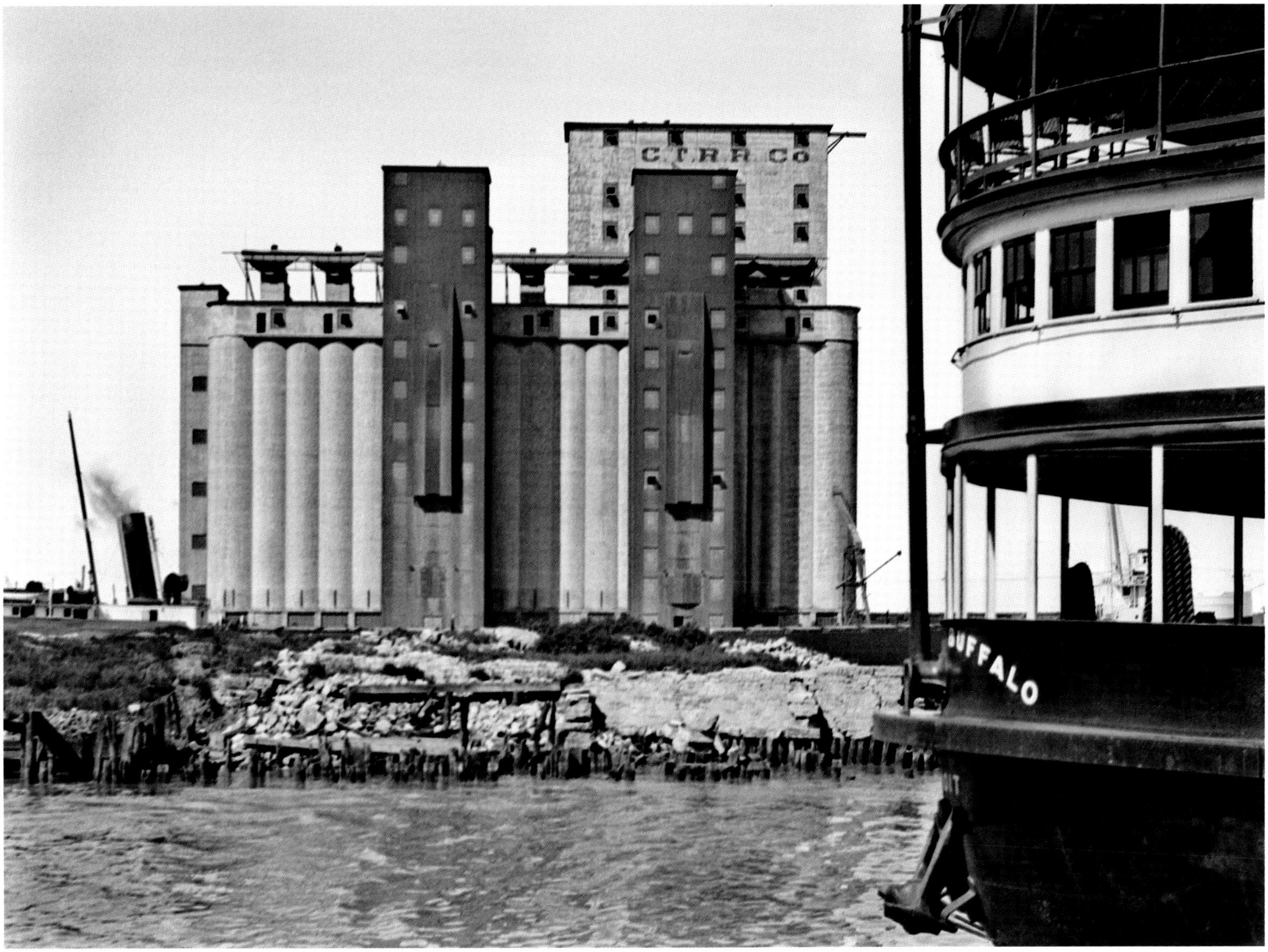

Grain Elevators and Ferry, Buffalo, New York, 1926

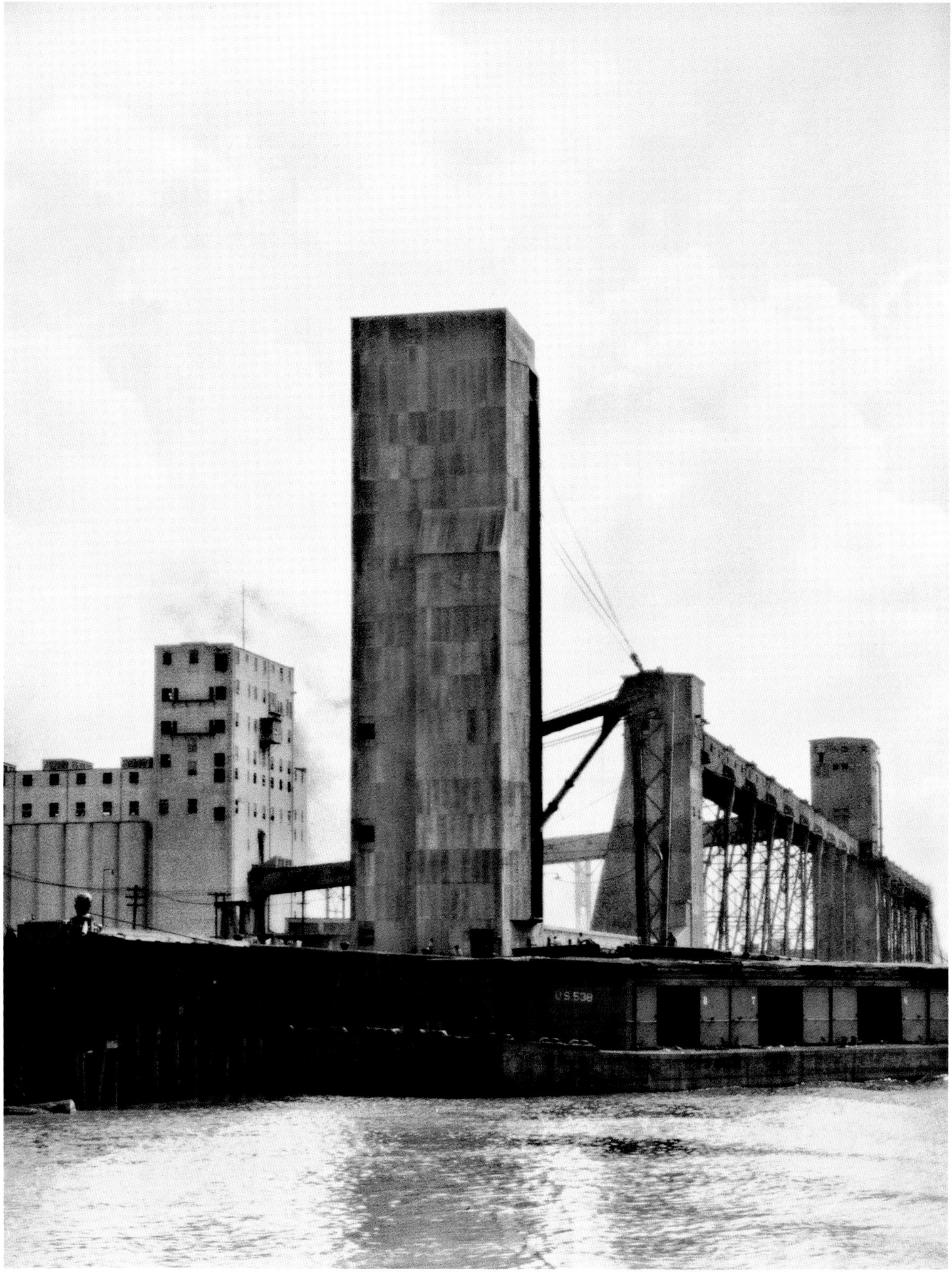

Elevator on the Mississippi, New Orleans, Louisiana, 1926

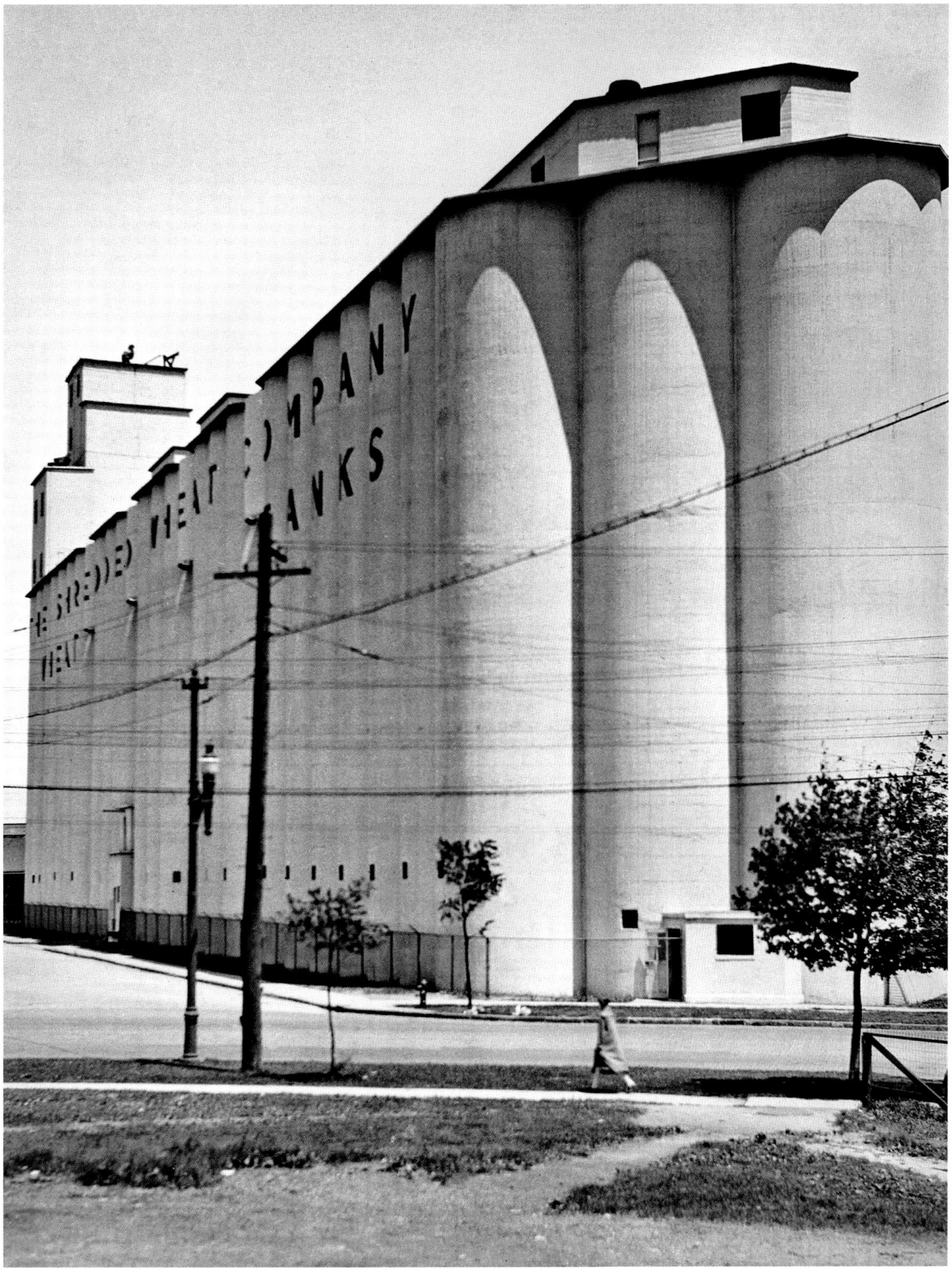

The Shredded Wheat Company's Grain Elevator at Niagara Falls, New York, 1926

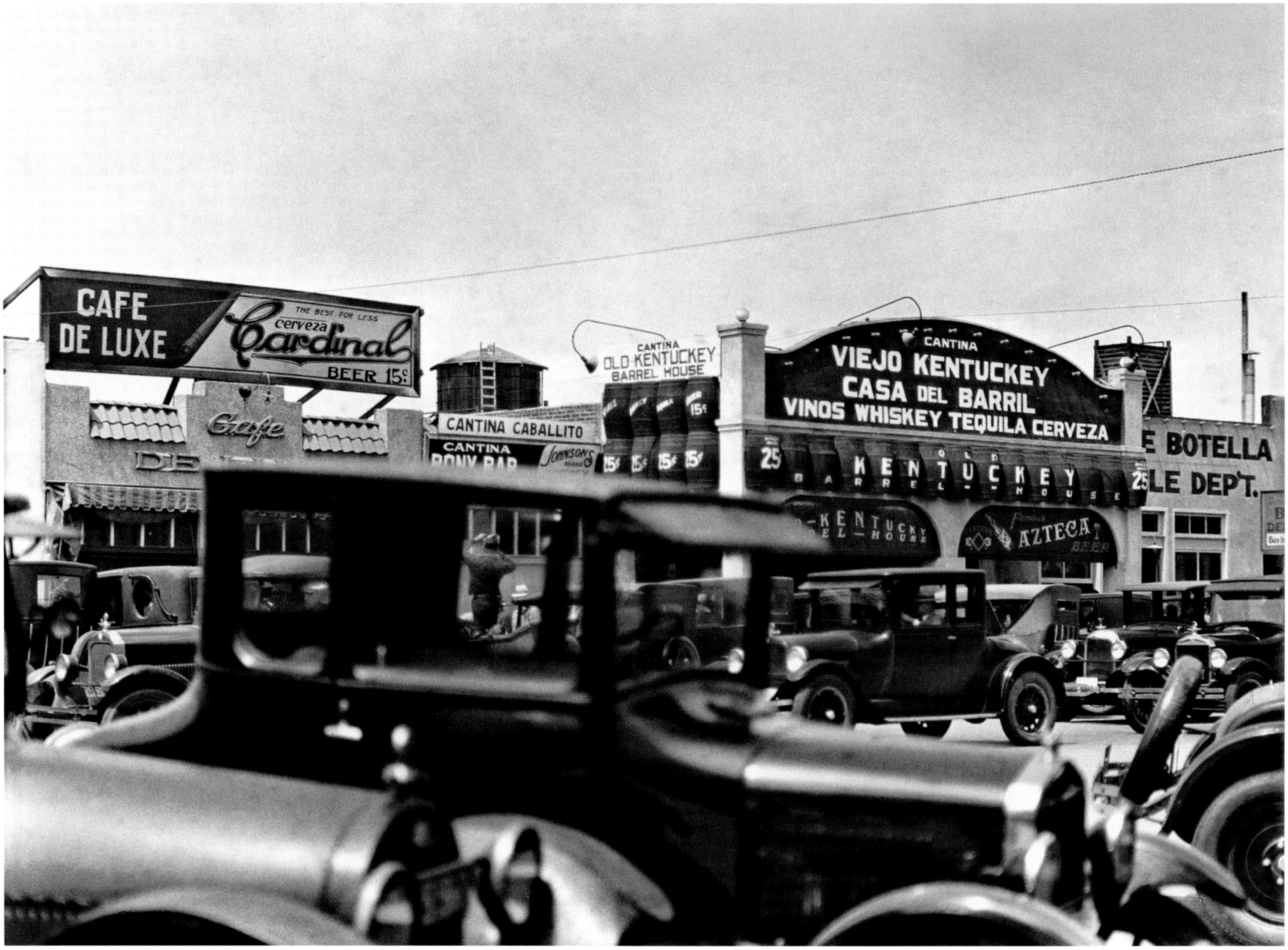

Street Scene, Tijuana, Mexico, 1926

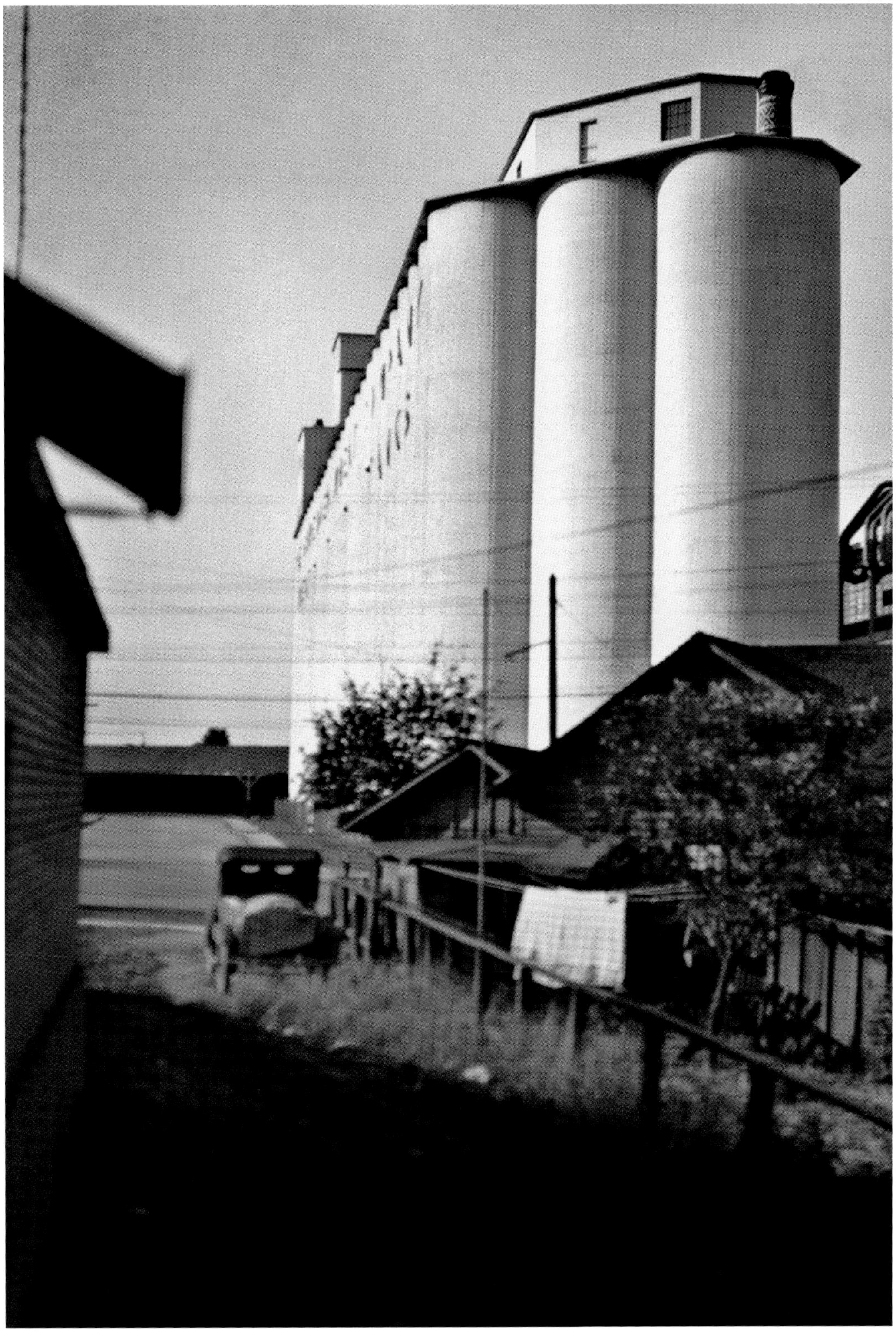

Grain Elevator and Car, Niagara Falls, New York, 1926

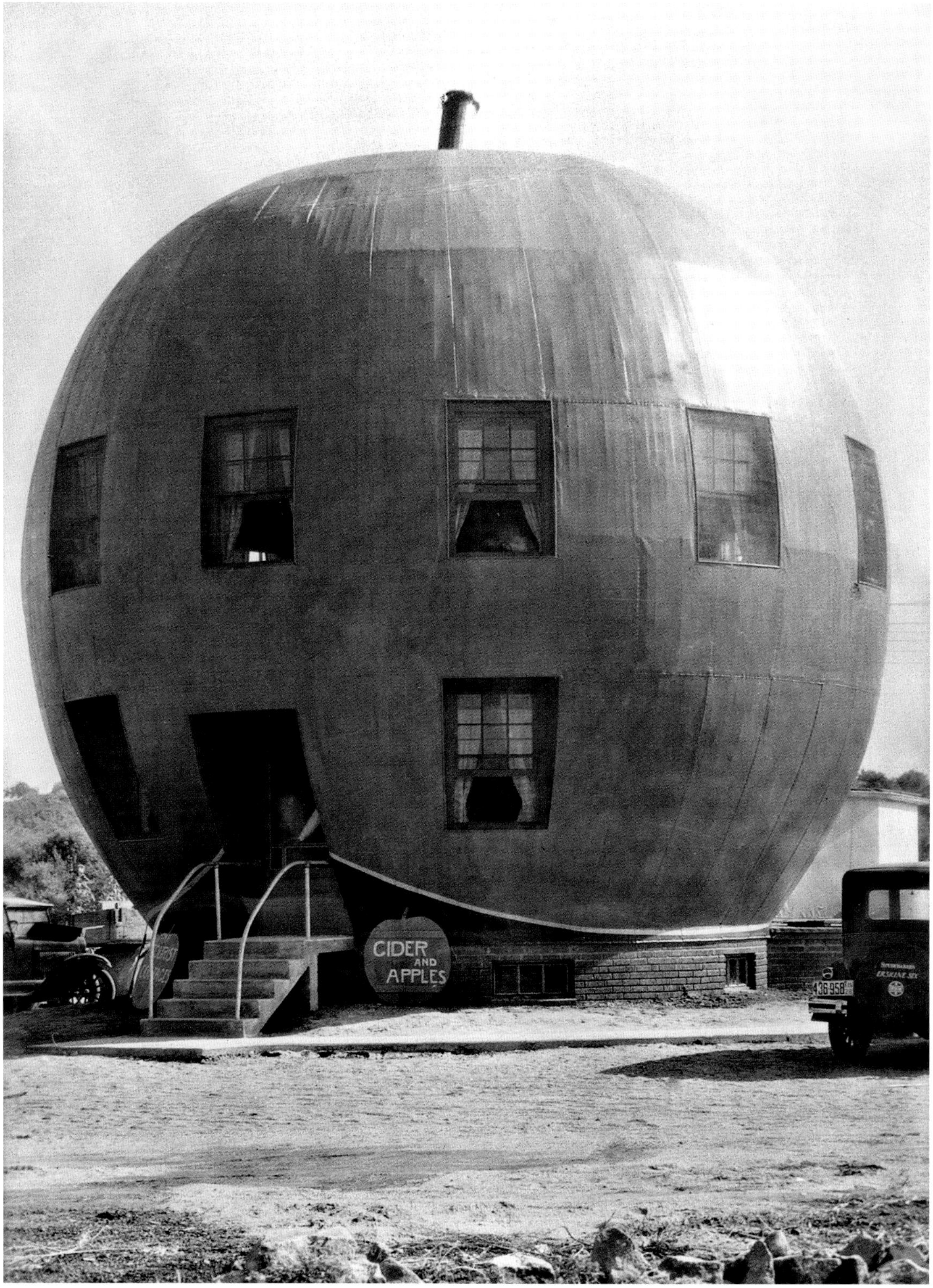

The Big Red Apple Restaurant, near St. Joseph, Missouri, 1926

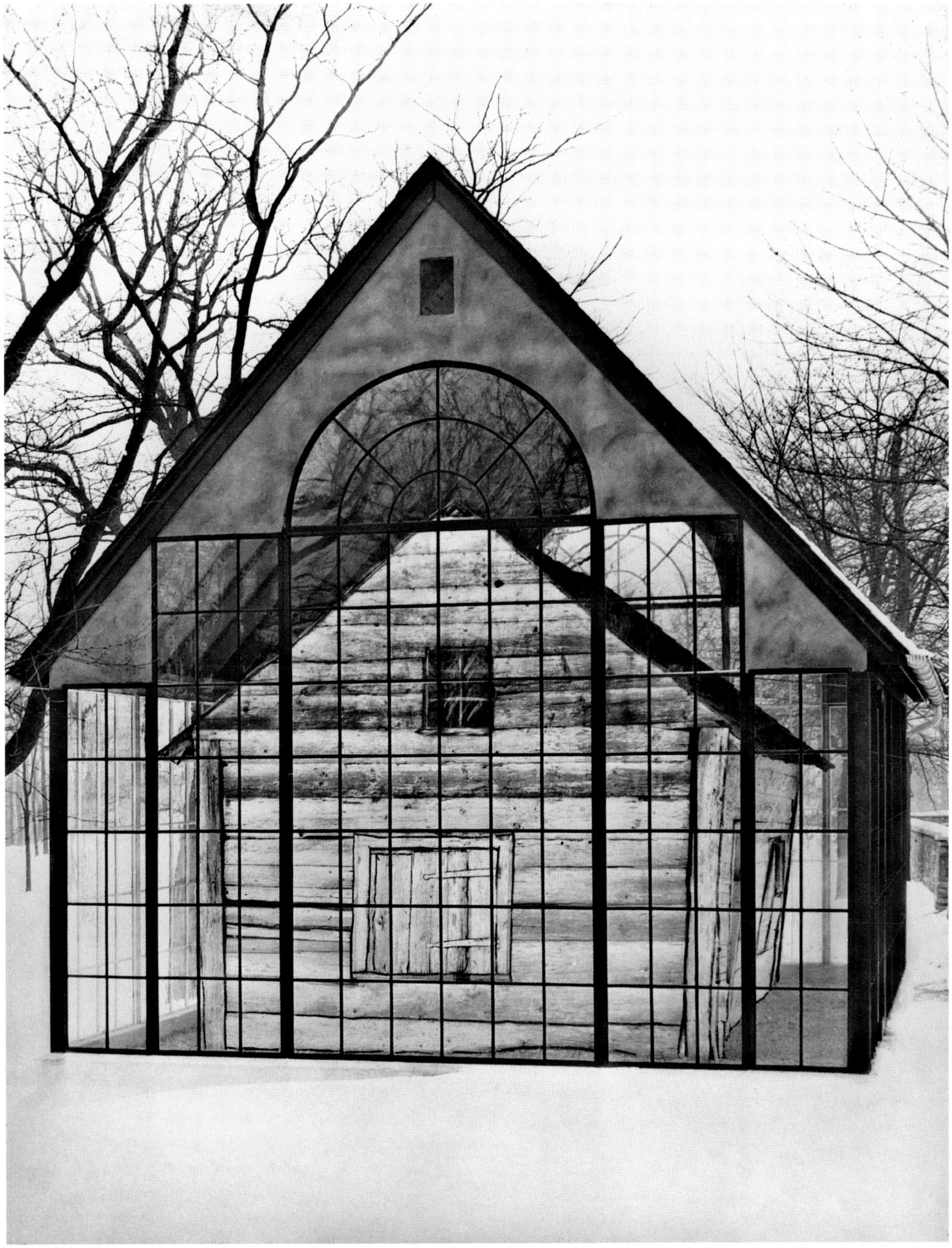

Enclosed Presbyterian Church, Derry, Pennsylvania, 1926

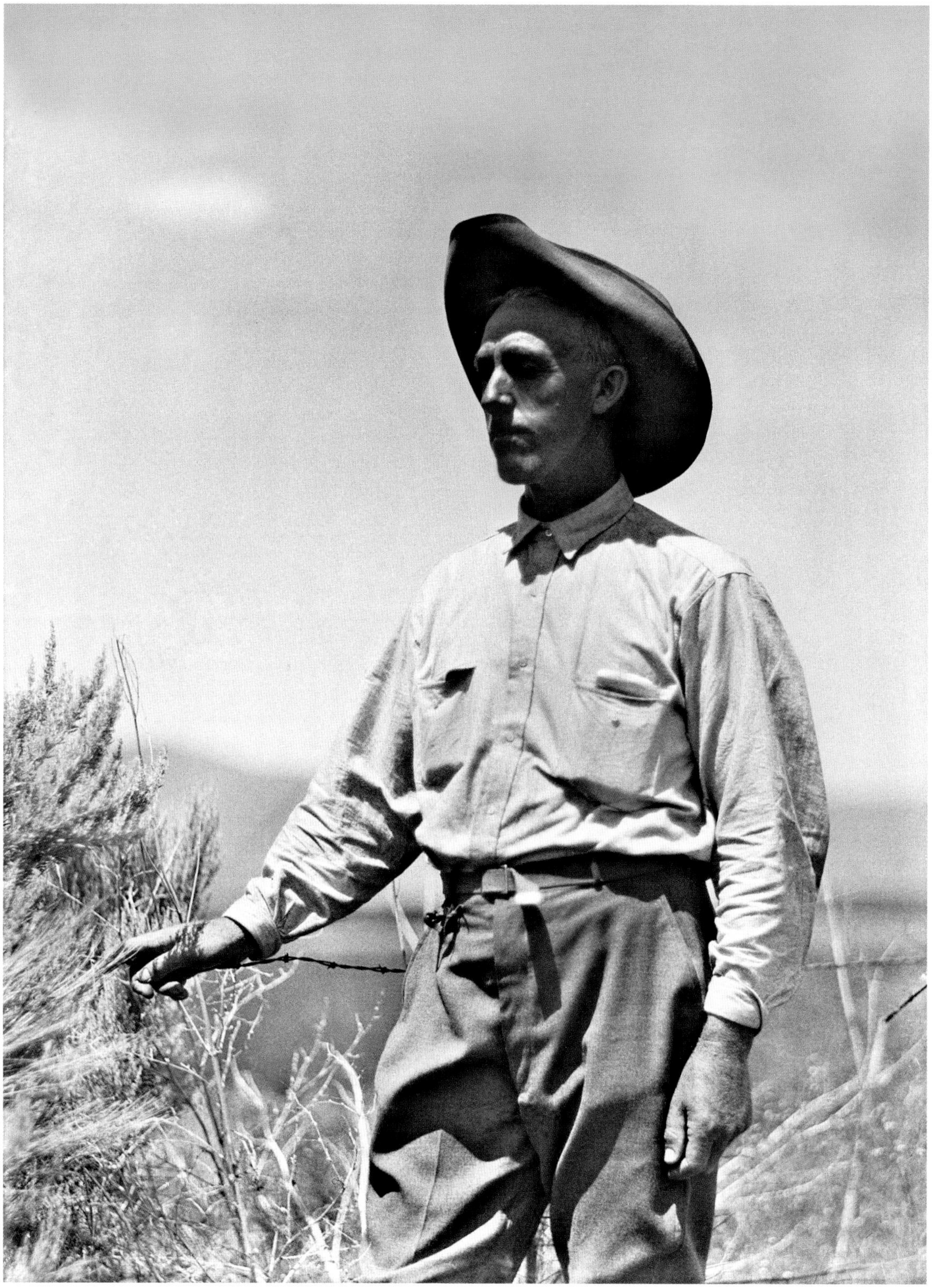

Son of Utah, 1926

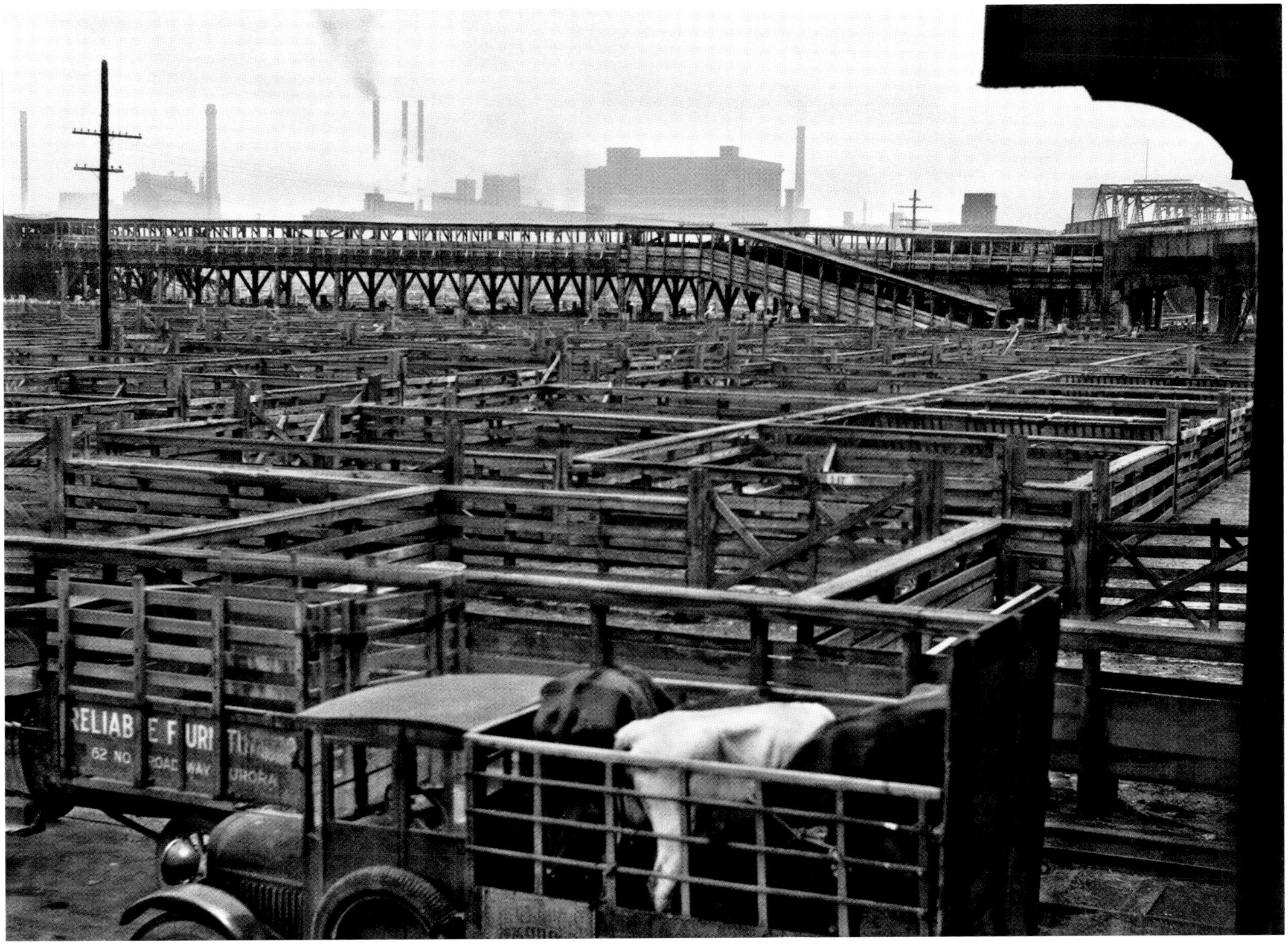

Stockyards, Chicago, Illinois, 1926

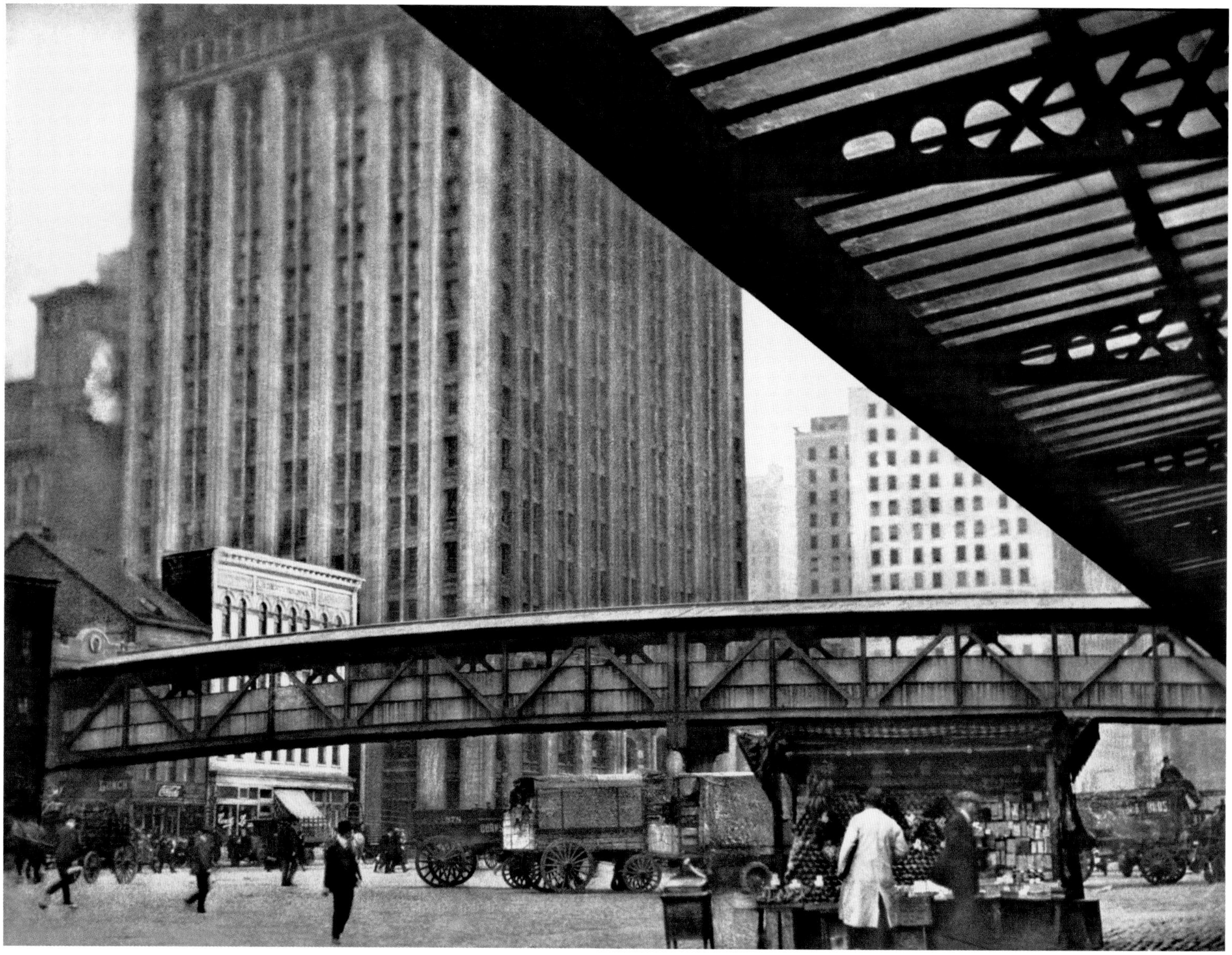

In the West Street District, New York City, 1921

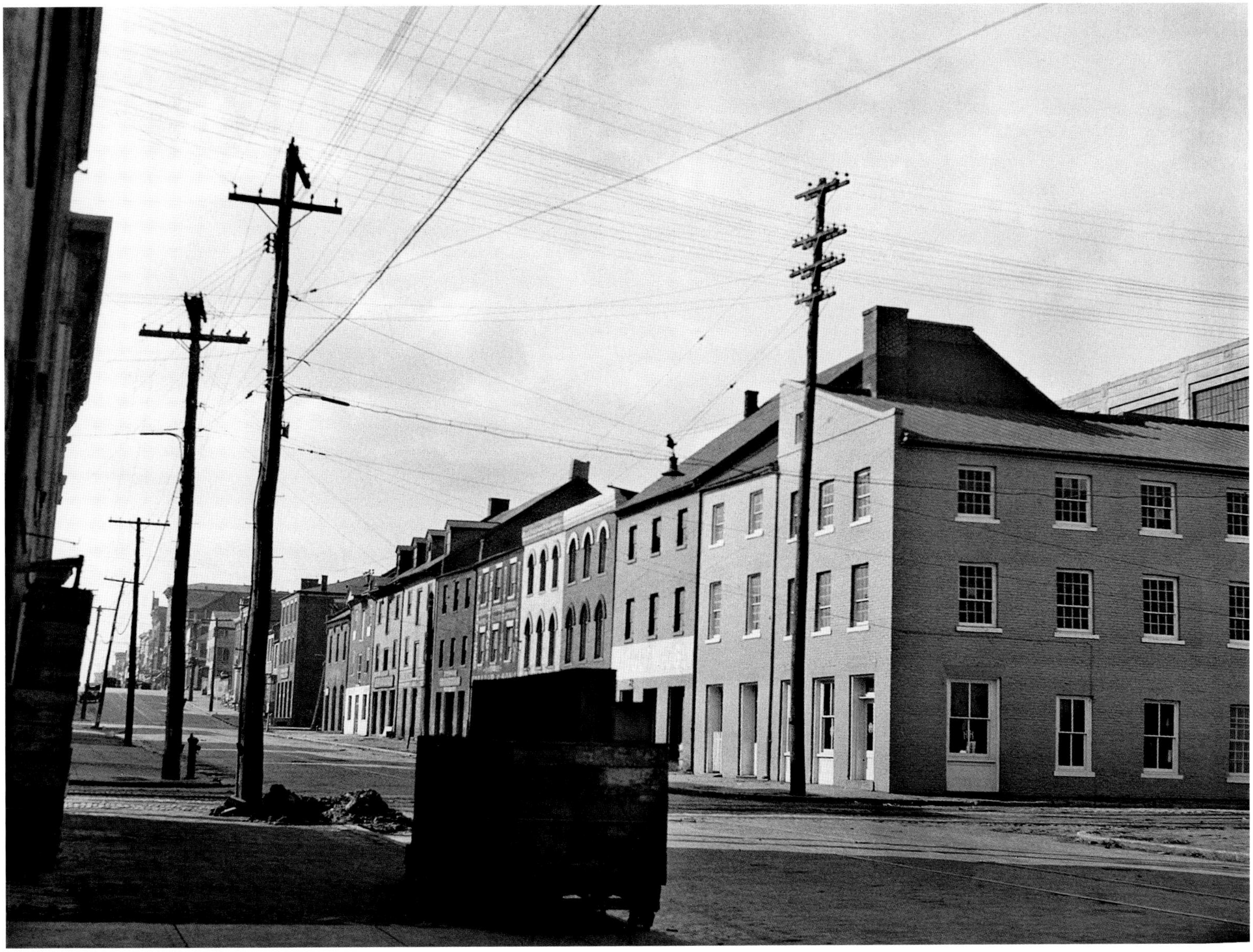

Alexandria, Virginia, 1926

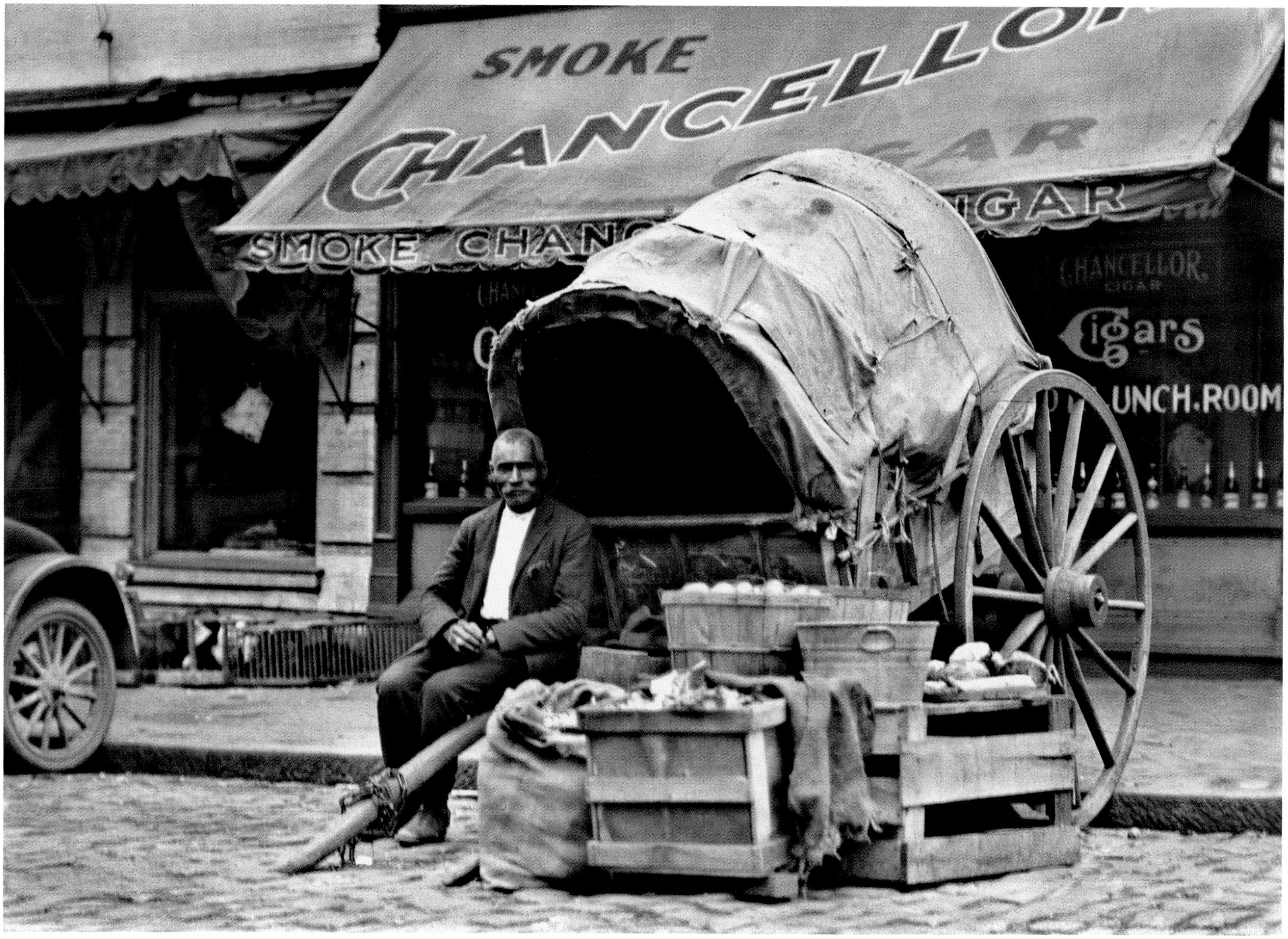

Fruit Vendor, Richmond, Virginia, 1926

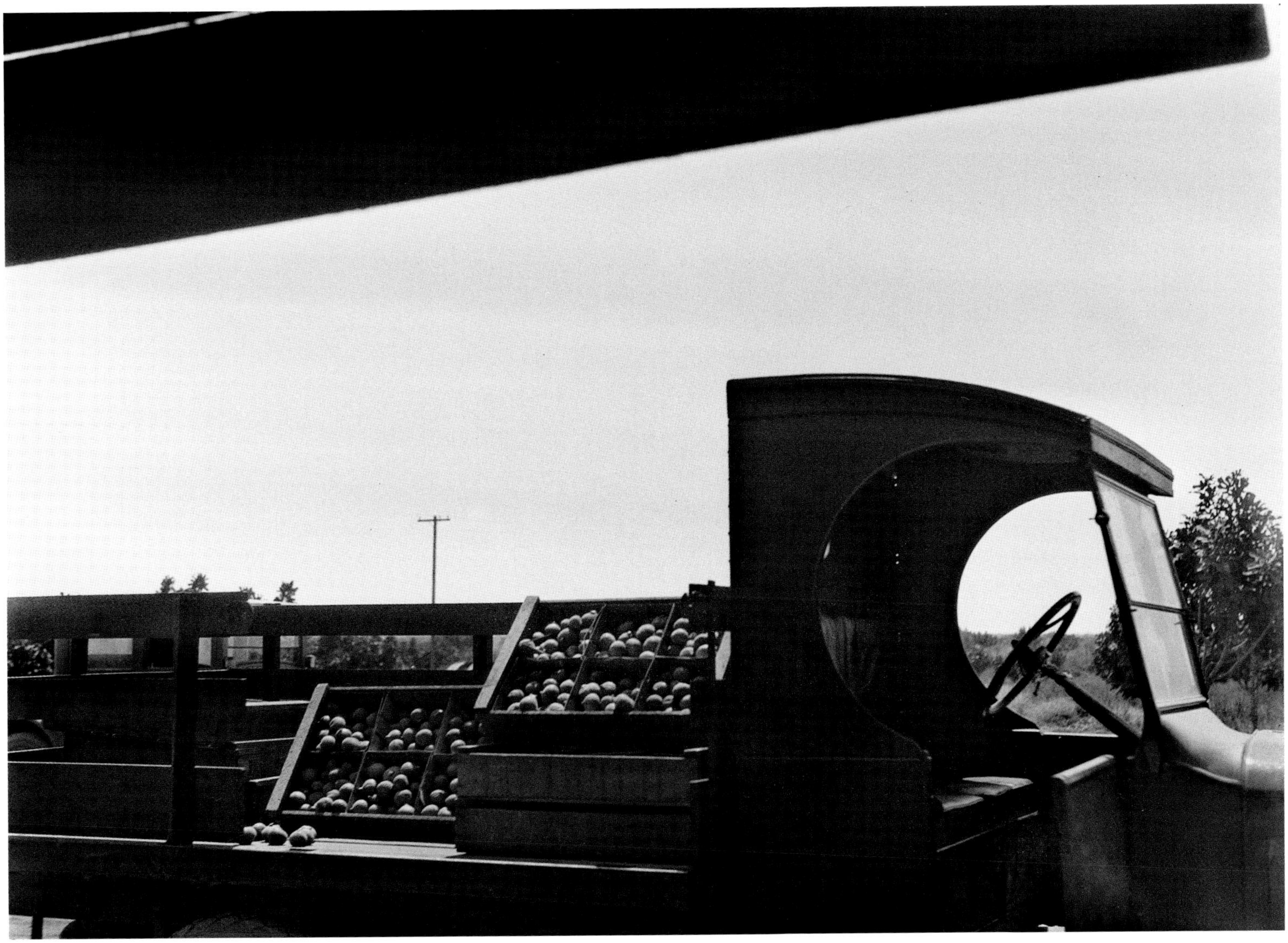

Truck Loaded with Figs, California, 1926

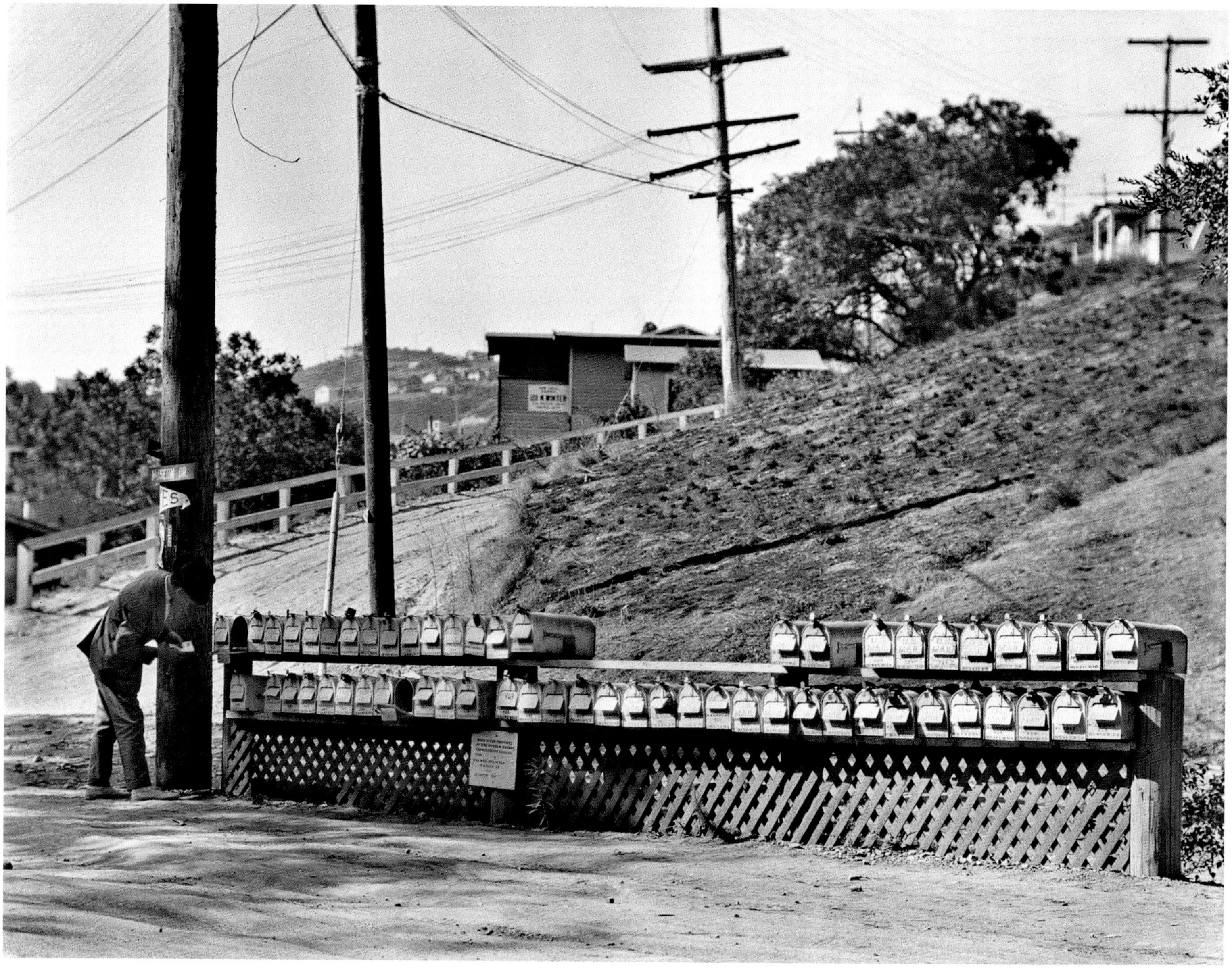

Mailboxes, Los Angeles, California, 1926

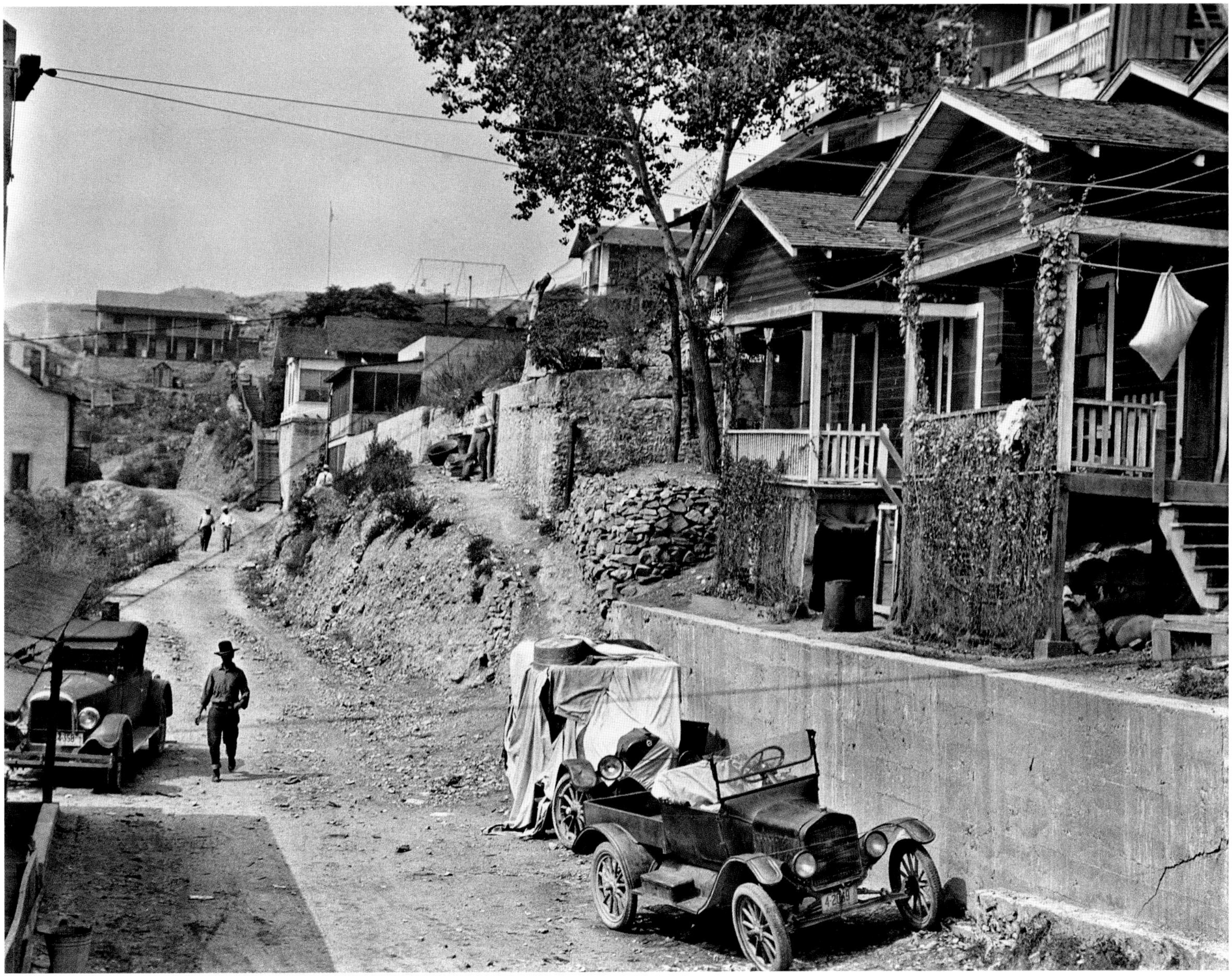

Street Scene, Superior City, Arizona, 1926

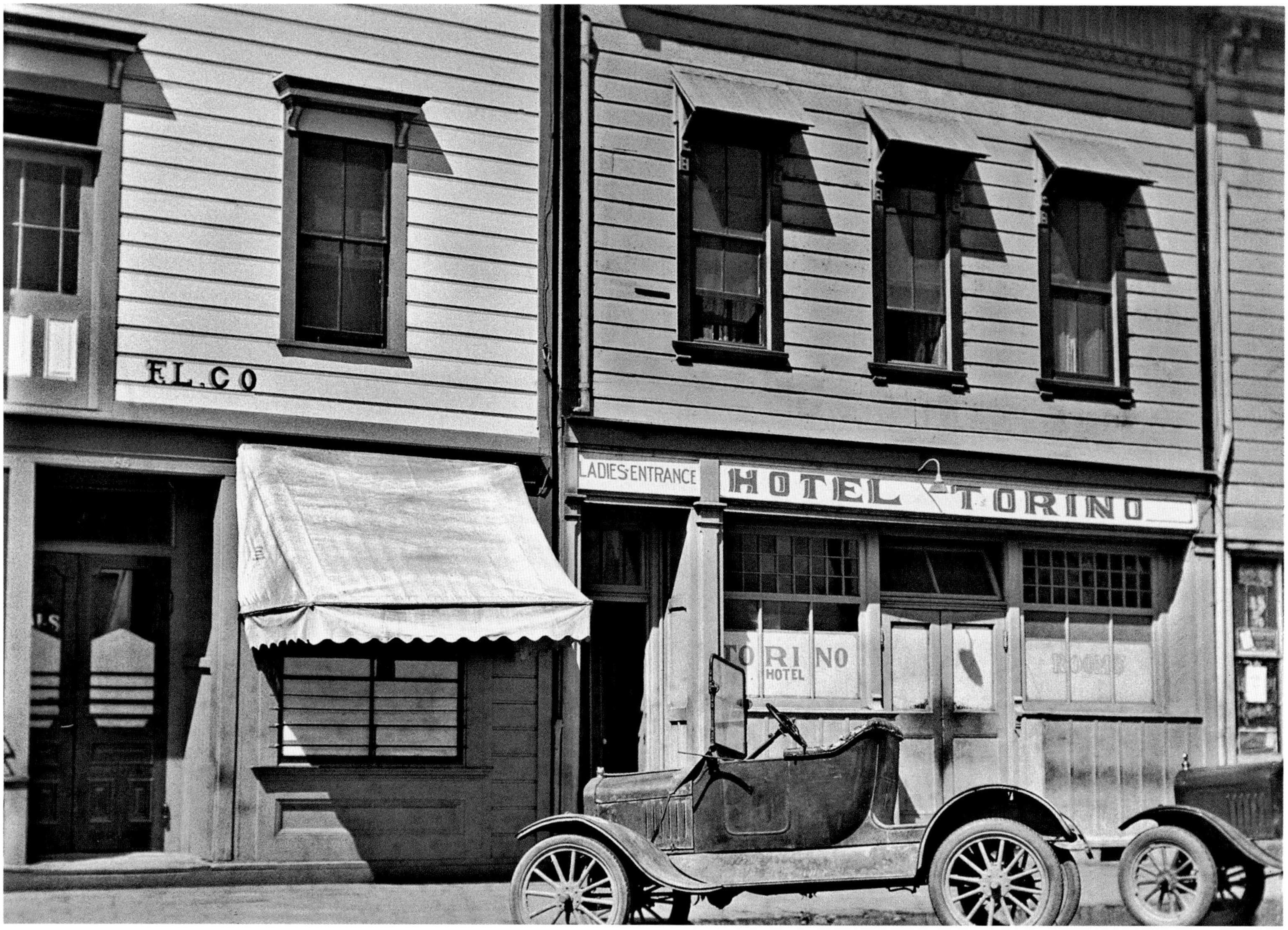

Hotel Torino, California, 1926

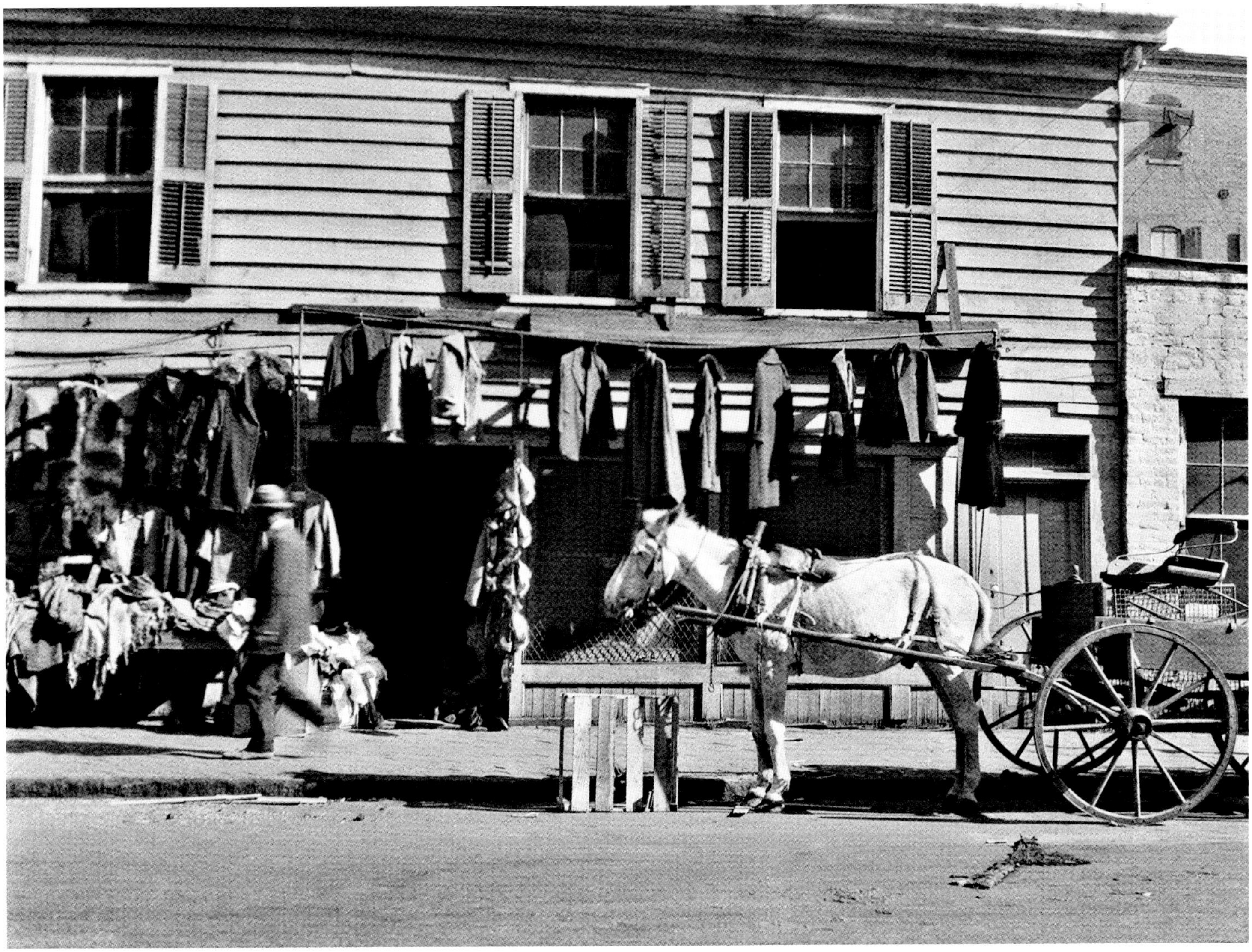

Used Clothing Store, Tennessee, 1926

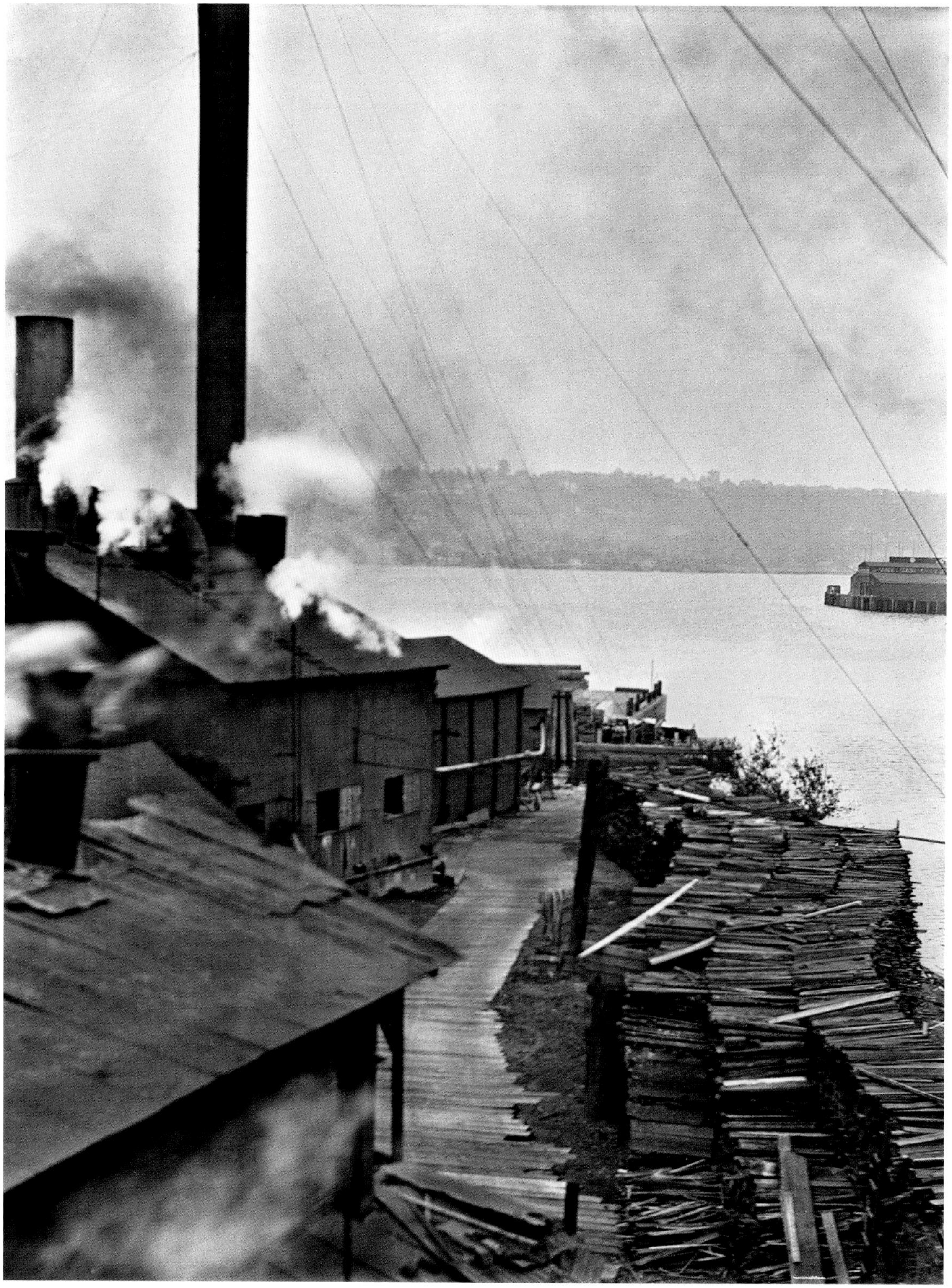

Lumber Mill, Waterfront, Seattle, Washington, 1926

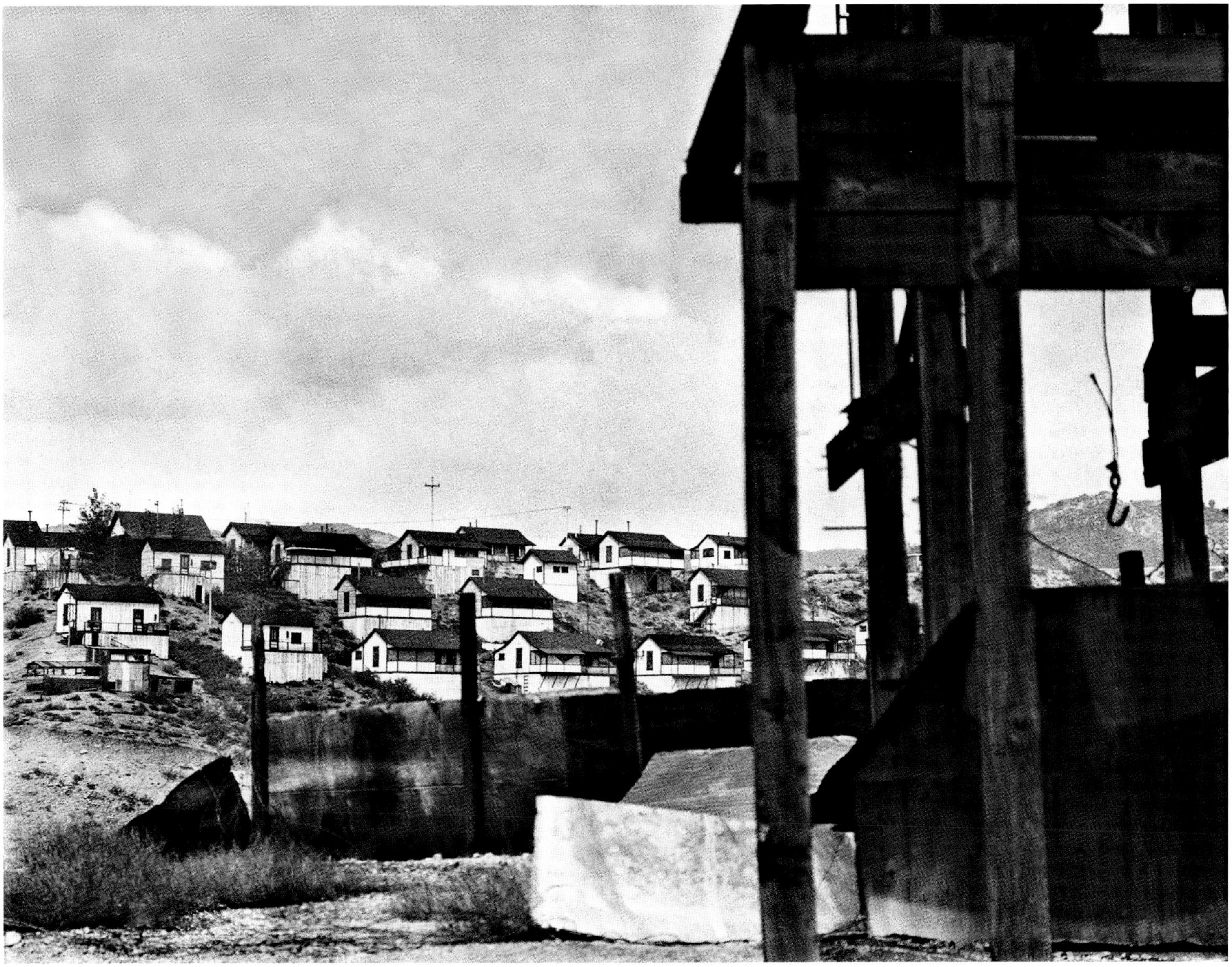

Hillside View, Superior City, Arizona, 1926

Dower House, West Chester, Pennsylvania, 1926

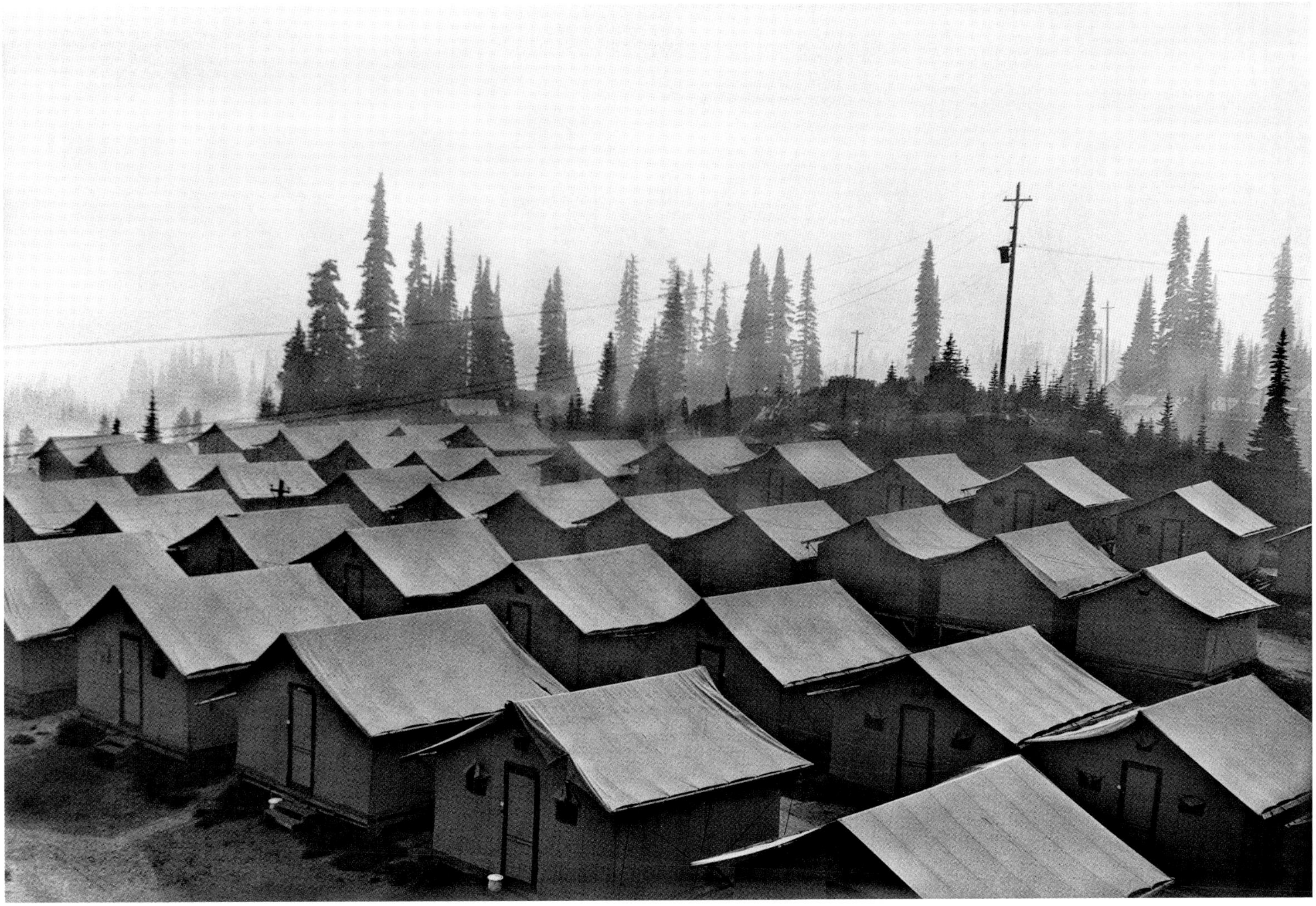

Paradise Valley, Washington, 1926

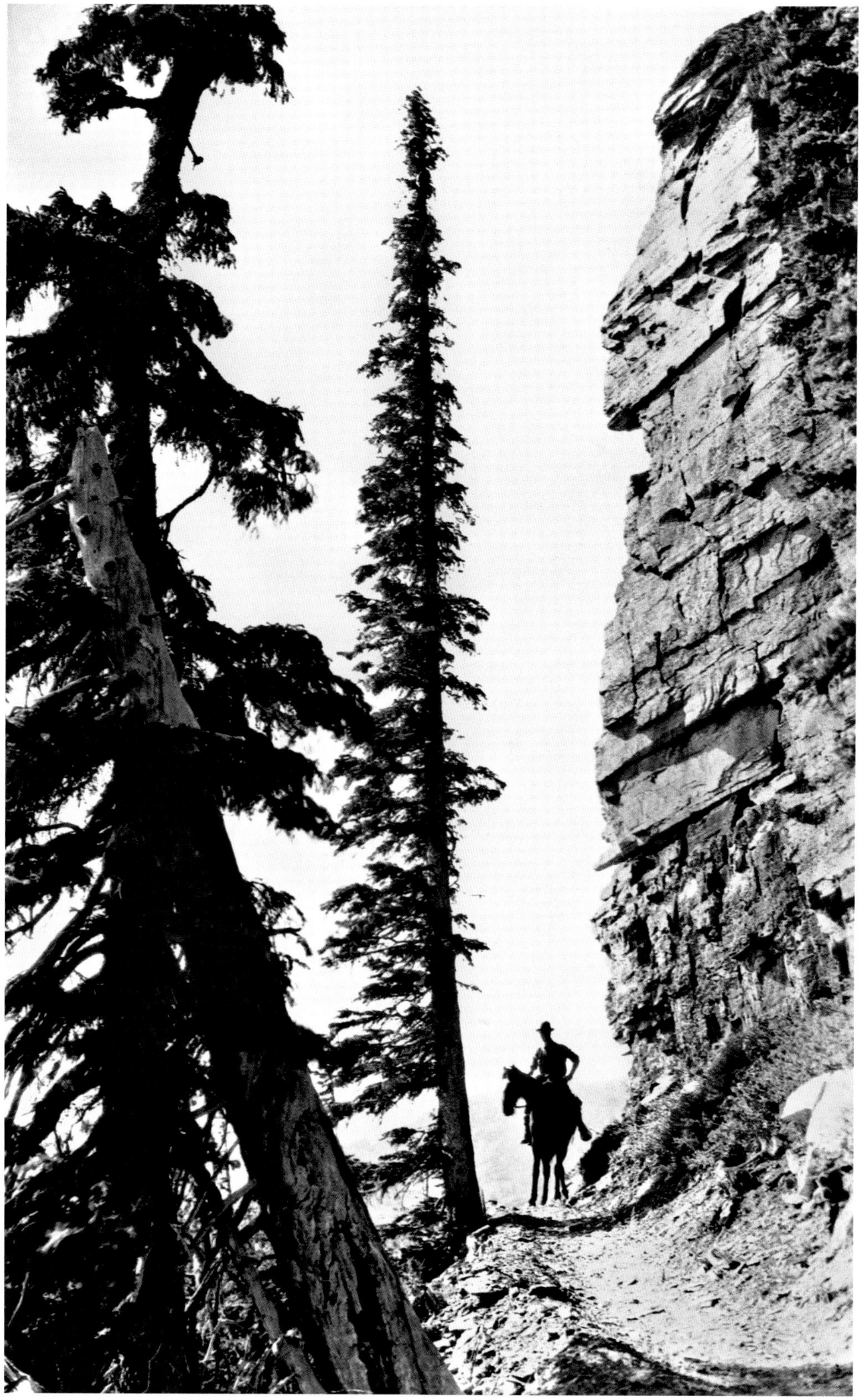

Rocky Mountains, Colorado, 1926

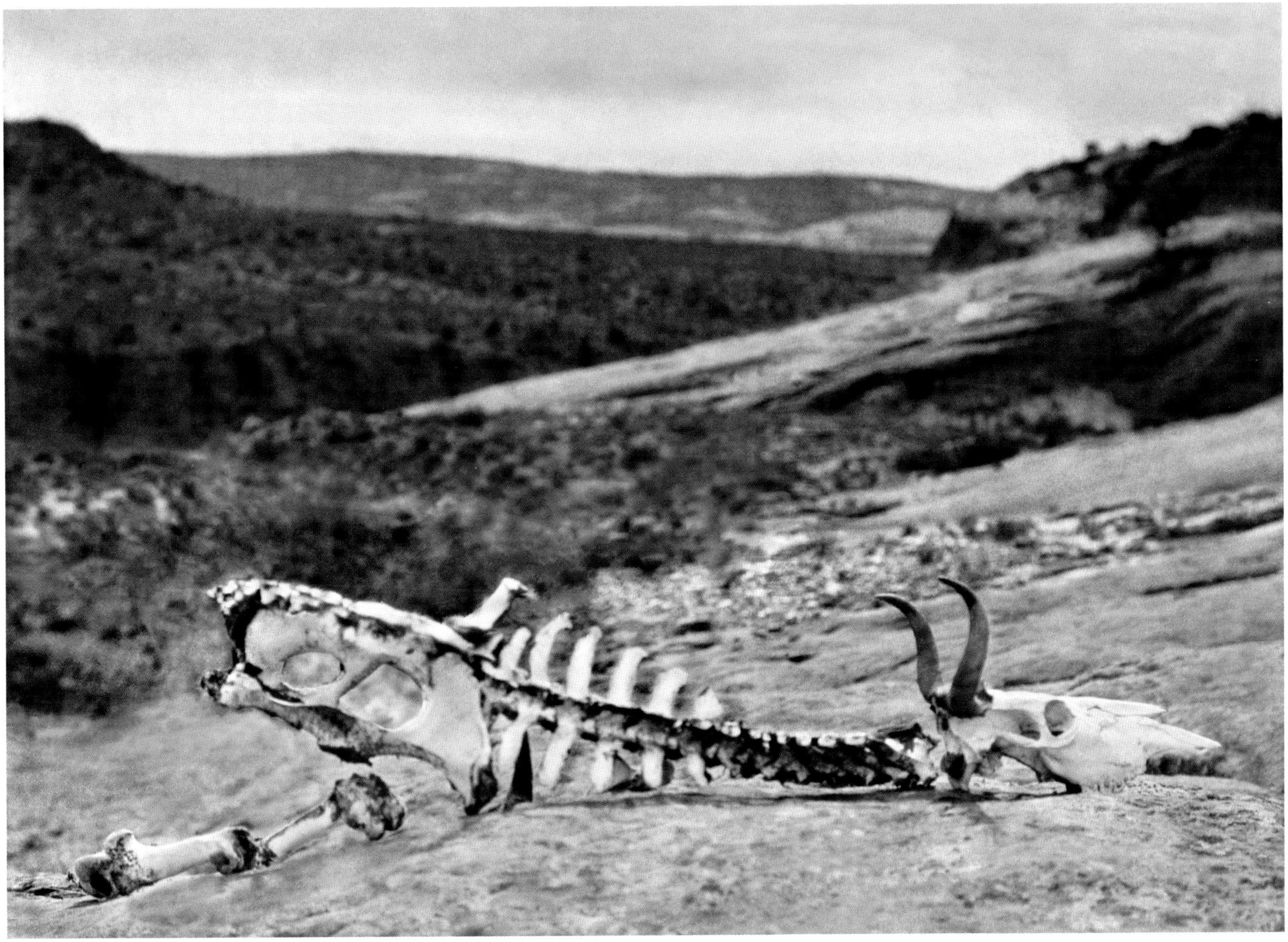

Skeleton, Desert Hills, Arizona, 1926

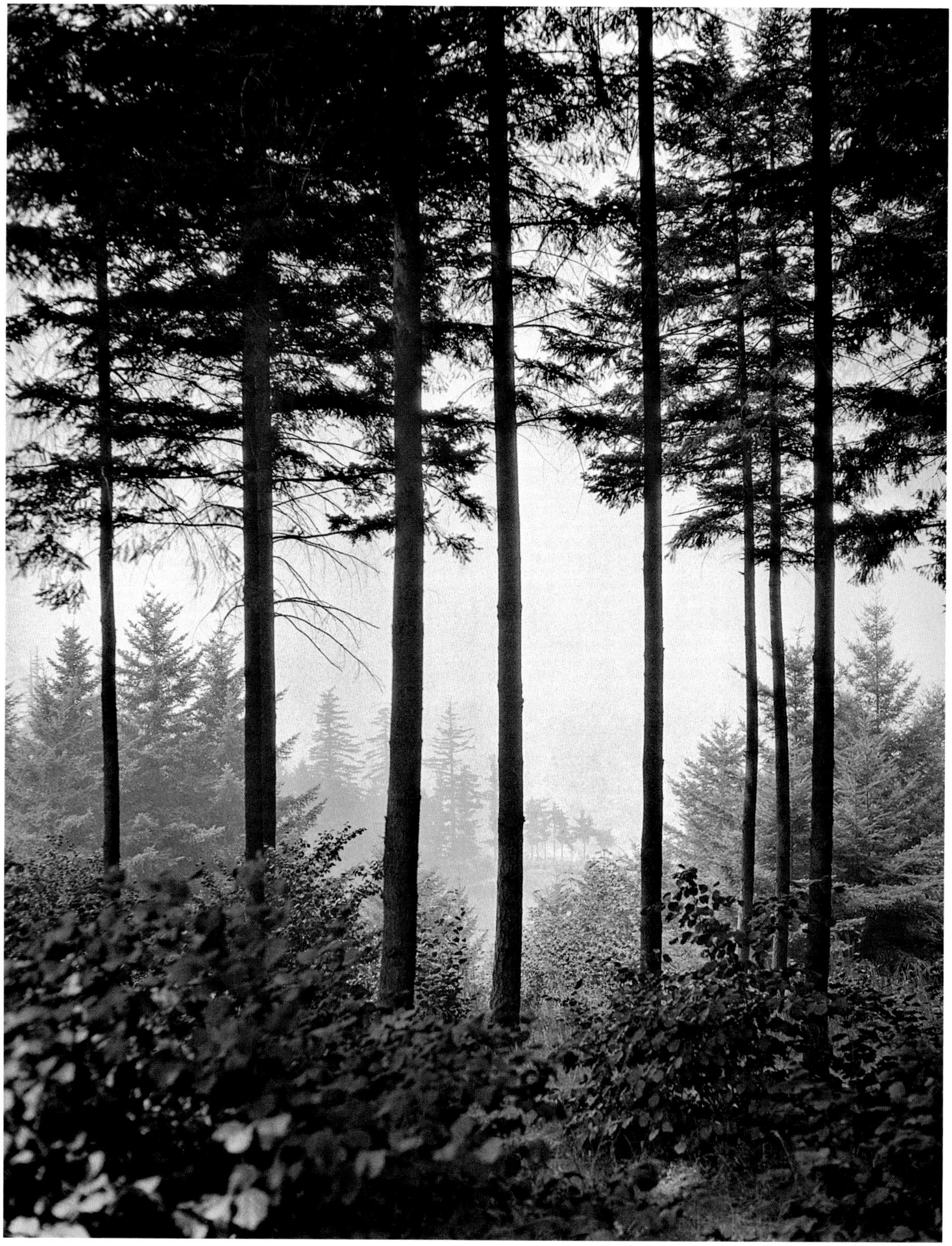

Mount Tabor, Portland, Oregon, 1926

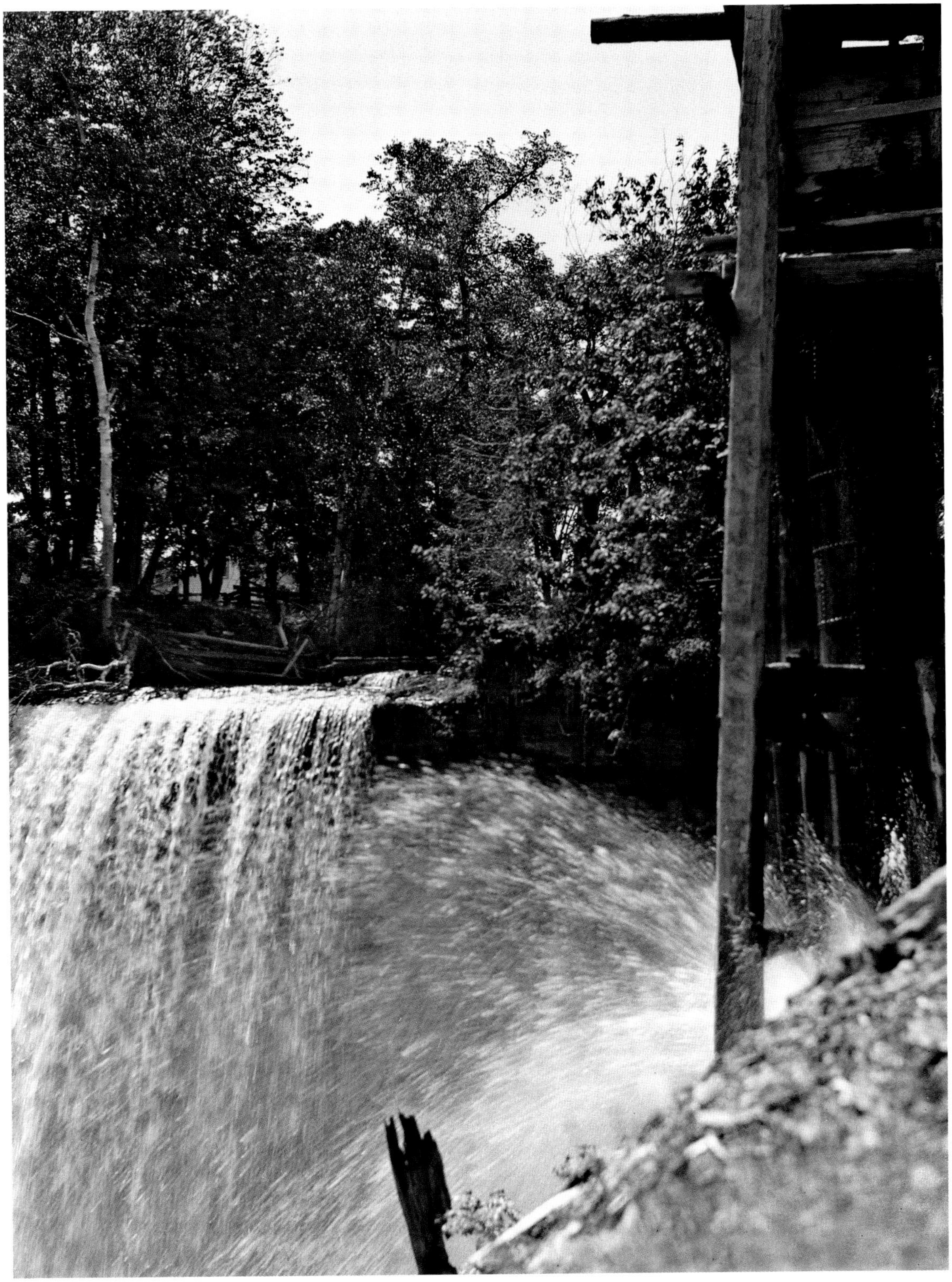

Bridal Veil Falls, Ontario, Canada, 1926

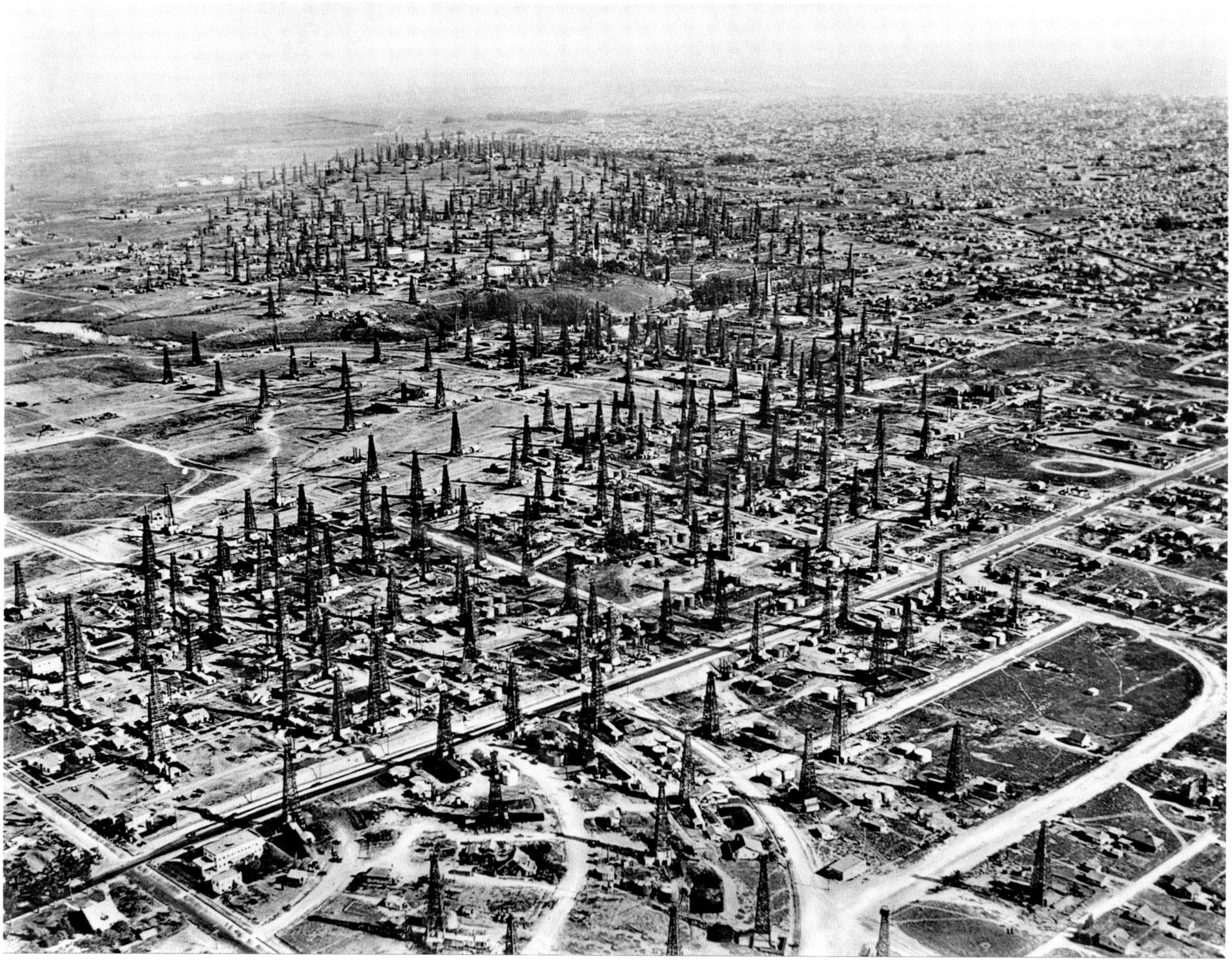

Signal Hill Oil Field, Los Angeles, California, 1926

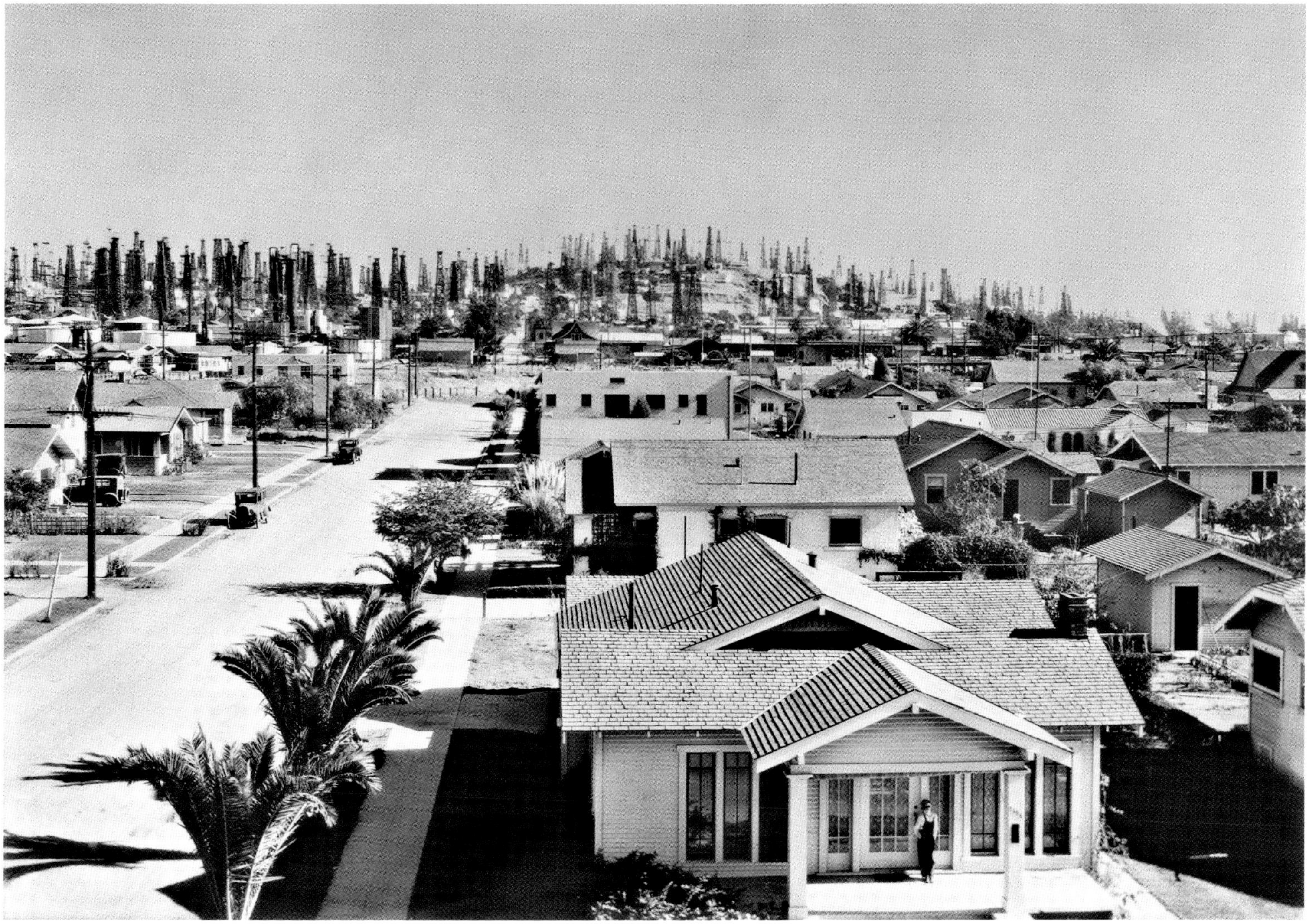

Houses at Signal Hill, Los Angeles, California, 1926

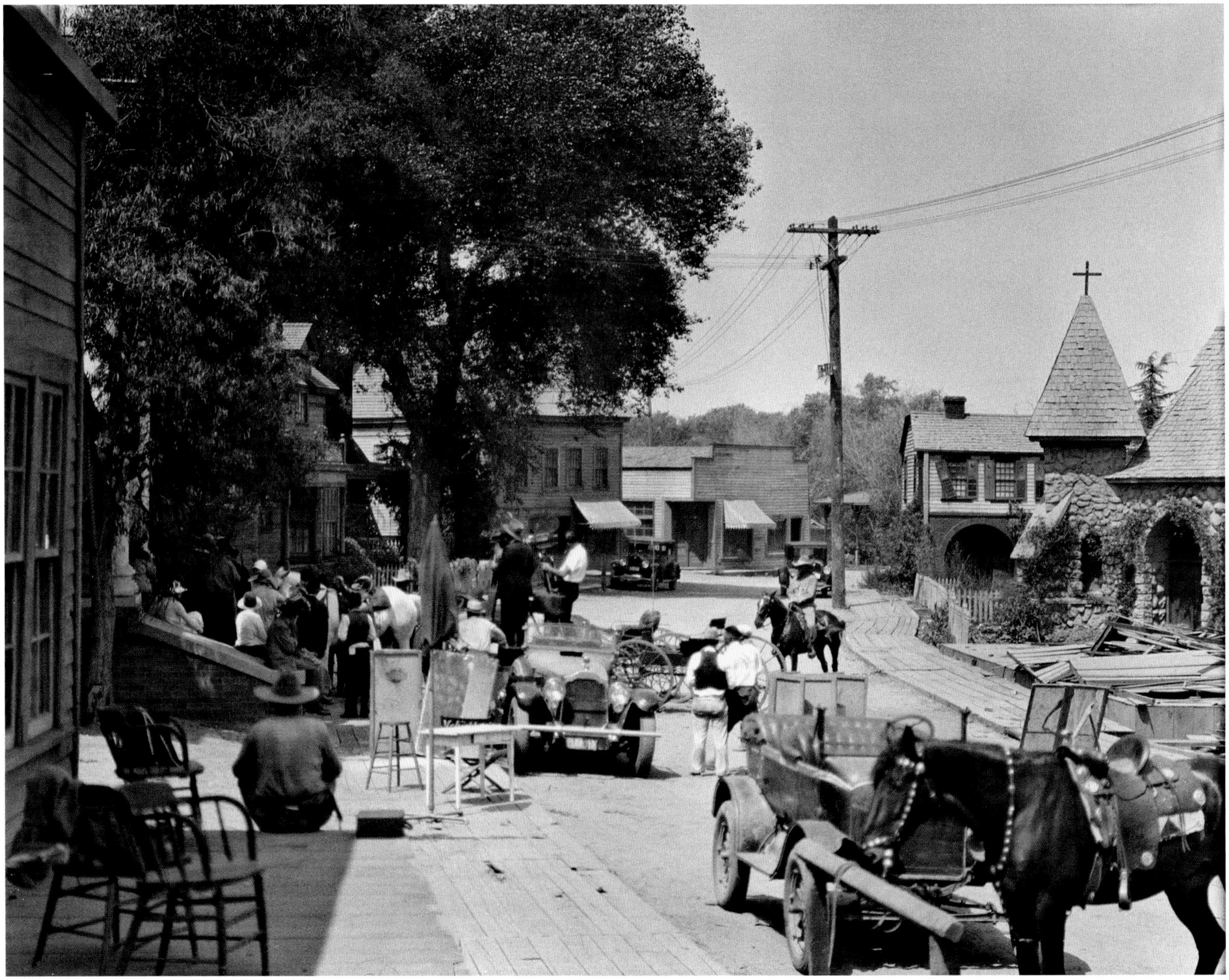

On the Set at Universal City, Los Angeles, California, 1926

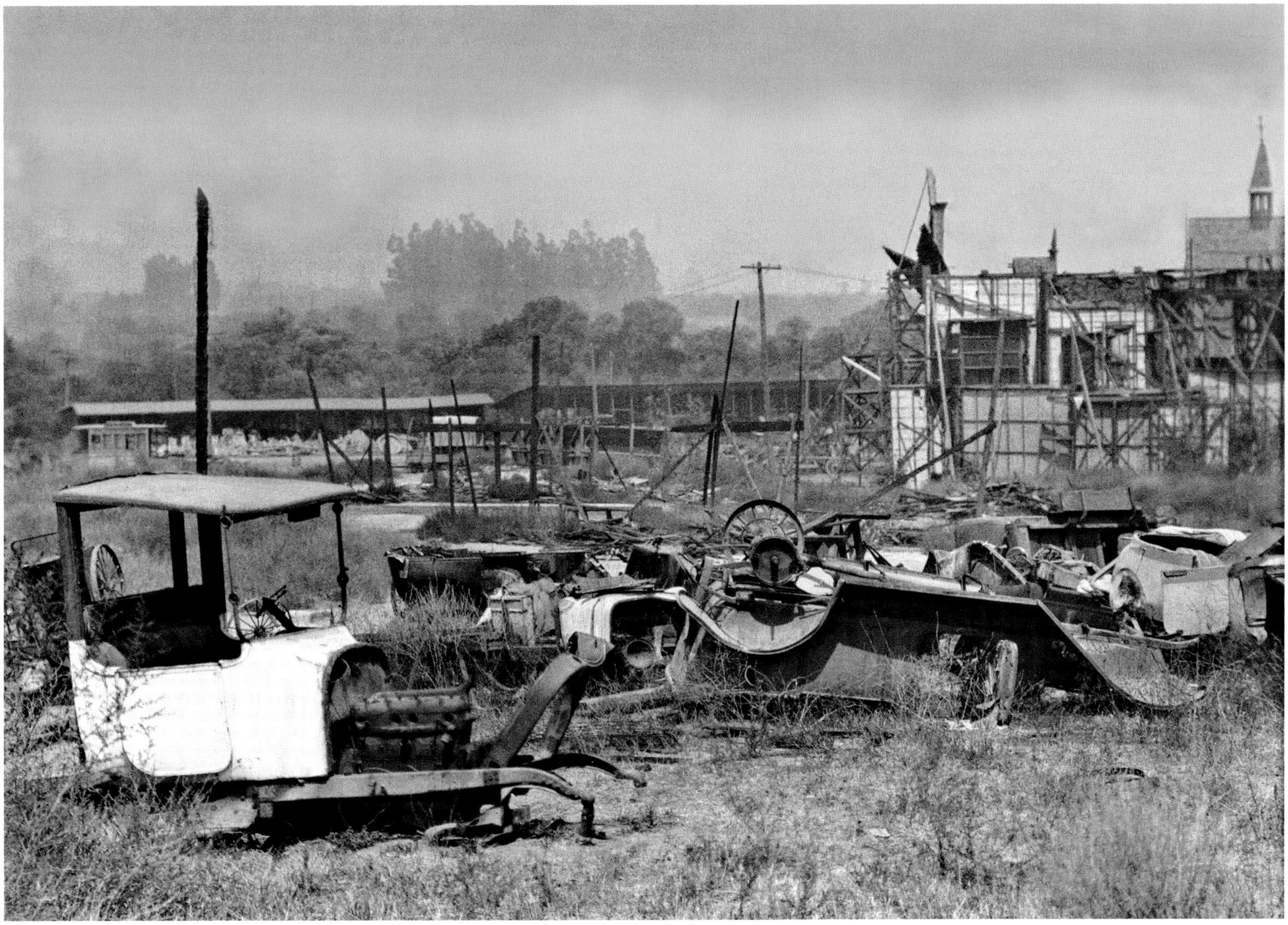

The Backlot, Universal City, Los Angeles, California, 1926

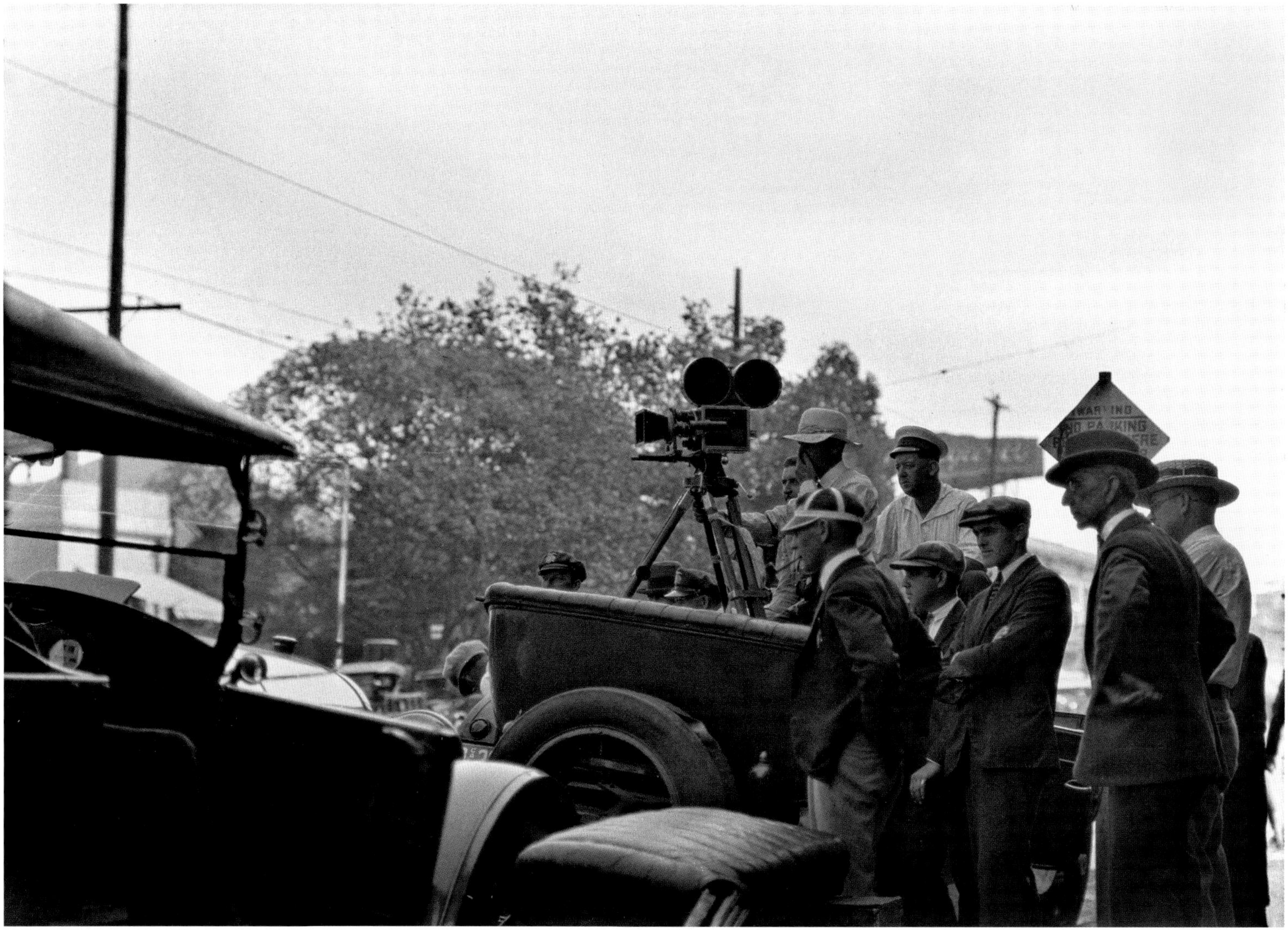

Film Crew, Los Angeles, California, 1926

The El Capitan Theater, Hollywood Boulevard, Los Angeles, California, 1926

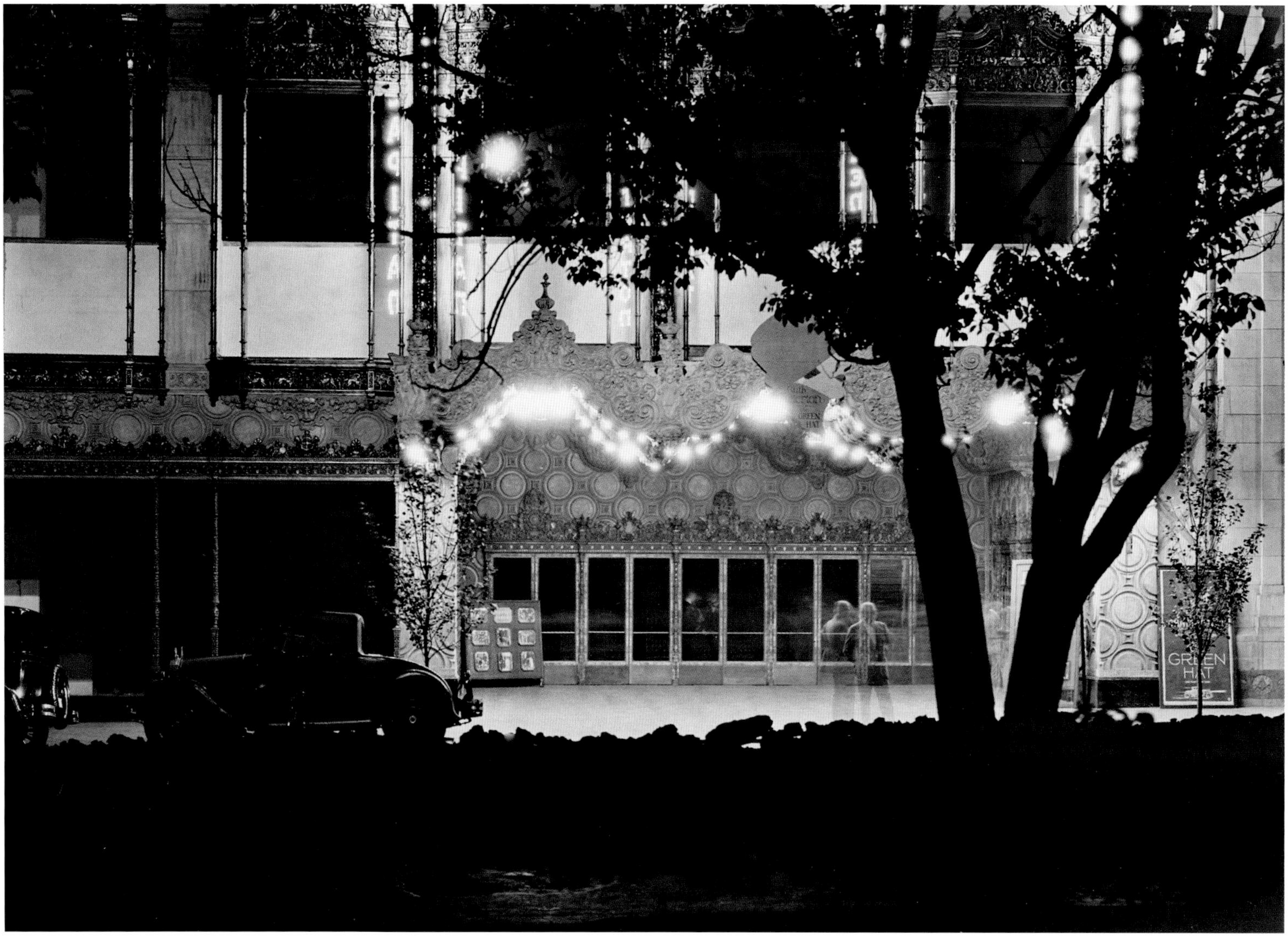

Night Scene in Hollywood, Los Angeles, California, 1926

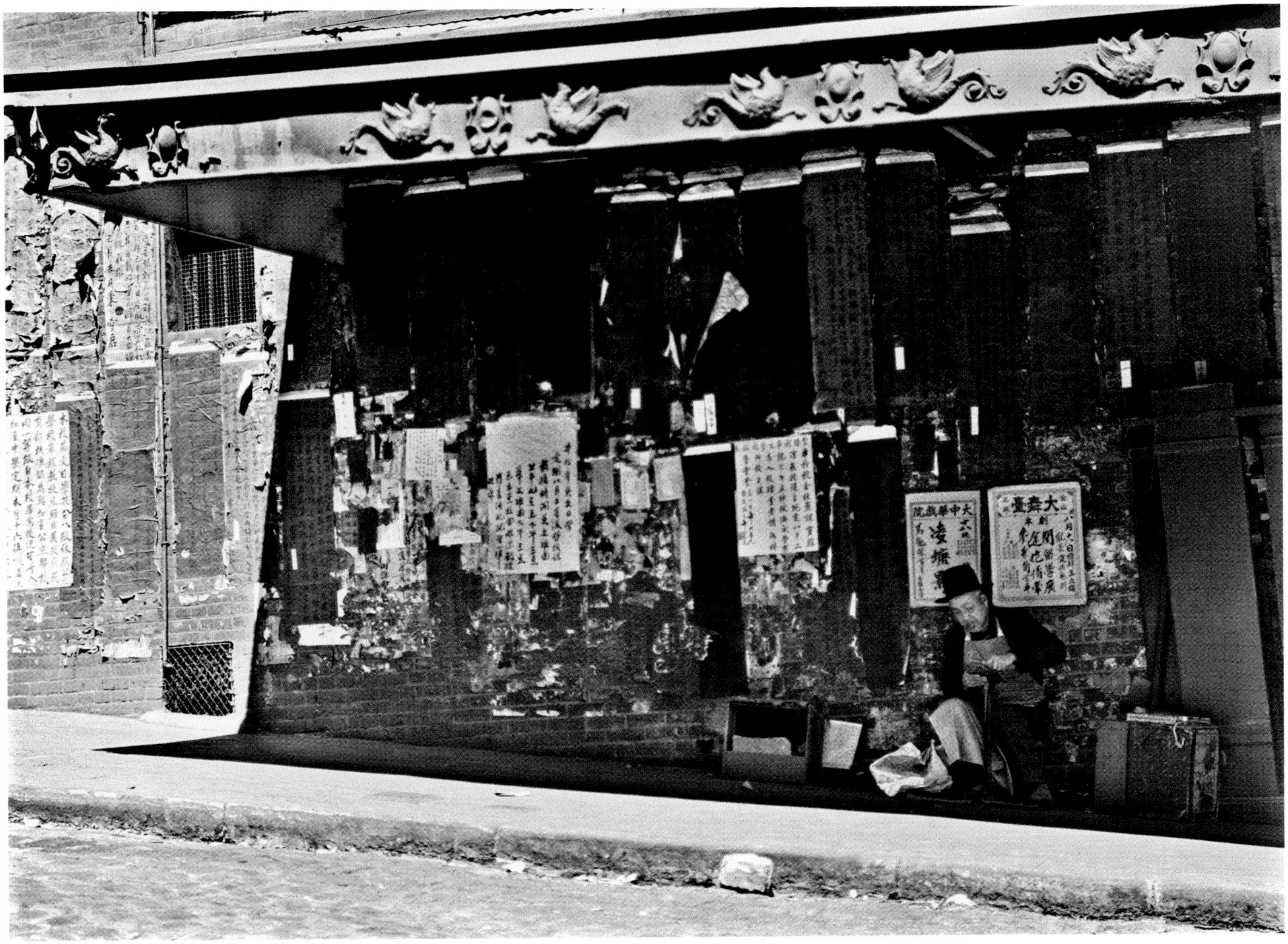

Man Seated Outside Store, Chinatown, San Francisco, California, 1926

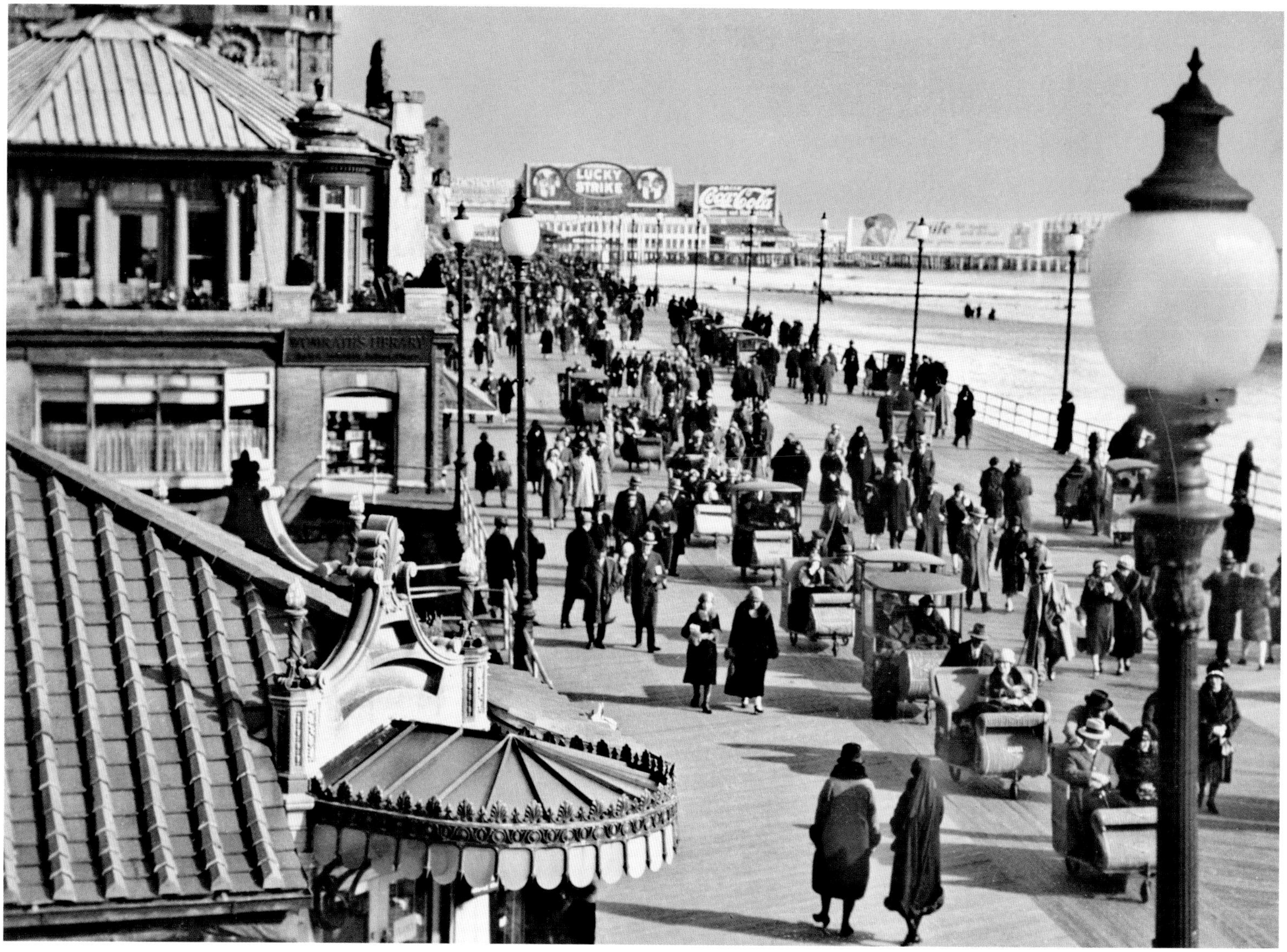

The Boardwalk, Atlantic City, New Jersey, 1926

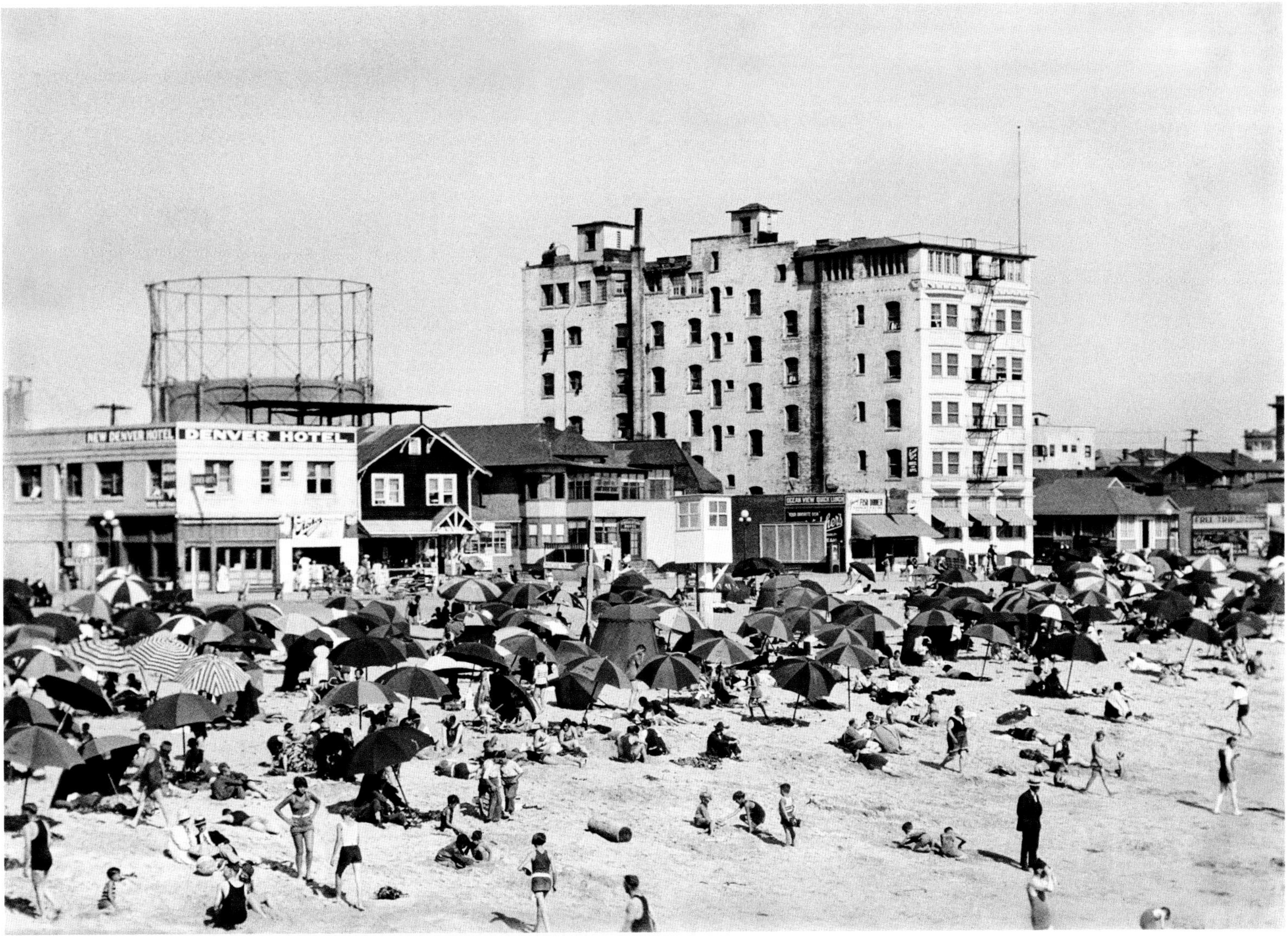

Venice Beach, Los Angeles, California, 1926

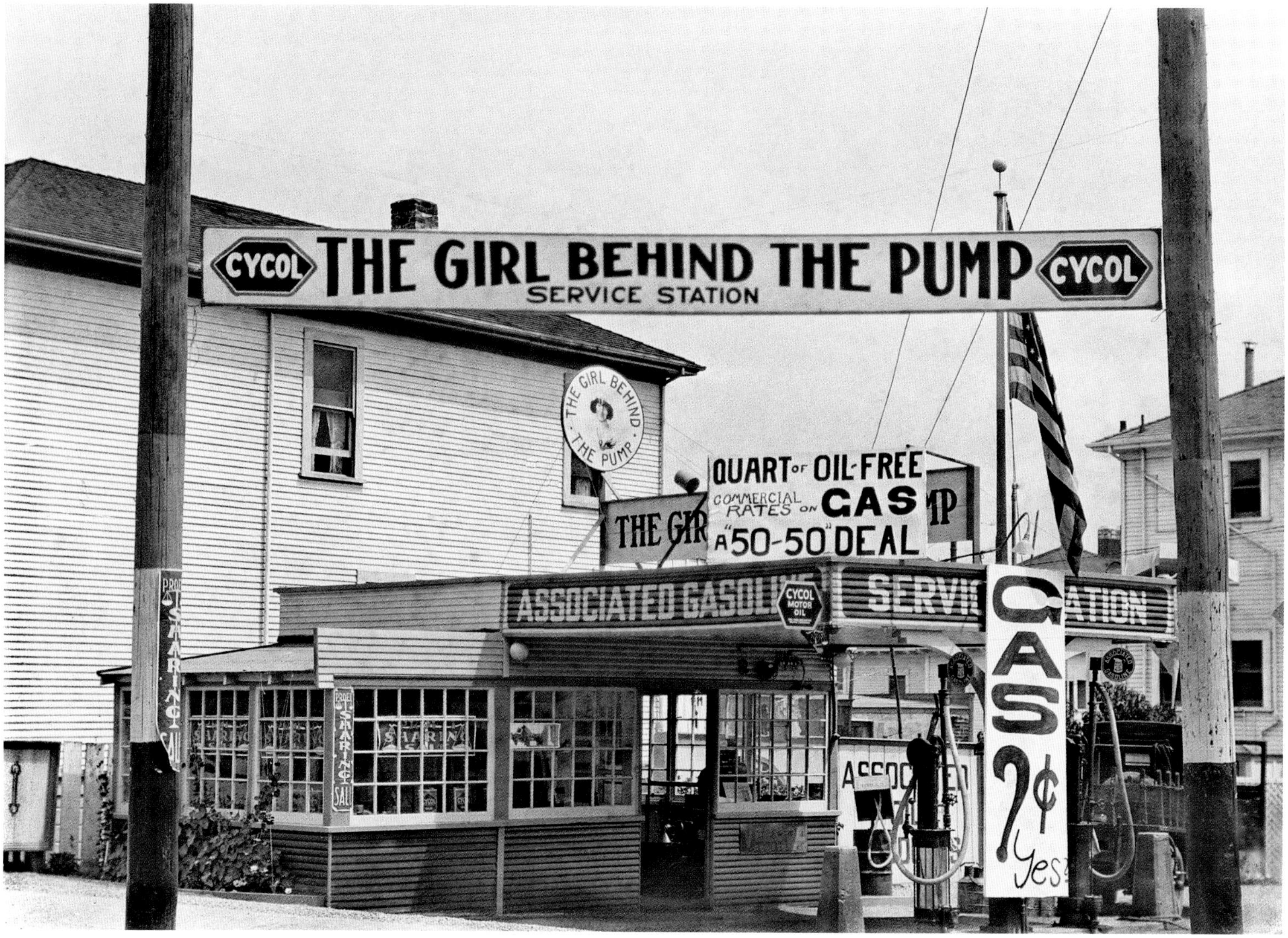

"The Girl Behind the Pump," Pacific Coast Highway, Los Angeles, 1926

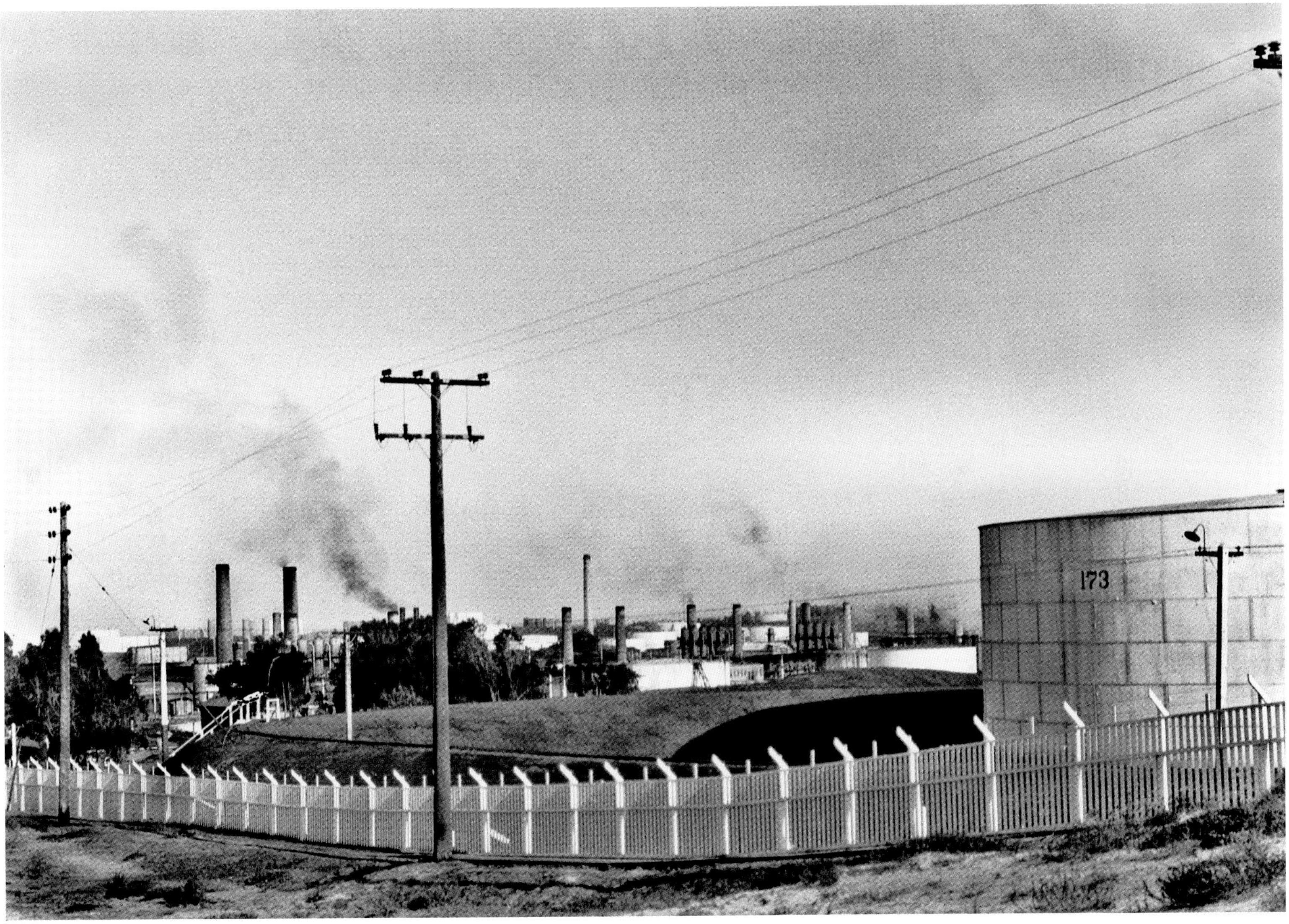

Oil Storage Tanks, Los Angeles, California, 1926

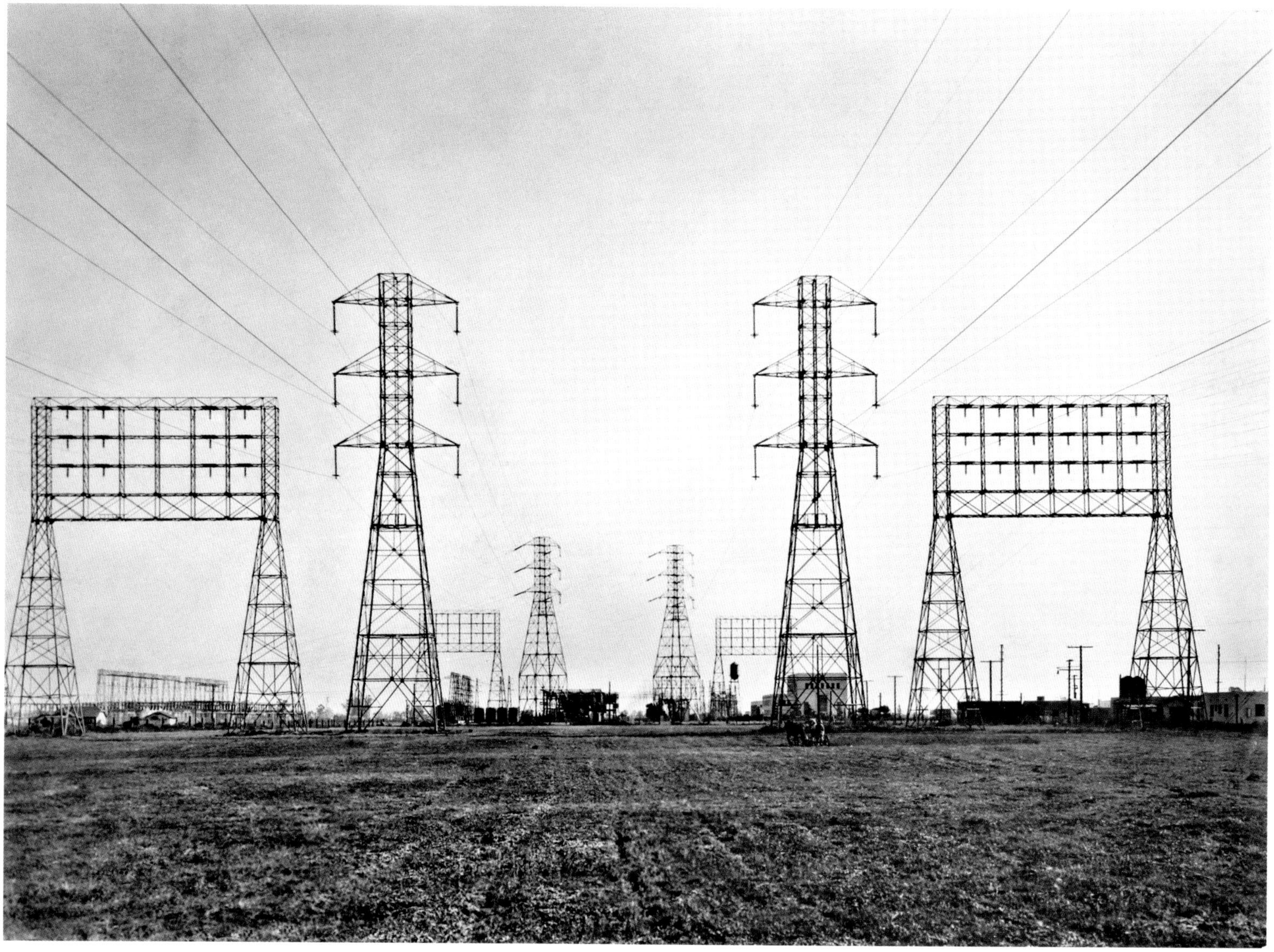

Edison Wireless, Electrical Pylons, Los Angeles, California, 1926

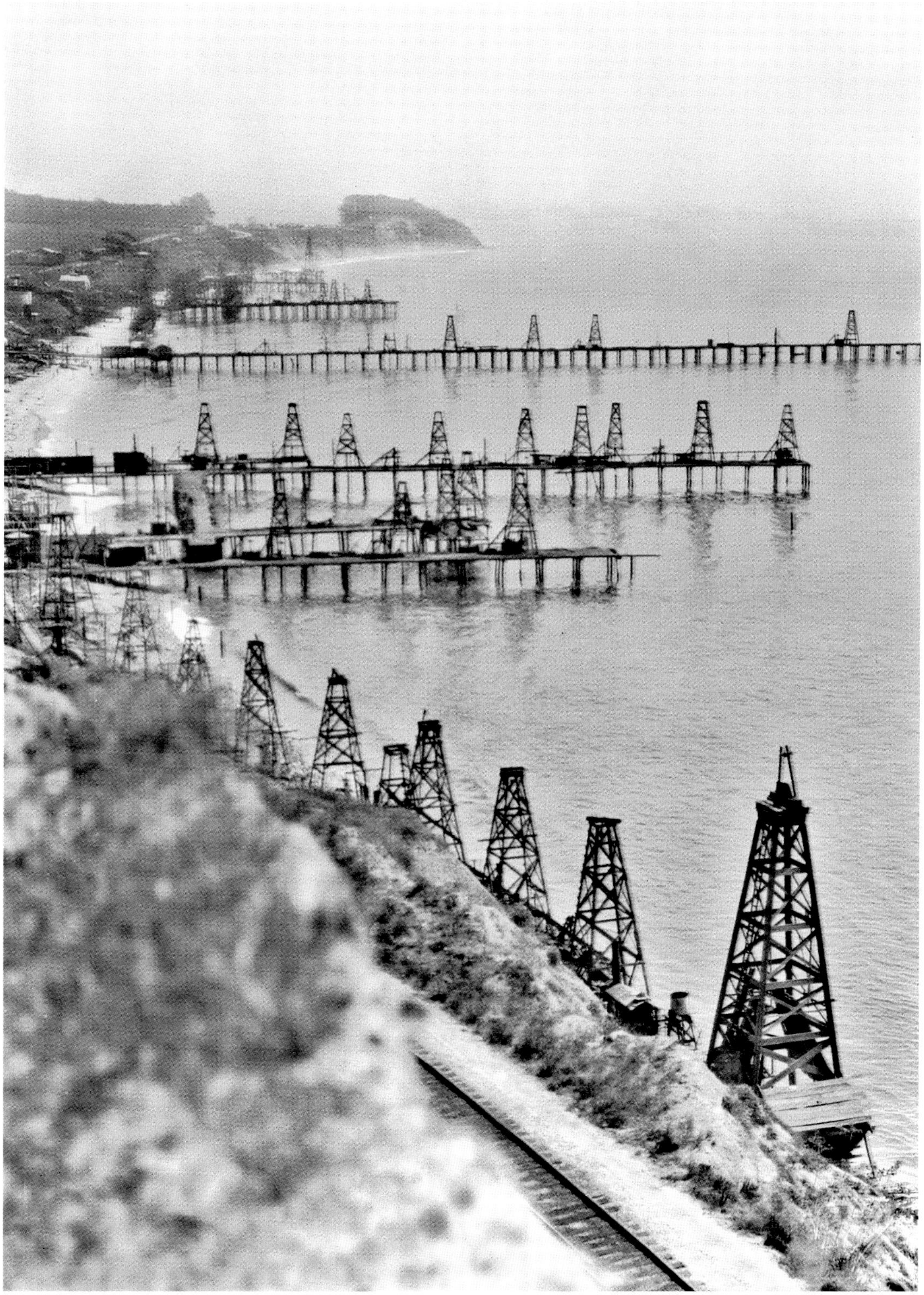

Oil Fields on the California Coast, 1926

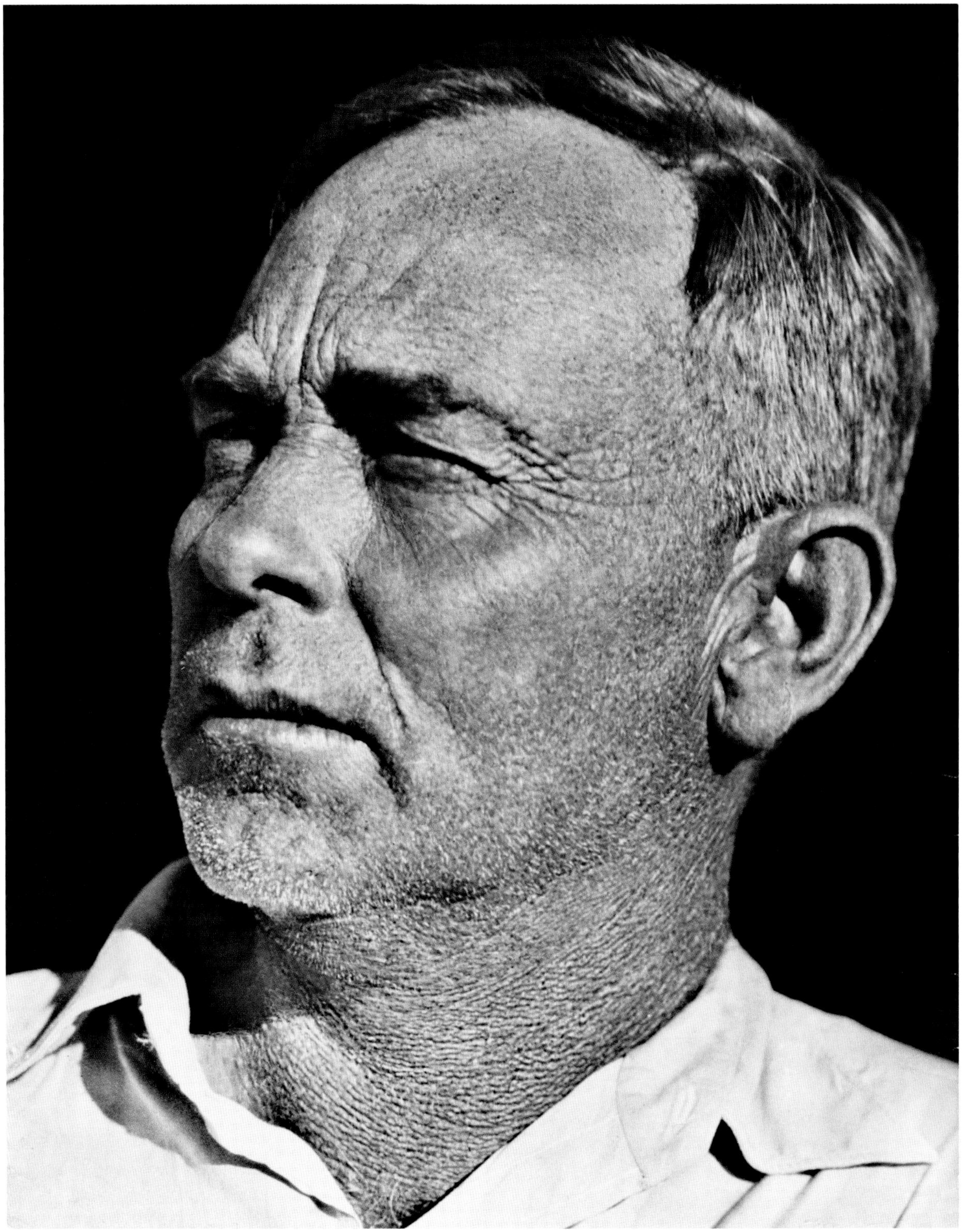

Mr. Richardson, California, 1926

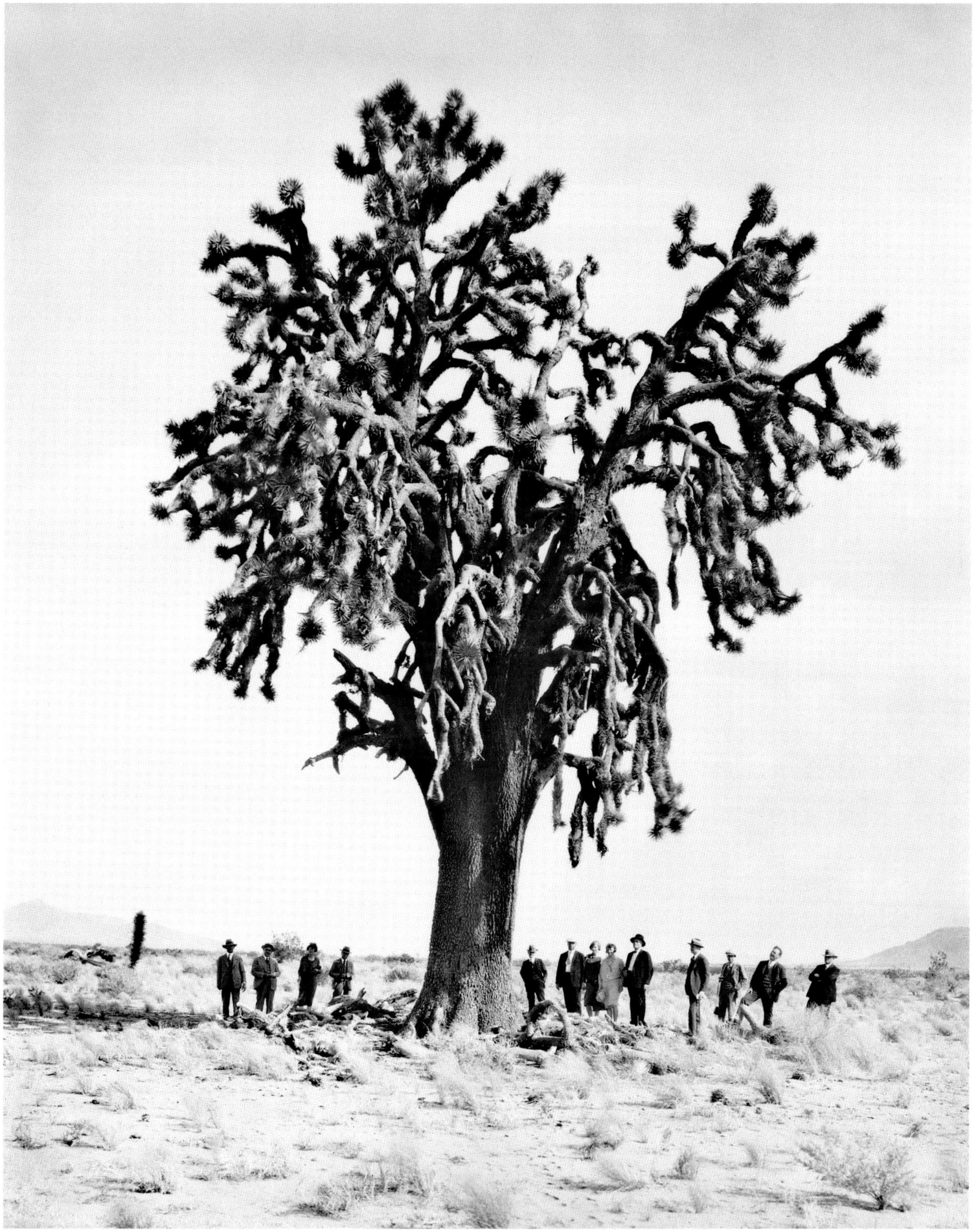

Tourists, Joshua Tree National Park, California, 1926

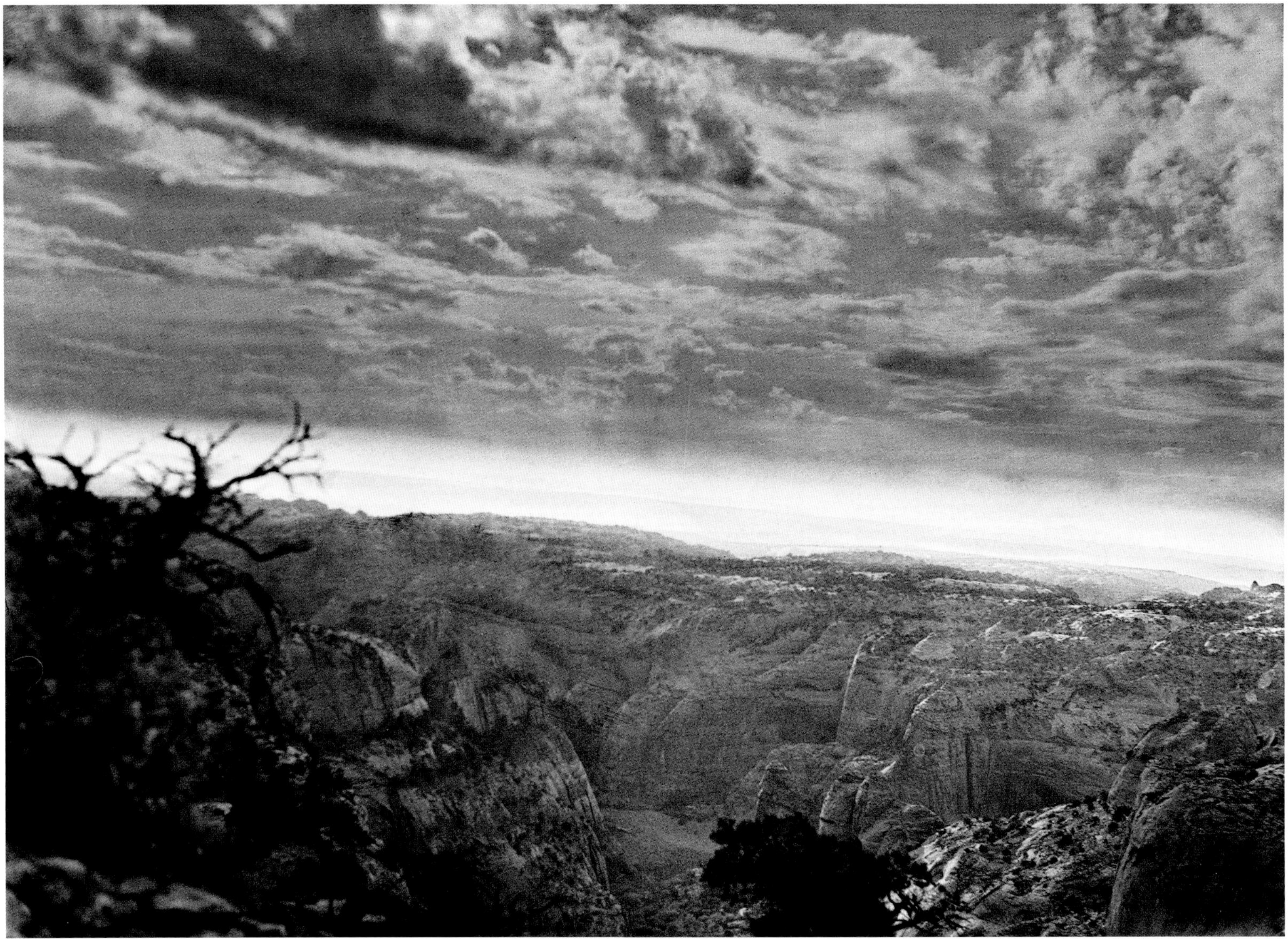

Painted Desert, Arizona, 1926

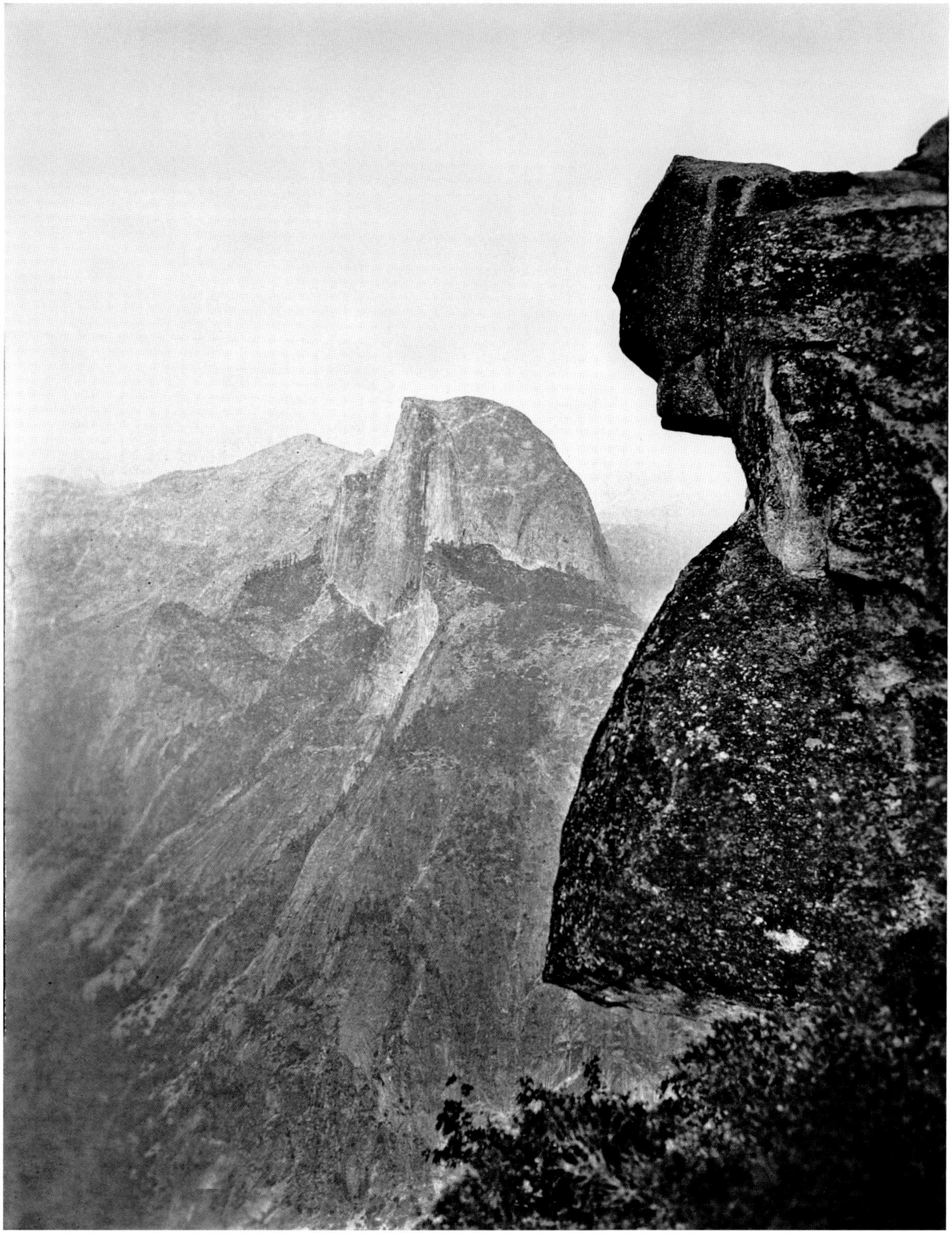

Half Dome and the Sierra Nevada from Glacier Point, Yosemite, California, 1926

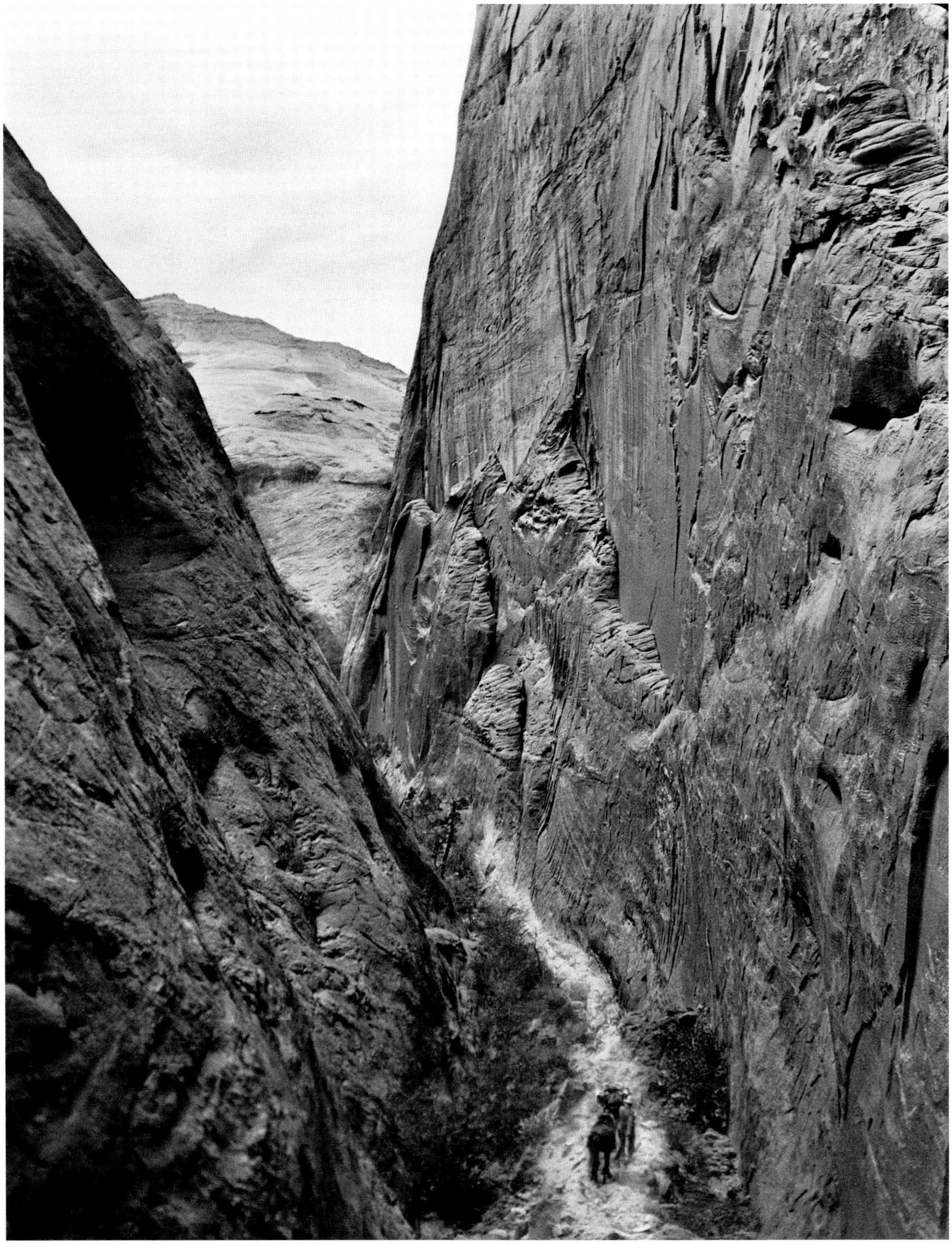

Traveler on the Rainbow Trail, Arizona, 1926

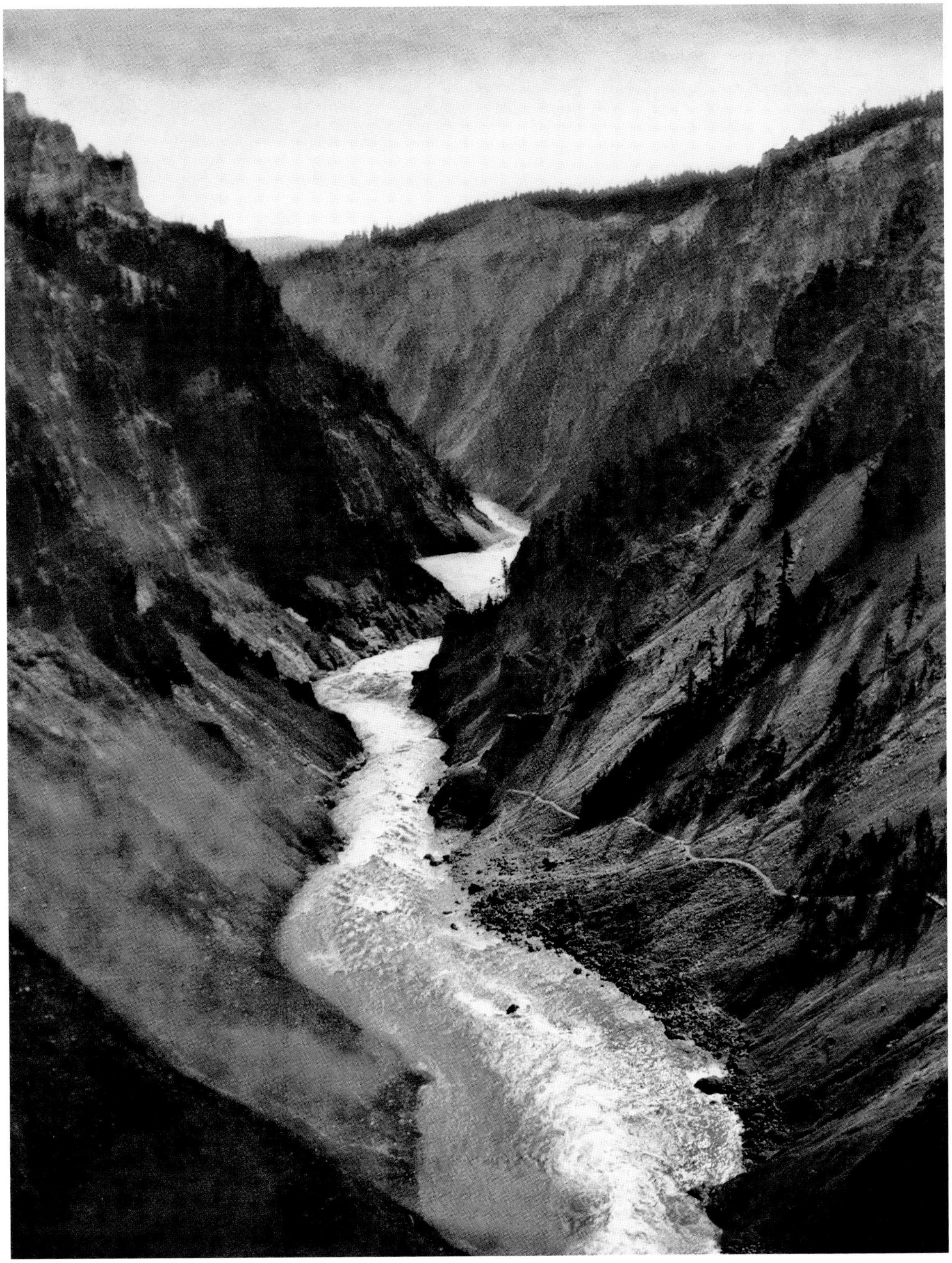

Canyon of Yellowstone, Yellowstone Park, Wyoming, 1926

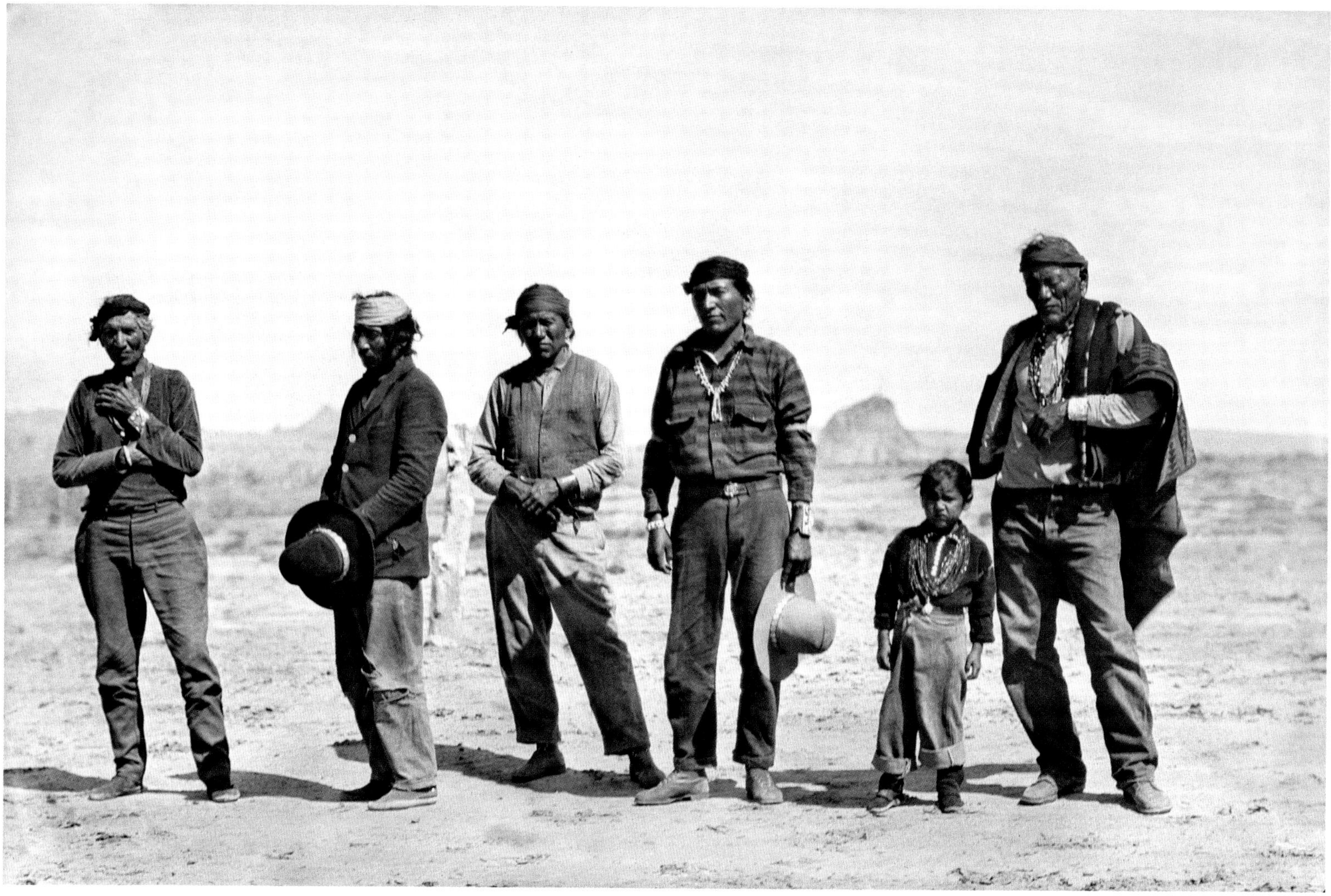

Navajo Indians, Arizona, 1926

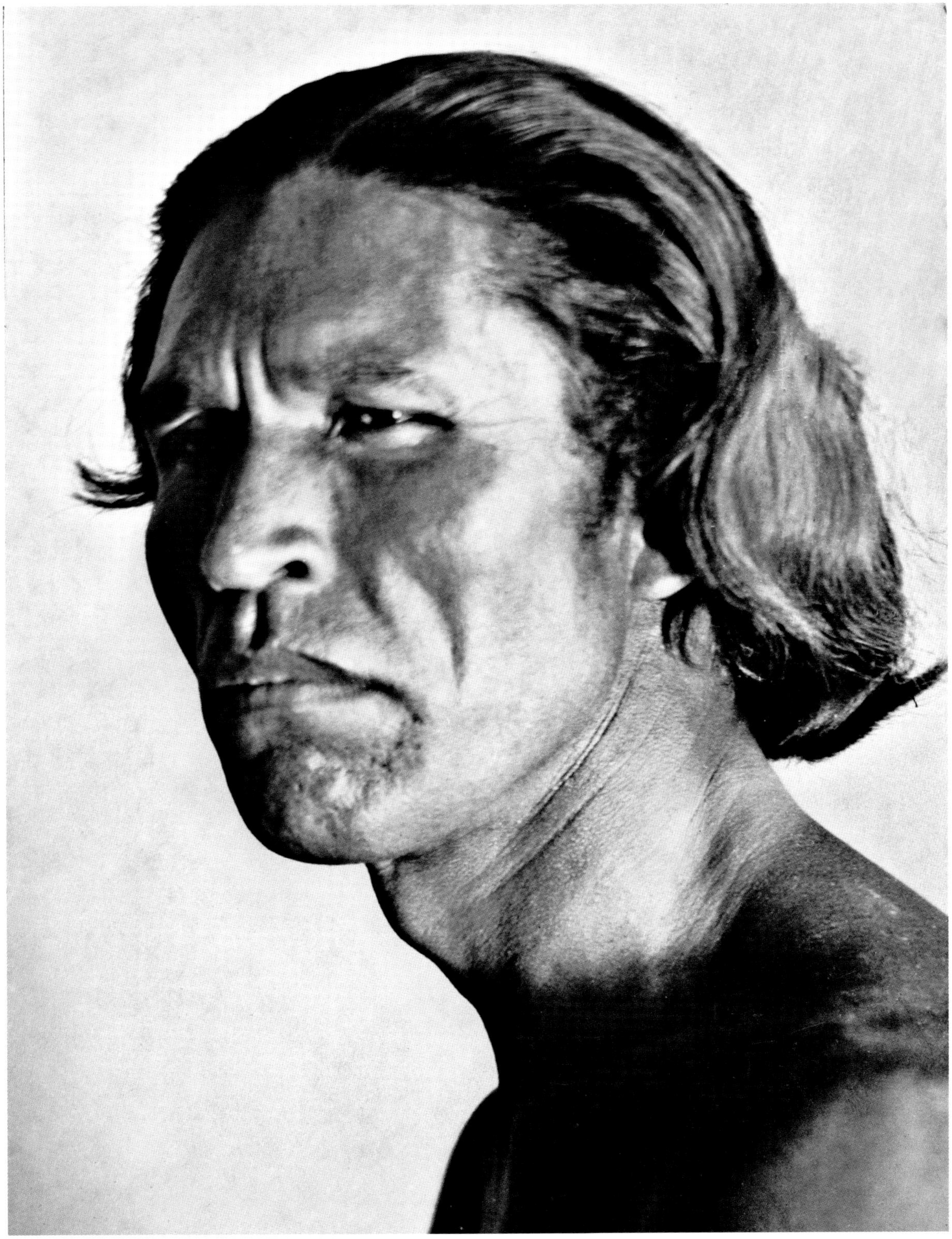

Yakima Indian, Washington, 1926

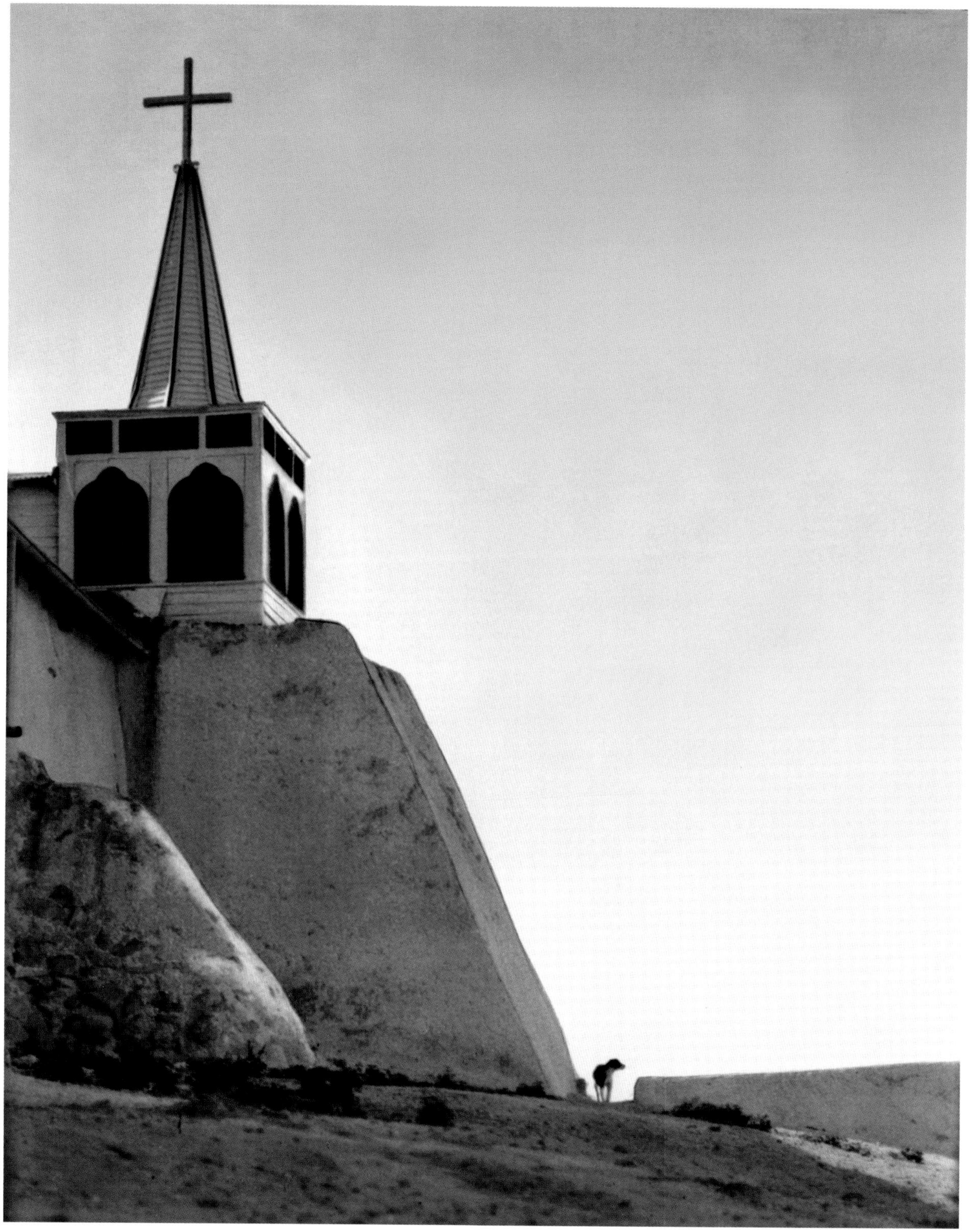

Church at Isleta, New Mexico, 1926

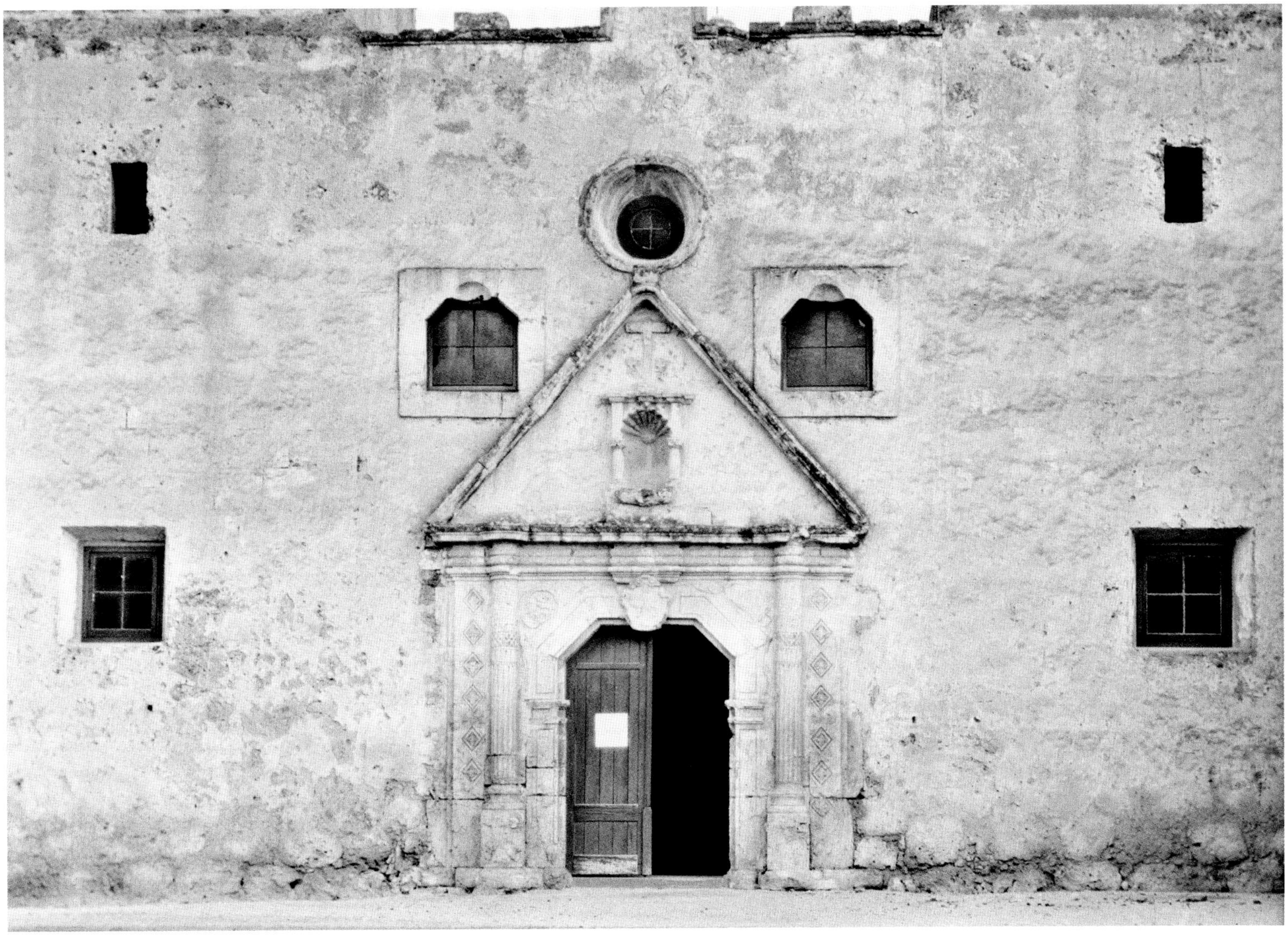

Mission Nuestra Senora de la Purisma Concepcion, San Antonio, Texas, 1926

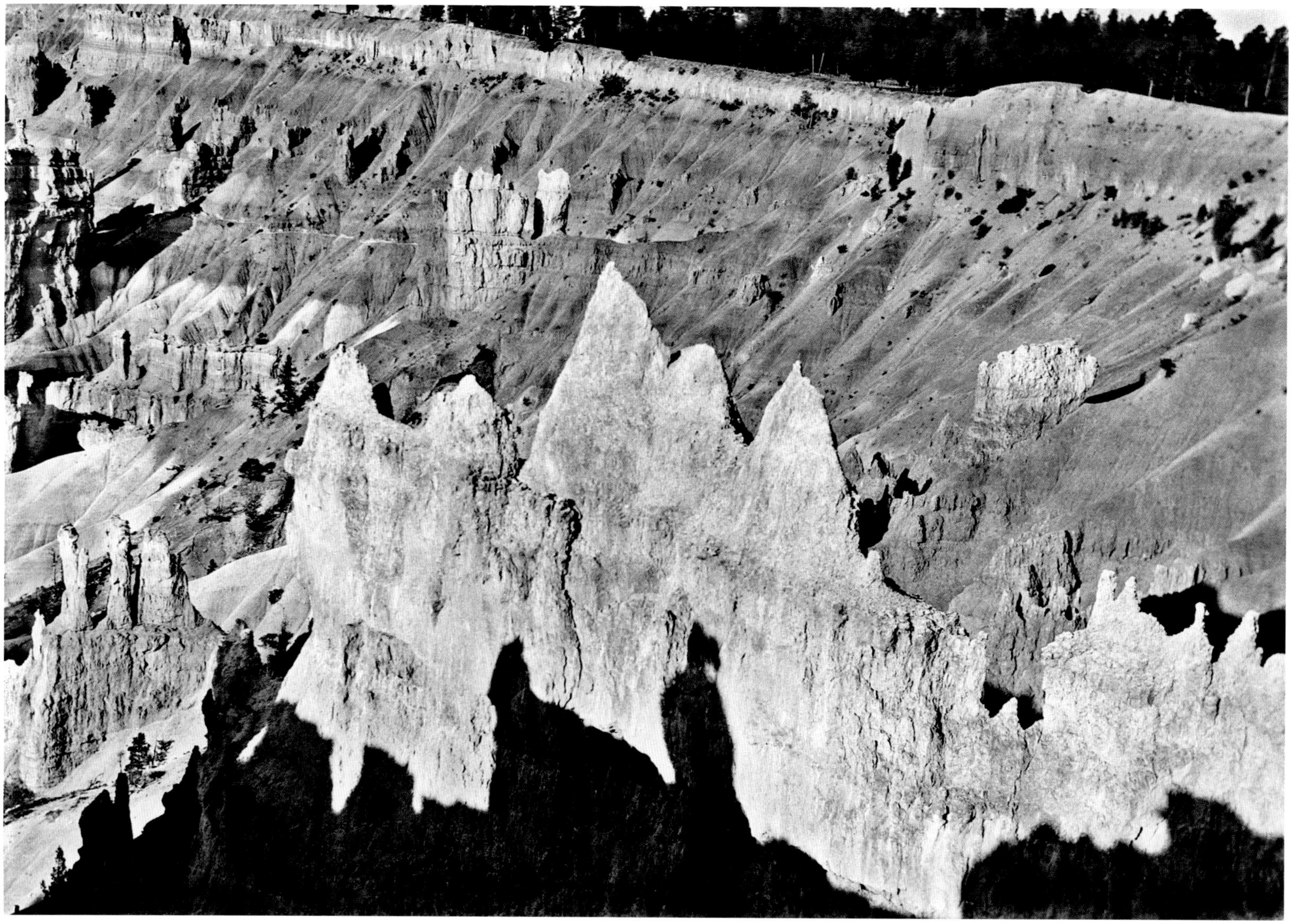

Bryce Canyon, Utah, 1926

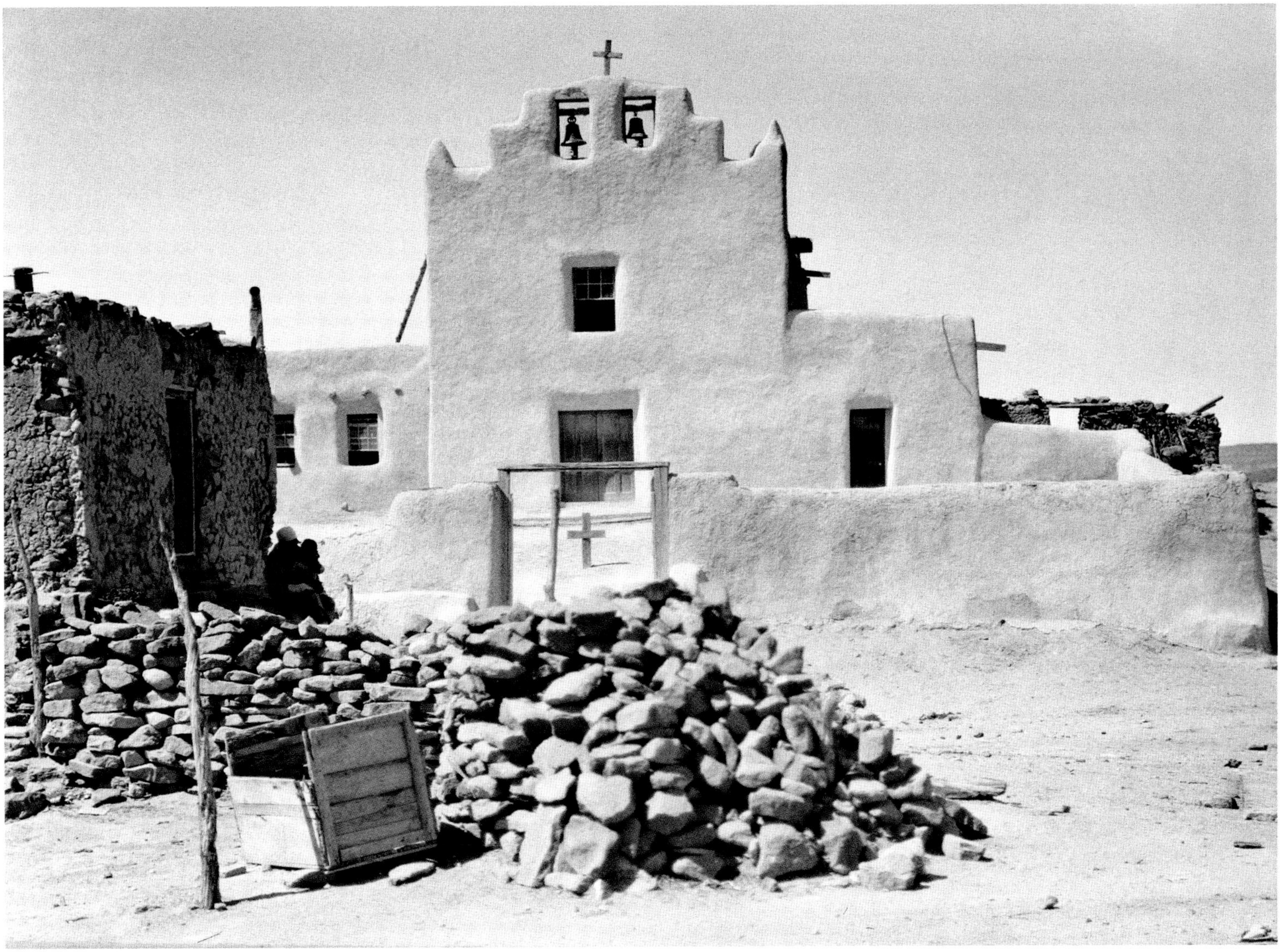

Acoma Pueblo Mission, New Mexico, 1926

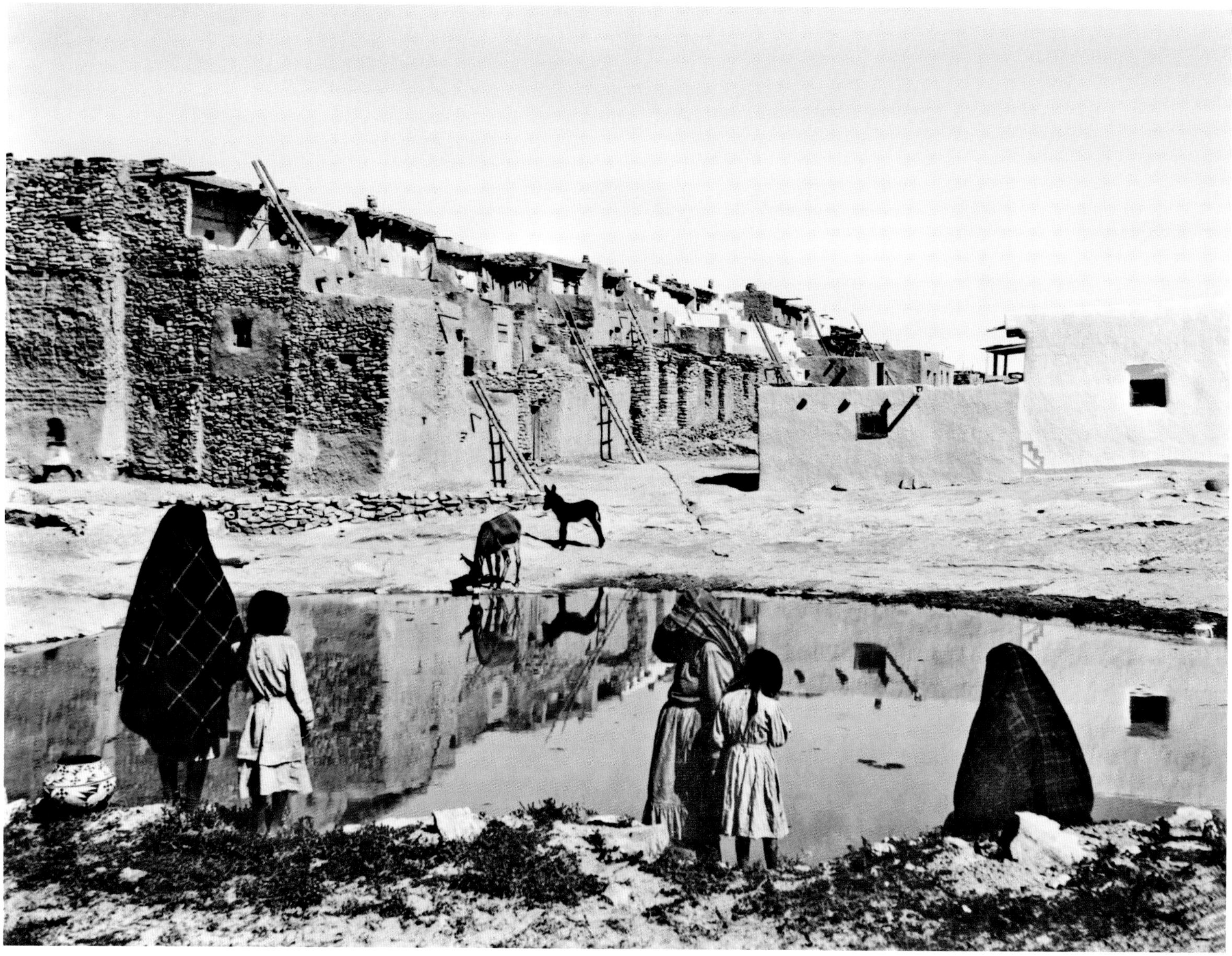

Acoma Pueblo, New Mexico, 1926

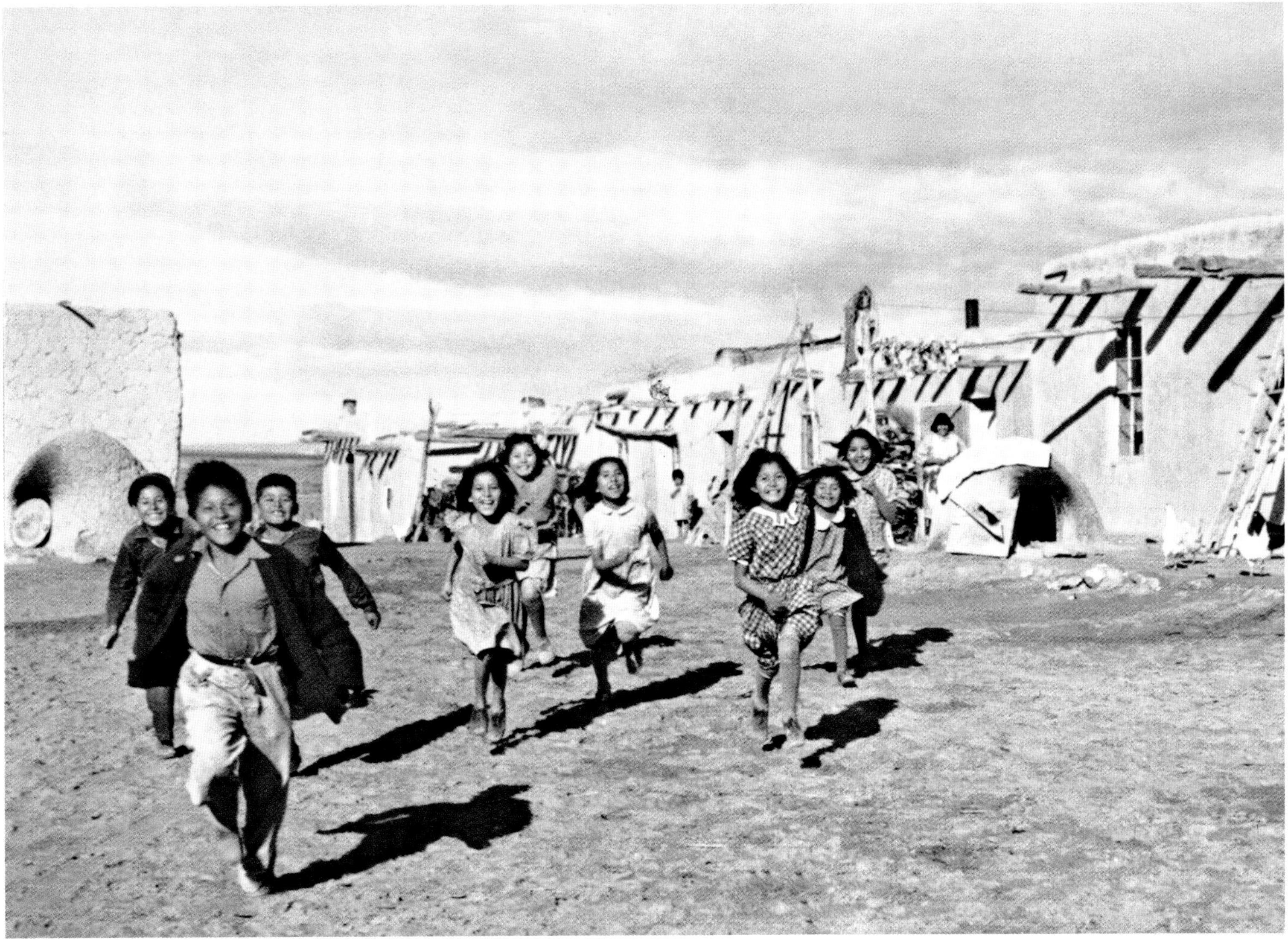

Children, Zuni Pueblo, New Mexico, 1926

ACKNOWLEDGMENTS

I am deeply indebted to Graham Howe of Curatorial Assistance for his tremendous insight and guidance, and to Pam Moffat for help in the Hoppé Archive. Pam Roberts also provided invaluable advice. I am also grateful to Claudia Sorsby for editing early drafts of this essay. The Getty Research Institute and Beinecke libraries provided research assistance. I am extremely grateful to Jim Mairs and Austin O'Driscoll of Norton and to Don Kennison, Katy Homans and Philipp Scholz Rittermann for making this handsome book a reality. Thanks go to Bruce Silverstein of Silverstein Photography gallery, New York, whose understanding of the importance of E. O. Hoppé's work led to the creation of this book.

— P. P.

NOTES

1. Hoppé, *Hundred Thousand Exposures* (London and New York: Focal Press, 1945), p. 186.

2. "First Exhibition of Photographic Prints by E. O. Hoppé," Gallery Guide, Belmaison Galleries, John Wanamaker, New York, 1921.

3. *Hundred Thousand Exposures,* p. 35

4. Hoppé, draft of autobiography, p. 1. Hoppé Archive no. 0005.

5. E. O. Hoppé, "Credo," *Britain Today,* 1954, p. 23. Hoppé Archive no. 1253-0003. Hoppé published this credo repeatedly over the course of his career, beginning in the 1920s.

6. See Hoppé, "The Changing American Face," *The Graphic,* September 7, 1921, p. 19; "Does the American Face Resemble the Indians?" *Saint Louis Globe Dispatch,* April 17, 1921, p. 13; or "The Camera Reveals New Racial Tendencies," *Photography,* 4:46, June 1936, p. 2.

7. Hoppé Archive no. 1713.

8. Hoppé, draft autobiography, p. 4. Hoppé Archive no. 0003.

9. Hoppé, draft autobiography, chapter 5, p. 7. Hoppé Archive no. 0001.

10. Hoppé, *Romantic America* (New York: Westerman [Orbis Terrarum series], 1927), p. 5.

11. Hoppé, "Skyscrapers and Women: The Psychology of American Beauty: Environment, Intellect, and Evolution," *Eye,* April 26, 1927, pp. 146–47.

12. Ibid., p. 146.

13. Margaret M. Lukes, "American Beauty Achieves a Distinct Type," *Montreal Standard,* June 19, 1927, unpaginated, Hoppé Archive no. 0772.

14. Unidentified excerpt from a German-language publication, p. 542. Hoppé Archive no. 0785. Translation is the author's.

15. Hoppé, draft autobiography, chapter 6, p. 8. Hoppé Archive no. 0003.

16. Bill Jay, "Emil Otto Hoppé, 1878–1972," *Visual Communication* 11:2, Spring 1985, p. 6.

17. See, for example, "Some Works of Mr. E. O. Hoppé," *The Studio,* pp. 106–110, undated excerpt in the Hoppé Archive, no. 1701. Hoppé was also a contributor and editor of the short-lived art magazine *Colour,* launched in 1914 in which some of his drawings were published. See Terence Pepper, "E. O. Hoppé Chronology," *Visual Communication* 11:2, Spring 1985, p. 42.

18. Hoppé, draft autobiography, chapter 1, p. 2. Hoppé Archive no. 0001.

19. Ibid., chapter 1, p. 1. Hoppé Archive no. 0001. Hoppé settled on the title *Hundred Thousand Exposures* later; in the first draft he proposes *Close-Ups and Long-Shots,* or *Both Sides of the Lens.*

20. Hoppé was a wonderful storyteller and not immune to changing his tales for dramatic effect. He cultivated a certain mythology with regard to the early years of his studio, and accounts of the precise chronology of events vary somewhat depending on the publication.

21. Draft autobiography, chapter 1, p. 2. Hoppé Archive no. 0001. Again these details do not appear in the published version.

22. A number are preserved in the Royal Photographic Society Collection, National Museum of Photography, Film, and Television, Bradford, England.

23. *Hundred Thousand Exposures,* p. 13. The camera manufacturer is named only in the unpublished draft. In *Hundred*

Thousand Exposures he also mentions a camera given to him as a birthday present but does not elaborate.

24. See Alfred Lichtwark, *die Bedeutung der Amateur-Photographie* (Hamburg: Wilhelm Knapp, 1894).

25. Stone was an amateur photographer and Member of Parliament. The connection between Stone's National Photographic Record Association, intended to document the many regional customs of Britain, and Hoppé's concurrent effort to create extensive "typological" portraits seems quite direct. It is also likely to have influenced Hoppé's American work.

26. See, for example, Phillip Prodger and Patrick Daum eds., *Impressionist Camera: Pictorial Photography in Europe 1878–1918,* (London and New York: Merrell, 2006).

27. Hoppé, "The Soul of the Camera," *The Patrician,* 1920, p. 182.

28. Mark Haworth-Booth, *Hoppé's London* (London: Guiding Light, 2006), p. 5.

29. Hoppé, "The 'Seeing' Eye," undated journal clipping, pp. 13–14, Hoppé Archive, no. 1260.

30. Ferenc Berko and Karl Steinroth, *Ferenc Berko: Sixty Years of Photography—The Discovering Eye* (Zurich: Edition Stemmle, 1995), p. 76.

31. Although differential focus was one of the favorite subjects of Peter Henry Emerson (1856–1936), he never went as far as Hoppé in obscuring both foreground and background.

32. Hoppé, "Pictorial Photography Assessed Without Prejudice," *Photographic Journal,* section A, July 1955, p. 137.

33. Ibid., p. 138.

34. Ibid.

35. In his autobiography Hoppé proudly related Cameron's use of his studio in the days when it belonged to John Everett Millais.

36. Nancy Hall-Duncan, "E. O. Hoppé," *E. O. Hoppé, 100,000 Exposures* (New York: Photo Center Gallery, 1982).

37. The similarities between Hoppé's photographs and those of Adams's associate William Dassonville (1879–1957) are even more striking, strongly suggesting the possibility that the two might have met.

38. Hall-Duncan, pp. 9–10.

39. Unpublished correspondence, Gertrude Käsebier to E. O. Hoppé, March 15, 1921, Hoppé Archive no. 1716.

40. Ibid., December 18, 1926, Hoppé Archive no. 1717.

41. Hoppé published his credo in various publications throughout his career, beginning in the 1920s. Here I quote from E. O. Hoppé, "Credo," *British Journal of Photography* 118:580, October 1, 1971, p. 71.

42. Unpublished correspondence, Alfred Stieglitz to Max Weber, March 17, 1921, Max Weber Papers, Archives of American Art, Washington, D.C. With thanks to Pam Roberts for providing this and the following references.

43. Ibid.

44. Unpublished correspondence, E. O. Hoppé to Max Weber, March 21, 1921, Max Weber Papers.

45. Unpublished correspondence, Max Weber to E. O. Hoppé, March 22, 1921, Max Weber Papers.

46. Hoppé, "Photography," undated newspaper clipping, p. 221. Hoppé Archive no. 1256.

PHOTO CREDITS

Figure 1: Walker Evans, *Phillipsburg, New Jersey*, 1935.
Library of Congress, Prints and Photographs Division, FSA/OWI Collection.

Figure 3: Paul Strand, *Sandwich Man, New York,* 1916 © 1971 Aperture Foundation Inc., Paul Strand Archive.

Figure 8: Charles Sheeler, *Criss-Crossed Conveyors, Ford Plant,* 1927 © The Lane Collection.
Photograph courtesy of the Museum of Fine Arts, Boston.

Figure 10: Edward Hopper, *House by the Railroad,* 1925. Digital image © The Museum of Modern Art.
Licensed by Scala/Art Resource, New York.

Figure 13: Alfred Stieglitz, *From the Shelton, West,* 1935. Saint Louis Art Museum, given anonymously.

Figure 14: Alvin Langdon Coburn, *Woolworth Building, New York,* ca. 1912. Courtesy George Eastman House.

Figure 16: Edward Weston, *Power Lines, Lincoln Boulevard, Los Angeles,* ca. 1930.
Courtesy of the Center for Creative Photography.

Figure 18: Ansel Adams, *From Glacier Point,* ca. 1923.
Courtesy of the Center for Creative Photography. © The Ansel Adams Publishing Rights Trust.

Figure 21: Edward Steichen, *Milk Bottles,* 1915. Reprinted with permission of Joanna T. Steichen.

INDEX